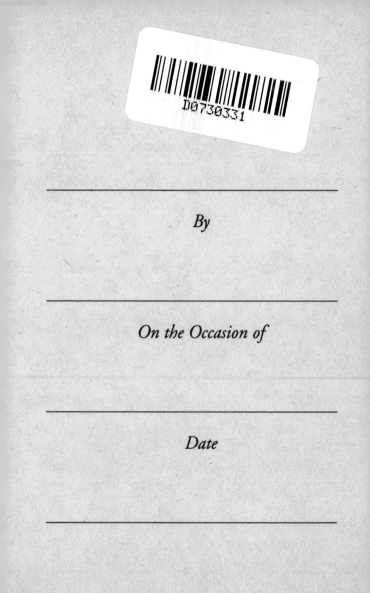

_By_

On the Occasion of

Date

GRANT ME WISDOM

Daily Devotional Insights from Matthew Henry

COMPILED AND UPDATED BY TONI SORTOR

BARBOUR
PUBLISHING

ISBN 1-59310-374-3

Cover image © PhotoDisc

Published by Barbour Publishing, Inc., P.O. Box 719, Uhrichsville, Ohio 44683, www.barbourbooks.com

Our mission is to publish and distribute inspirational products offering exceptional value and biblical encouragement to the masses.

ecpa Member of the
Evangelical Christian
Publishers Association

Printed in the United States of America.
5 4 3 2 1

Contents

Introduction

Many modern Christians have heard Matthew Henry's name. Some know he wrote a commentary on the Bible. But considerably fewer have actually read his work.

Matthew Henry's writings are certainly worth reading, though, and this book, *Grant Me Wisdom—Daily Devotional Insights from Matthew Henry,* makes them readily accessible to the modern Christian. Carefully drawn from Henry's massive *Commentary on the Whole Bible,* this devotional book takes his most practical thoughts and puts them into a one-a-day format for a year's worth of inspiring reading.

Though he lived three centuries ago, Matthew Henry's writings still speak to the Christian reader seeking insight into the Scriptures. For the modern reader's benefit, *Grant Me Wisdom—Daily Devotional Insights from Matthew Henry* features a light editing of Henry's original words and the use of the New King James Version of the Bible. Selections are categorized by monthly topics, including faith, prayer, Bible study, devotion and commitment, intimacy with God, worship, relationships, fruits of the Spirit, Christian duty, spiritual warfare, the Great Commission, and anticipating Christ's return.

Whether you're already familiar with the work of Matthew Henry or this is your first exposure to this great Christian leader, we hope you'll find challenge and encouragement from his writings.

THE EDITORS

Know Your Own Mind

Examine yourselves as to whether you are in the faith.
Test yourselves. Do you not know yourselves,
that Jesus Christ is in you?—
unless indeed you are disqualified.
2 CORINTHIANS 13:5

What the apostle Paul says here of the duty of the Corinthians to examine themselves is applicable to the great duty of all who call themselves Christians: to examine themselves concerning their spiritual state. We should examine whether we are in the faith, because it is a matter in which we may be easily deceived and where a deceit is highly dangerous. As with the goats in Jesus' parable in Matthew 25, He shall say to them, " 'Depart from Me, you cursed' " (v. 41). Every word has terror in it, like that of the trumpet at Mount Sinai, waxing louder and louder, every accent more and more doleful, and exclusive of comfort. In this world they were often called to come to Christ, to come for life and rest, but they turned a deaf ear to His calls; justly, therefore, those who would not come to Him are bid to depart from Christ. It is the hell of hell to depart from Christ.

We are therefore concerned to prove our own selves, to put the question to our own souls, whether Christ is in us or not; and Christ *is* in us, unless we are reprobates: so that either we are true Christians or we are great cheats, and what a reproachful thing it is for a man not to know himself, not to know his own mind!

The Grace of Faith

Now faith is the substance of things hoped for,
the evidence of things not seen.
For by it the elders obtained a good testimony.
HEBREWS 11:1–2

The grace of faith is the substance of things hoped for. Faith and hope go together, and the same things that are the object of our hope are the object of our faith. We are of a firm persuasion and expectation that God will perform all that He has promised to us in Christ. Believers in the exercise of faith are filled with unspeakable joy and full of glory. Faith is the evidence of things not seen. Faith demonstrates to the eye of the mind the reality of those things that cannot be discerned by the eye of the body. It is designed to serve the believer instead of sight and to be to the soul all that the senses are to the body.

True faith is an old grace and has the best plea to antiquity: It is not a new invention, a modern fancy. The eldest and best men who ever were in the world were believers. They were an honor to their faith, and their faith was an honor to them. It started them doing the things that were of good report.

Adhere to the Truth

But you must continue in the things which
you have learned and been assured of,
knowing from whom you have learned them,
and that from childhood you have known the Holy Scriptures,
which are able to make you wise for salvation
through faith which is in Christ Jesus.
2 TIMOTHY 3:14–15

As good men, by the grace of God, grow better and better, so bad men, through the subtlety of Satan and the power of their own corruptions, grow worse and worse. It is not enough to learn what is good, but we must continue in it and persevere in it until the end. If Timothy would adhere to the truth as he had been taught it, this would arm him against the snares and insinuations of seducers.

It is a great happiness to know the certainty of the things wherein we have been instructed. Consider who taught you—not evil men and seducers, but good men who had themselves experienced the power of the truths they taught you. "Knowing especially the firm foundation upon which you have built. That from a child you have known the Holy Scriptures."

Those who would acquaint themselves with the things of God must know the Holy Scriptures. It is a great happiness to know the Holy Scriptures from our childhood. The age of childhood is the learning age; and those who would get true learning must get it out of the Scriptures. They must not lie neglected and seldom or never looked into.

Converting Grace

For by grace you have been saved through faith,
and that not of yourselves; it is the gift of God,
not of works, lest anyone should boast.

EPHESIANS 2:8–9

There is no room for any man's boasting of his own abilities and power or as though he had done anything that might deserve such immense favors from God. God Himself is the author of this great and happy change. Love is His inclination to do us good, considered simply as creatures: Mercy respects us as apostate and miserable creatures. That love of God is great love, and that mercy of His is rich mercy. Every converted sinner is a saved sinner. The grace that saves them is the free, undeserved goodness and favor of God, and He saves them not by the works of the law, but through faith in Christ Jesus. Both that faith and that salvation are the gifts of God.

Grace in the soul is a new life in the soul. Grace unlocks and opens all and enlarges the soul. A regenerate sinner becomes a living soul, being born of God. It is in Him that we live. We who were buried are raised up. When He raised Christ from the dead, He in effect raised up all believers together with Him, and when He placed Him at His right hand in heavenly places, He advanced and glorified them in and with Him.

A Pardon Is Purchased

"For God so loved the world that
He gave His only begotten Son,
that whoever believes in Him
should not perish but have everlasting life."
JOHN 3:16

In order to redeem and save us, it pleased God to give His only begotten Son. He gave Him—that is, He gave Him up to suffer and die—for us. His enemies could not have taken Him if His Father had not *given* Him. By sacrificing His Son, God showed His love to the world. He loved the world so really, so richly. Behold, and wonder, that the great God should love such a worthless world, that the holy God should love such a wicked world. The Jews thought that the Messiah would be sent in love only to their nation, but Christ tells them that He came in love to the whole world, Gentiles as well as Jews. Through Him there is a general offer of life and salvation for all. God loved the world so much that He sent His Son with this fair proposal: Whosoever believes in Him shall not perish. Salvation had been of the Jews, but now Christ is known as salvation to the ends of the earth. Here is the great gospel duty: to believe in Jesus Christ. Here is the great gospel benefit: That whoever believes in Christ shall not perish. God has taken away their sin, and they shall not die. A pardon has been purchased, and those who believe are entitled to the joys of heaven: They shall have everlasting life.

Walk with Christ

As you therefore have received Christ Jesus the Lord,
so walk in Him, rooted and built up in Him
and established in the faith, as you have been taught,
abounding in it with thanksgiving.

COLOSSIANS 2:6–7

All Christians have, in profession at least, received Jesus Christ the Lord, consented to Him, taken Him for theirs in every relation and every capacity. The great concern of those who have received Christ is to walk in Him. We must walk with Him in our daily course of life and keep up our communion with Him. The more closely we walk with Christ, the more we are rooted and established in the faith. If we walk in Him, we shall be rooted in Him; and the more firmly we are rooted in Him, the more closely we shall walk in Him: "Rooted and built up. . .as you have been taught." A good education has a good influence upon our establishment. We must be established in the faith, as we have been taught, abounding therein. And this with thanksgiving.

"Beware lest anyone cheat you through philosophy and empty deceit, according to the tradition of men, according to the basic principles of the world, and not according to Christ" (v. 8). The Jews governed themselves by the traditions of their elders. The Gentiles mixed their maxims of philosophy with Christian principles. Both alienated their minds from Christ. Those who pin their faith on other men's sleeves have turned away from following Christ. As the Old Testament priesthood had its perfection in Christ, so did the kingdom of David. Jesus the Christ is the Lord and head of all the powers in heaven and on earth.

Our Adoption by Faith

For you are all sons of God
through faith in Christ Jesus.
GALATIANS 3:26

The great privilege that real Christians enjoy under the gospel is that they are no longer servants, but sons. They are admitted into the family of God and have a right to all the privileges of His children. They come to obtain this privilege by faith in Christ Jesus. This faith in Christ was what they professed in baptism. Having thus become members by Christ, they also became the children of God. Baptism is the solemn rite of admission into the Christian church. Being baptized into Christ, we are baptized into His death; as He died and rose again, so we should die to sin and walk in newness of life. It would be a great advantage to us to remember this more often.

This privilege of being the children of God is now enjoyed in common by all real Christians. The old law made a difference between Jew and Greek, between slave and free, and between male and female, but this is not true now. We all stand on the same level and are all one in Christ Jesus. All who sincerely believe in Christ, of whatever nation, or sex, or condition, whoever they are, are accepted by Him and become the children of God through faith in Him.

Living by Faith

*"I have been crucified with Christ;
it is no longer I who live, but Christ lives in me;
and the life which I now live in the flesh
I live by faith in the Son of God,
who loved me and gave Himself for me."*

GALATIANS 2:20

Paul saw that justification was not to be expected by the works of the law and that there was no further need of the temple sacrifices, since they were done away with through Christ, by His offering Himself as a sacrifice for us. But though he was thus dead to the law, Paul did not look upon himself as without law. He was dead to the law so he might live for God. The doctrine of the gospel, instead of weakening the bond of duty, strengthened and confirmed it. Though Paul was dead to the law, it was only in order to live a new and better life with God. As he was dead to the law, so he was alive through Jesus Christ (v. 20). He is crucified, and yet he lives; the old man is crucified, but the new man is living. Sin is mortified and grace quickened. Paul has the comforts and the triumphs of grace, yet that grace is not from himself, but from another. He is crucified with Christ, and yet Christ lives in him. He is interested in the death of Christ, so as to die to sin, and yet interested in the life of Christ, so as to live for God. He lives in the flesh and yet lives by faith. To outward appearance, he lives as other people do, yet he has a higher and nobler principle that supports him, that of faith in Christ. Those who have true faith live by that faith.

The Author of Our Faith

Therefore we also, since we are surrounded by
so great a cloud of witnesses, let us lay aside every weight,
and the sin which so easily ensnares us,
and let us run with endurance the race that is set before us,
looking unto Jesus, the author and finisher of our faith,
who for the joy that was set before Him endured the cross,
despising the shame, and has sat down
at the right hand of the throne of God.
HEBREWS 12:1–2

Christians have a race to run. This race is set before them; it is marked out for them both by the Word of God and the examples of the faithful servants of God, that cloud of witnesses that encompasses the faithful. This race must be run with patience and perseverance. Faith and patience are the conquering graces and therefore must always be cultivated.

Christians have a greater example to encourage them than any who have been mentioned before. Jesus, the author and finisher of their faith, is the great leader and precedent of our faith. He is the finisher of grace and of the work of faith in the souls of His people, and He is the judge and the rewarder of their faith.

We must look to Jesus; we must set Him continually before us as our example. We must consider Him and meditate much upon Him. We shall find that as His sufferings far exceeded ours, so His patience far excels ours.

There is a tendency in the best of us to grow weary and to faint under our trials and afflictions. The best way to prevent this is to look to Jesus. Faith and meditation will bring us fresh supplies of strength, comfort, and courage.

Witnesses of Faith

"To Him all the prophets witness that,
through His name, whoever believes in Him
will receive remission of sins."
ACTS 10:43

The Christian faith is built on the foundation of the apostles and prophets and the testimony given by them. Peter, as foreman of the apostles, speaks for the rest, saying that God commanded them to preach to the people and to testify concerning Christ. Their testimony is God's testimony, and they are His witnesses to the world. In addition, all the prophets give witness of Him. Out of the mouth of these two clouds of witnesses, the prophets and the apostles, this Word is established.

We are all accountable to Christ as our Judge. Jesus is ordained by God to be the Judge of the living and the dead (v. 42). He is empowered to prescribe the terms of salvation, that rule by which we must be judged. God has assured us of this, in that He has raised Jesus from the dead, so that it is the great concern of every one of us to make Him our friend. If we believe in Jesus, we shall all be justified by Him. The prophets gave witness to this, that through His name, whosoever believed in Him shall receive remission of sins. This is the great thing we need, without which we are undone. This remission of sins lays a foundation for all the favors and blessings that are available from God. If sin is pardoned, all is well and shall end everlastingly well.

Adoption and Regeneration

*But as many as received Him, to them He gave the right
to become children of God, to those who believe in His name.*
JOHN 1:12

The true Christian receives Christ and believes in His name. Believing in Christ's name is receiving Him as a gift from God. We must receive His doctrine as true and good, and we must receive the image of His grace and impressions of His love as the governing principle of our affections and actions. The true Christian's dignity and privilege are twofold.

First, the privilege of adoption. Before, the adoption pertained to the Jews only, but now, by faith in Christ, Gentiles are the children of God. To them He gave a right, the unspeakable privilege of all good Christians: They are the children of God. If they are the children of God, they become so, are *made* so. God calls them His children, and they call Him Father. The privilege of adoption is entirely owing to Jesus Christ, who gave this power to them who believe on His name. The Son of God became the Son of man, that the sons and daughters of men might become the sons and daughters of God Almighty.

Secondly, the privilege of regeneration. All the children of God are born again; all who are adopted are regenerated. We do not become the children of God the way we become the children of our natural parents. Grace does not run in the blood. This regeneration is not produced by the natural power of our own will. It is the grace of God that makes us willing to be His. This new birth is due to the Word of God as the means and to the Spirit of God as the great and sole author. True believers are born of God.

The Only Way to Salvation

Then he [the jailer] called for a light...
and fell down trembling before Paul and Silas...
and said, "Sirs, what must I do to be saved?"
So they said, "Believe on the Lord Jesus Christ,
and you will be saved, you and your household."

ACTS 16:29–31

They gave the jailer the same directions they did to others, the sum of the whole gospel, the covenant of grace in a few words: "Believe on the Lord." Not only would the jailer be rescued from eternal ruin, but brought to eternal life and blessedness. Though a persecutor, his heinous transgressions would all be forgiven and his hard, embittered heart softened and sweetened by the grace of Christ. We must approve the method God has taken of reconciling the world to Himself by a Mediator and accept Christ as He is offered to us. This is the only sure way to salvation: no other way of salvation than by Christ and no danger of coming short if we take this way. It is the gospel that is to be preached to every creature.

The apostles proceeded to instruct him and his family in the doctrine of Christ, speaking the Word to all who were in his house. Masters of families should take care that all under their charge partake of the means of knowledge and grace and that the Word of the Lord is spoken to them, for the souls of the poorest servants are as precious as those of their masters and are bought with the same price.

The jailer and his family were immediately baptized. The Spirit of grace worked such a strong faith in them that Paul and Silas knew by the Spirit that a work of God had been done in them.

The Bread of Life

"I am the bread of life.
He who comes to Me shall never hunger,
and he who believes in Me shall never thirst."
JOHN 6:35

Christ often spoke of Himself as the bread of life that came down from heaven. What did His hearers make of this claim?

When they heard of the bread of God that gives life, they heartily prayed for it (v. 34). I take this request to be made, though ignorantly, yet honestly, and to be well meant. General and confused notions of divine things produce some kind of desires toward them. Those who have an indistinct knowledge of the things of God make inarticulate prayers for spiritual blessings.

But when they understood that by this bread of life Jesus meant *Himself,* they despised it. This comes immediately after that solemn declaration that Christ had made of God's will and His own undertaking concerning man's salvation (vv. 39–40). One would think that when they heard God had thus visited them, they would have bowed their heads and worshiped, but on the contrary, they quarreled with what Christ said. What offended them was Christ's asserting His origin was from heaven (vv. 41–42). They knew His extraction on earth. " 'Is not this Jesus, the son of Joseph, whose father and mother we know' " (v. 42)? They took it amiss that He should say He came down from heaven when He was one of them.

If

Jesus said to him,
"If you can believe,
all things are possible to him who believes."

MARK 9:23

" 'If You can do anything, have compassion on us and help us' "
(v. 22), begged the father of the possessed child. The answer
Christ gave to this plea checked the weakness of the father's
faith. The sufferer put it upon Christ's power, but Christ turns
it upon him and makes the man question his own faith and
will have him impute any disappointment to a lack of faith on
his own part. He graciously encourages the strength of his desire: "All things are possible to him who believes the almighty
power of God, to which all things are possible." In dealing with
Christ, much is put on our believing and very much promised
to it. Can you believe? Do you dare to believe? If you can, it is
possible that your hard heart may be softened, your spiritual
diseases may be cured, and that, weak as you are, you may be
able to hold out to the end.

The poor man cried out, "Lord, I believe; my cure shall
not be prevented by the want of faith. Lord, I believe." He
adds a prayer for grace to enable him more firmly to rely on
Christ to save: " 'Help my unbelief' " (v. 24). Those who complain of unbelief must look up to Christ for grace to help
them against it, and His grace shall be sufficient for them.
"Help out what is wanting in my faith with Your grace, the
strength of which is perfected in our weakness."

Believing without Seeing

Jesus said to him,
"Thomas, because you have seen Me,
you have believed.
Blessed are those who have not seen
and yet have believed."

JOHN 20:29

Christ acknowledges that Thomas is a believer. No sooner did Thomas consent to Christ than Christ let him know that he believes. He upbraids him for his former incredulity. He had been so backward to believe and came so slowly to his own comforts. Those who in sincerity have come to Christ see a great deal of reason to lament that they did not do it sooner. If no evidence must be admitted but that of our own senses, and we must believe nothing but what we ourselves are eyewitnesses of, how can the world be converted to the faith of Christ?

Jesus commends the faith of those who believe on easier terms. Thomas, as a believer, was truly blessed, but even more blessed are those who have not seen Christ's miracles and especially His resurrection. Blessed are those who do not see these and yet believe in Christ. This faith is more praiseworthy than theirs who saw and believed. It shows a better quality of mind in those who do believe. He who believes upon sight has his resistance conquered by a sort of violence, but he who believes without it is more noble. It is a greater instance of the power of divine grace. Flesh and blood contribute more to their faith who see and believe than to those who see not and yet believe.

Our Resurrection

"I am the resurrection and the life.
He who believes in Me, though he may die, he shall live.
And whoever lives and believes in Me shall never die."

JOHN 11:25–26

Martha believed that at Jesus' prayer God would give anything, but Jesus wanted her to know that by His word He could *work* anything. It is an unspeakable comfort to all Christians that Jesus Christ is the resurrection and life and will be that to them. Resurrection is a return to life; Christ is the author of that return and that life to which it is a return.

Promises are made to those who believe in Jesus Christ. The condition of the latter promise is, "Whoever lives and believes in Me," by which may be understood natural life. Whoever lives in this world, if he believes in Christ, shall live by Him. Or this may be applied to the spiritual life. He who lives and believes is by that faith born again to a heavenly and divine life. Here is the promise of a blessed resurrection. Though the body is dead because of sin, yet it shall live again. The body shall be raised as a glorious body. Here also is the promise of a blessed immortality. He who lives and believes shall never die. That spiritual life shall never be extinguished, but perfected in eternal life. The mortality of the body shall at length be swallowed up, but the life of the soul shall immediately at death be swallowed up by immortality. Martha was hoping that her brother would be raised to life in this world. Before Christ gave her hope for this, He directed her thoughts to another life, another world.

Believe in the Name

These things I have written to you who
believe in the name of the Son of God,
that you may know that you have eternal life,
and that you may continue to believe in
the name of the Son of God.
1 JOHN 5:13

Sound Christian believers are secured against sin that leads to death. The new nature and the inhabitation of the divine Spirit thereby prevent the admission of such unpardonable sin. They are fortified against the devil's destructive attempts. They are on God's side in opposition to the world. Mankind is divided into two great parties, one that belongs to God and one that belongs to wickedness. Christian believers belong to God. On the contrary, the rest, being by far the most numerous, are wicked. May the God of the Christian world continually demolish the devil's dominion and bring souls into the kingdom of His dear Son!

The Son of God has come into our world, and we have seen Him and know Him. He has revealed to us the true God. He has opened our minds to understand that revelation, and we are assured that it is the true God that Jesus revealed to us. The Son leads us to the Father, and we are in both, in the love and favor of both. In union with either, much more with both, we are united to the true God and eternal life.

The apostle warns that since you know the true God and are in Him, let your light and love guard you. Flee from false gods. God redeemed you by His Son, who has pardoned your sins and given you eternal life. Cling to Him in faith, love, and constant obedience.

The Power of Faith

"I say to you, if you have faith as a mustard seed,
you will say to this mountain,
'Move from here to there,' and it will move;
and nothing will be impossible for you."

MATTHEW 17:20

Our Lord Jesus takes this occasion to show us the power of faith. Some make the comparison to refer to the quality of the mustard seed, which is, when bruised, sharp and penetrating. "If you have an active, growing faith, not dead, flat, or insipid, you will not be baffled." But it rather refers to the quantity: "If you had but a grain of true faith, though so little that it were like that which is the least of all seeds, you would do wonders." The faith required here is that which had for its object that particular revelation by which Christ gave His disciples power to work miracles in His name. It was a faith in this revelation that they were defective in. Perhaps their Master's absence might occasion some doubts concerning their power to do this. It is good for us to be diffident of ourselves and our own strength, but it is displeasing to Christ when we distrust any power derived from or granted by Him.

If you have ever so little of this faith, in sincerity you shall say to the mountain: Move. Nothing shall be impossible for you. They distrusted the power they had received, and so they failed. An active faith can move mountains—not of itself, but by virtue of a divine power engaged by a divine promise.

The Grace of Love

And now abide faith, hope, love, these three;
but the greatest of these is love.
1 CORINTHIANS 13:13

Here the apostle discusses charity, or love—true love to God and man. Without this, the most glorious gifts are nothing. (1) Tongues: It is the charitable heart, not the voluble tongue, that is acceptable with God; (2) Prophecy: The understanding of mysteries and knowledge without charity are as nothing; (3) Miraculous faith: One dram of charity is of much greater worth than all the faith of this sort. Saving faith is always found with charity, but the faith of miracles may be without it; (4) The outward acts of charity: There may be an open and lavish hand without a liberal and charitable heart; and (5) Suffering: If we sacrifice our lives for the faith, this will do us no good without charity.

Faith, hope, and love are the three principal graces, of which love is the chief. Faith fixes on the divine revelation and assents to that. Hope fastens on future happiness and waits for that. But love fastens on the divine perfections themselves. These will all shine forth in the most glorious splendors in another world, and there will love be made perfect. There we shall perfectly love God, and there we shall perfectly love one another. When faith and hope are at an end, true love will burn forever with the brightest flame. Where God is to be seen as He is, face-to-face, love is in its greatest height, and only there will it be perfected.

Hold onto Faith

Did you receive the Spirit by the works of the law,
or by the hearing of faith? Are you so foolish?
Having begun in the Spirit,
are you now being made perfect by the flesh?
GALATIANS 3:2–3

The apostle is dealing here with those who, having embraced the faith of Christ, still continued to seek justification by the works of the law. They did not adhere to the gospel way of justification, as they had been taught. Several things proved the folly of these Christians.

Jesus Christ had clearly been set forth and crucified among them. They had the doctrine of the cross preached to them and the sacrament of the Lord's Supper administered to them. He appeals to the experiences they had had of the working of the Spirit on their souls. He asks how they came by these gifts and graces. Was it by the works of the law or the hearing of faith? If they were truthful, they would say it was the latter. They had begun well, but now they expected to be advanced to higher degrees of perfection by adding their observance of the law to faith in Christ. Instead of being an improvement on the gospel, this was really a perversion of it. They were so far from being more perfect Christians that they were in danger of becoming no Christians at all.

The apostle had ministered the Spirit to them and wrought miracles among them. Did he do so by the works of the law or by the hearing of faith? They very well knew that it was the latter and could not be excused for forsaking such a clear doctrine.

Christian Unity

There is one body and one Spirit,
just as you were called in one hope of your calling;
one Lord, one faith, one baptism;
one God and Father of all,
who is above all,
and through all, and in you all.

EPHESIANS 4:4–6

The seat of Christian unity is in the heart or spirit. It does not lie in one set of thoughts or one form and mode of worship, but in one heart and one soul. This we should endeavor to keep.

Consider how many unities there are. There should be one heart, for there is one body and one spirit. Two hearts in one body would be monstrous. If there is only one body, all that belong to that body should have one heart. If we belong to Christ, we are all actuated by one and the same Spirit and therefore should be one. There is one Christ that they all hope in and one heaven that they are all hoping for; therefore, they should be of one heart. One Lord, that is, Christ. One faith, that is, the gospel or the same grace of faith whereby all Christians are saved. One baptism, by which we profess our faith. One God, who owns all the true members of the church for His children. And He is above all, and through all, by His providence upholding them, and in all believers by His Spirit.

Spiritual Warfare

*Taking the shield of faith with which
you will be able to quench all
the fiery darts of the wicked one.*

EPHESIANS 6:16

Christians must see that they are stout-hearted. Those who have so many battles to fight and who, on their way to heaven, must dispute every pass with the sword have need of a great deal of courage. A soldier can be ever so well armed, but if he does not have a good heart, his armor will stand him in little stead. Spiritual strength and courage are very necessary for our spiritual warfare. We do not have sufficient strength on our own; all our sufficiency is from God. In His strength we must go forth and go on. We must call in grace and help from heaven to enable us to do what we cannot do alone.

Faith is all to us in an hour of temptation. The breastplate secures the vitals, but with a shield we may turn every way. Faith is like a shield, a sort of universal defense. Our enemy the devil endeavors to make us wicked. His temptations are called fiery darts, an allusion to poisonous darts. Violent temptations, by which the soul is set on fire, are the darts that Satan shoots at us. Faith is the shield with which we must quench these darts, that they may not hit us or at least that they may not hurt us.

Spiritual Armor

But let us who are of the day be sober,
putting on the breastplate of faith and love,
and as a helmet the hope of salvation.

1 THESSALONIANS 5:8

Our spiritual enemies are many and mighty and malicious. We need to arm ourselves against their attempts, and this spiritual armor consists of the three great graces of Christians: faith, love, and hope. We must live by faith, and this will keep us watchful and sober. Faith will be our best defense against the assaults of our enemies. We must have a heart inflamed with love. True and fervent love of God and the things of God will keep us watchful and sober.

We must make salvation our hope. This good hope of eternal life will be a helmet to defend the head and hinder our being intoxicated with the pleasures of sin, which are but for a season. The apostle shows what grounds Christians have to hope for this salvation. He says nothing of their meriting it. No, the doctrine of our merits is altogether unscriptural and antiscriptural. Our hopes are to be grounded in God's appointment, because God appointed us to obtain salvation. If we would trace our salvation to the first cause, that is God's appointment. On this we build unshaken hope, especially when we consider Christ's merit and grace, and that salvation is by our Lord Jesus Christ, who died for us. Our salvation therefore is owning to and our hopes of it are grounded in Christ's atonement as well as God's appointment.

Not All Have Faith

And that we may be delivered from
unreasonable and wicked men;
for not all have faith.
But the Lord is faithful,
who will establish you
and guard you from the evil one.
2 THESSALONIANS 3:2–3

Those who are enemies of the preaching of the gospel are unreasonable and wicked men. There is the greatest absurdity in the world, as well as impiety. Godly and faithful ministers are like standard-bearers, who are most attacked. Many do not believe the gospel; no wonder they are restless in their endeavors to oppose the gospel and disgrace the ministers of the Word; and too many have neither common faith nor honesty. There is no confidence that we can safely put in them, and we should pray to be delivered from those who have no conscience of honor.

Paul encourages the Thessalonians to trust in God. What good may we expect from the grace of God? Establishment and preservation from evil. We stand no longer than God holds us up. We have as much need of the grace of God for our perseverance to the end as for the beginning of the good work.

What encouragement have we to depend on the grace of God? He is faithful to His promises. Once the promise is made, performance is sure and certain. He is a faithful God and a faithful friend. Let it be our care to be true and faithful in our promises and to our relations with this faithful God.

The Rewards of Faith

For to this end we both labor and suffer reproach,
because we trust in the living God,
who is the Savior of all men,
especially of those who believe.
1 TIMOTHY 4:10

What encouragement do we have to proceed in the ways of godliness? Will the profit balance the loss? Here is another of Paul's faithful sayings worthy of acceptance—that all our labors and losses in the service of God will be abundantly rewarded, so that though we lose for Christ, we shall not lose by Him.

Toil and trouble are to be expected by us in this world, not only as men, but as saints. Those who labor and suffer reproach in the service of God may depend on the living God that they shall not lose by it. He is the Savior of all men. Now, if He is the Savior of all men, we may infer that He will be the rewarder of those who seek and serve Him. The salvation He has in store for those who believe is sufficient to reward them for all their services and sufferings. The life of a Christian is a life of labor and suffering. The best we can expect to suffer in the present life is reproach for our well doing, for our work of faith and labor of love.

God's Faithfulness

*Let us hold fast the confession of
our hope without wavering,
for He who promised is faithful.*

HEBREWS 10:23

The faithful must draw near to God and in a right manner. They must draw near in conformity to God and communion with Him, still endeavoring to get nearer and nearer, until they come to dwell in His presence. We need a true heart. God is the searcher of hearts, and He requires truth in the inward parts. We need full assurance of faith. We should lay aside all sinful distrust. Without faith it is impossible to please God. We will be cleansed from guilt and whatever evils the consciences of men are subject to by reason of sin. Our bodies must be washed with pure water, the water of baptism or the sanctifying virtue of the Holy Spirit, cleansing us from the filthiness of the flesh as well as of the spirit.

Our spiritual enemies will do what they can to wrest our faith and hope out of our hands, but we must hold fast without wavering. Those who begin to waver are in danger of falling away. He who promised is faithful. There is no fickleness with Him, and there should be none with us. We must depend more on His promises to us than on our promises to Him.

Be Strong in Your Faith

Watch, stand fast in the faith,
be brave, be strong.
1 CORINTHIANS 16:13

The Corinthians were in manifest danger on many accounts. Their feuds ran high, the irregularities among them were very great, and there were deceivers among them. In such dangerous circumstances it was their concern to watch. If a Christian would be secure, he must be on his guard. Paul advises them to stand fast in the faith. A Christian should be fixed in the faith of the gospel. It is by this faith alone that he will be able to keep his ground in an hour of temptation; it is by this that we must overcome the world, both when it fawns and when it frowns. He advises them to act like men and be strong.

Professed Christians may bring upon themselves the most dreadful destruction. Many who have His name much in their mouths have no true love for Him in their hearts. And none love Him in truth who do not love His laws and keep His commandments. True faith in Christ will always be productive of sincere love for Him. Those who do not love Him cannot be believers in Him.

Faith Heals

Jesus turned around, and when He saw her He said,
"Be of good cheer, daughter;
your faith has made you well."
And the woman was made well from that hour.

MATTHEW 9:22

This woman's disease was of such a nature that her modesty would not allow her to speak openly to Christ for a cure, as others did, but she believed Him to have such an overflowing fullness of healing virtue that the very touch of His garment would cure her. Christ allowed this bashful patient to steal a cure unknown to anyone else, though she could not think how to do it unknown to Him. Now she was well content to be gone, for she had what she came for. But Christ was not willing to let her go. The triumphs of her faith must be to her praise and honor. He turned and discovered her. He called her "daughter," for He spoke to her with the tenderness of a father, and He bid her to be of good cheer, telling her that her faith had made her whole. Her bodily cure was the fruit of faith, of her faith, and that made it a happy, comfortable cure indeed.

Active Faith

But without faith it is impossible to please Him,
for he who comes to God must believe that He is,
and that He is a rewarder of those who diligently seek Him.
HEBREWS 11:6

We cannot please God without a faith that helps us to walk with God, an active faith. God has prescribed means and ways whereby He may be found. Those who would find God must seek Him diligently, and once they have found Him, they will never repent the pains they have spent in seeking Him.

Through Noah's faith, he and his house were saved when a whole world of sinners was perishing about them. His holy fear condemned their vain confidence, his faith condemned their unbelief, and his obedience condemned their contempt. Good examples will either convert sinners or condemn them. This is the best way the people of God can take to condemn the wicked: not by harsh and censorious language, but by a holy, exemplary conversation.

Abraham put himself into the hand of God to send him wherever He pleased. All who are called resign their own will and wisdom to the will and wisdom of God. Though they know not always their way, they know their guide.

Faith Overcomes

For whatever is born of God overcomes the world.
And this is the victory that has overcome the world—
our faith. Who is he who overcomes the world,
but he who believes that Jesus is the Son of God?
1 JOHN 5:4–5

Faith is the cause of victory. In and by faith, we cling to Christ in opposition to the world. Faith receives and derives strength from the object of it, the Son of God, for conquering the world. It is the real Christian who is the true conqueror of the world; he who believes that Jesus came from God to be the Savior of the world. And he who so believes must by this faith overcome the world. He sees it must be a great part of the Savior's work and of his own salvation to be redeemed and rescued from this malignant world. He perceives that the Lord Jesus conquered the world, not for Himself only, but for His followers. He is possessed with a spirit and disposition that cannot be satisfied with the world, that looks beyond it. It is the Christian revelation that is the great means of conquering the world and gaining another that is blessed and eternal. The Savior designs not this world for the inheritance and portion of His saved company. It is the real Christian who is the proper hero, who vanquishes the world. Who in all the world but a believer of Jesus Christ can thus overcome the world?

Robes of Glory

For we walk by faith,
not by sight.
2 CORINTHIANS 5:7

There is a groaning of desire for the happiness of another life, and thus believers groan. The believer is willing to be absent from the body in order to be present with the Lord, to put off these rags of mortality and put on the robes of glory. Gracious souls are not found naked in the other world; no, they are clothed with garments of praise.

Believers have assurance of this future blessedness from the experience of the grace of God. All who are designed for heaven in the future are worked or prepared for heaven while they are here. The stones of that spiritual building above are squared and fashioned here below. No hand less than the hand of God can work this thing for us. The promise of the Spirit gave them this assurance.

Now believers are absent from the Lord. God is with us here; yet we are not with Him as we hope to be, for we walk by faith, not by sight. Faith is for this world, and sight is reserved for the other world. How comfortable and courageous we ought to be in the hour of death. They should be willing rather to die than live, when it is the will of God that they should put off this tabernacle, to close their eyes to all things in this world and open them in a world of glory. Faith will be turned into sight.

Pray Always

*Praying always with all prayer
and supplication in the Spirit,
being watchful to this end with all perseverance
and supplication for all the saints.*

EPHESIANS 6:18

Prayer must buckle on all the other parts of our Christian armor. We must join prayer with all these graces, and we must pray always. Not as though we were to do nothing else but pray, for there are other duties that are to be done in their place and season, but we should keep up constant times of prayer. We must pray on all occasions. We must intermix prayers with other duties and with common business. Though set and solemn prayer may sometimes be unseasonable, yet pious prayers can never be so. We must pray with all prayer and supplication, with all kinds of prayer. We must pray in the Spirit, by the grace of God's good Spirit. We must watch, endeavoring to keep our hearts in a praying frame and taking all occasions for the duty. This we must do with all perseverance. We must continue in it as long as we live in the world. And we must pray with supplication, not only for ourselves but for all saints. None are so much saints and in so good a condition in this world that they do not need our prayers, and they ought to have them.

Prayer and Confession

Confess your trespasses to one another,
and pray for one another,
that you may be healed.
The effective, fervent prayer of
a righteous man avails much.
JAMES 5:16

Christians are directed to confess their faults to one another. The confession here required is that of Christians to one another, where persons have tempted one another to sin or have consented in the same evil actions. So far as confession is necessary to our reconciliation with such as are at variance with us or for reparation of wrongs done to any, making our own spirits quiet and easy, so far we should be ready to confess our faults. And sometimes it may be of good use to Christians to disclose their peculiar weaknesses and infirmities to one another. Those who make confession of their faults should thereupon pray with and for one another.

The great advantage and efficacy of prayer are declared and proved. He who prays must be a righteous man. The prayer itself must be a fervent, in-wrought, well-wrought prayer. Such prayer avails much. It is of great advantage to ourselves, it may be very beneficial to our friends, and we are assured of its being acceptable to God.

Ask in Faith

If any of you lacks wisdom, let him ask of God,
who gives to all liberally and without reproach,
and it will be given to him.
But let him ask in faith, with no doubting,
for he who doubts is like a wave of the sea
driven and tossed by the wind.

JAMES 1:5–6

We should not pray so much for the removal of an affliction as for wisdom to make a right use of it. To be wise in trying times is a special gift of God. In what way is this to be obtained? Upon our asking for it. We have the greatest encouragement to do this. He to whom we are sent has it to give, and He is of a giving disposition. Nor is there any fear of His favors being limited to some, for He gives to all men. If you should say you want a great deal of wisdom, that a small portion will not serve your needs, He gives liberally; and lest you should be afraid of being put to shame for your folly, He upbraideth not. Ask when you will and as often as you will, you will meet with no upbraidings. The promise is: It shall be given him.

There is one thing necessary to be observed in our asking: There must be no wavering, no staggering at the promise of God through unbelief. Sincerity of intention and a steadiness of mind constitute another duty required under affliction. To be sometimes lifted up by faith and then thrown down again by distrust—this is very fitly compared to a wave of the sea that rises and falls, swells and sinks, just as the wind tosses it higher or lower, that way or this. The success of prayer is spoiled thereby.

Prayer and Illness

And the prayer of faith will save the sick,
and the Lord will raise him up.
And if he has committed sins,
he will be forgiven.
JAMES 5:15

We have particular directions given as to sick persons. It is
the duty of sick people to send for ministers and ask their assistance with their prayers. It is the duty of ministers to pray
over the sick, when this is desired and called for. Once the
sick were to be anointed with oil in the name of the Lord.
When miracles ceased, this institution ceased also. Some have
thought that it should not be wholly laid aside, but that where
there are extraordinary measures of faith in the person anointing and in those who are anointed, an extraordinary blessing
may attend the observance of this direction for the sick. There
is one thing to carefully be observed here: The saving of the
sick is not ascribed to the anointing with oil but to prayer.
Prayer over the sick must proceed from and be accompanied
with a lively faith. There must be faith both in the person praying and in the person prayed for. And, if he has committed sins,
they will be forgiven him. The great thing we should beg of
God for ourselves and others in the time of sickness is the pardon of sin. Sin is both the root of sickness and the sting of it.
If sin is pardoned, either the affliction will be removed in mercy
or we shall see there is mercy in the continuance of it.

Cry Out in Faith

He will be very gracious to you
at the sound of your cry;
when He hears it, He will answer you.
ISAIAH 30:19

At the sound of our cry, the cry of necessity, when it is most urgent and fervent, God will be gracious to us. When He hears it, nothing more is needed. At the first word, He will answer and say, "Here I am." Those who were disturbed in the possession of their estates shall again enjoy them quietly. When the danger is over, the people will dwell in Zion, at Jerusalem, as they used to do; they shall dwell safely, free from the fear of evil. Those who dwell in Zion, the holy city, will find enough there to wipe away tears from their eyes. This is grounded on two great truths. The Lord is a God of judgment. He is both wise and just in all the disposals of His providence, true to His word and tender of His people. Therefore, all those are blessed who wait for Him, who not only wait on Him with their prayers, but wait for Him with their hopes.

A Prayer-Hearing God

"Ask, and it will be given to you;
seek, and you will find; knock,
and it will be opened to you."
MATTHEW 7:7

Here is a precept in three words: *ask, seek, knock.* That is, in one word, "Pray, pray, and pray again." Ask as a beggar asks alms. Those who would be rich in grace must take to the poor trade of begging, and they shall find it a thriving trade. Ask; represent your wants and burdens to God. Ask as a traveler asks the way; to pray is to inquire of God. Seek as if seeking a thing of value that you have lost. Seek by prayer. Knock as he who desires to enter into the house knocks at the door. Sin has shut and barred the door against us, but by prayer we knock: "Lord, Lord, open to us." Christ knocks at our door and allows us to knock at His, which is a favor we do not allow to common beggars. Seeking and knocking imply something more than asking and praying. We must not only ask, but seek; we must second our prayers with our endeavors. We must, by the appointed means, seek that for which we ask, else we tempt God. We must not only ask, but knock; we must come to God's door, must ask importunately: not only pray, but plead and watch with God.

There is a promise added: Our labor in prayer, if we do indeed labor at it, shall not be in vain. When God finds a praying heart, He will be found a prayer-hearing God. He will give you an answer of peace.

Our Freedom to Call for Help

The LORD is near to all who call upon Him,
to all who call upon Him in truth.
He will fulfill the desire of those who fear Him.

PSALM 145:18–19

With respect to all those who are heavy laden under the burden of sin, if they come to Christ by faith, He will ease them, He will raise them. He is very ready to hear and answer the prayers of His people. In this appears the grace of His kingdom: that His subjects have not only the liberty of petitioning but all the encouragement that can be to petition. It was said that He satisfies the desire of every living thing; much more will He fulfill the desire of those who fear Him, for He who feeds His birds will not starve His babes. He will hear their call and will save them.

He will hear and help us if we worship and serve Him with a holy awe of Him. In all devotions, inward impressions must be answerable to the outward expressions, or else they are not performed in truth. He takes those under His special protection who have confidence in Him. The Lord preserves all those who love Him. The psalmist concludes (v. 21): "My mouth shall speak the praise of the LORD." When we have said what we can in praising God, there is still more to be said. As the end of one mercy is the beginning of another, so should the end of one thanksgiving be. While I have breath to draw, my mouth shall still speak God's praises. Let all flesh, all mankind, bless His holy name forever.

Where Do I Pray?

"But you, when you pray, go into your room,
and when you have shut your door,
pray to your Father who is in the secret place;
and your Father who sees in secret will reward you openly."
MATTHEW 6:6

Instead of praying publicly, go into some place of privacy and retirement. Isaac went into the field, Christ to the mountain, Peter to the housetop. No place is wrong if it answers the end. Yet if the circumstances are such that we cannot possibly avoid being taken notice of, we must not, therefore, neglect the duty, lest the omission is a greater scandal than the observation of it.

Instead of doing it to be seen of men, pray to your Father who is in secret. The Pharisees prayed to men, not to God. Pray to God, and let that be enough. Pray to Him as a Father, as your Father, ready to hear and answer, graciously inclined to pity, help, and comfort you. Pray to your Father who is in secret. He is there in your room when no one else is there, especially close to you in whatever you call on Him for.

Your Father sees in secret. There is not a secret or sudden breathing after God that He does not observe. He will reward you openly. They have their reward who pray openly, and you shall not lose yours for praying in secret. It is called a reward, but it is of grace, not of debt. Sometimes secret prayers are rewarded openly in this world by unusual answers to them, which manifest God's praying people in the consciences of their adversaries.

Persevering in Prayer

As for me, I will call upon God,
and the LORD shall save me.
Evening and morning and at noon I will pray,
and cry aloud, and He shall hear my voice.
PSALM 55:16–17

David persevered in his resolution to call upon God, being well assured that he should not seek Him in vain. "As for me, let them take what course they please to secure themselves, let violence and strife be their guards, prayer shall be mine; this I have found comfort in, and therefore this will I abide by: I will call upon God, and commit myself to Him, and the Lord shall save me. I will pray and cry aloud. I will meditate."

He will pray frequently, every day, and three times a day—evening, morning, and at noon. Those who think three meals a day little enough for the body ought much more to think three solemn prayers a day little enough for the soul and to count it a pleasure, not a task. It was Daniel's practice to pray three times a day, and noon was one of Peter's hours of prayer. David assured himself that God would in due time give an answer of peace to his prayers.

The Wicked Scorn God

*" 'Who is the Almighty, that we should serve Him?
And what profit do we have if we pray to Him?' "*
JOB 21:15

Job shows how the wicked abuse their prosperity and are confirmed and hardened by it in their impiety. God allows them to prosper, but let us not wonder at that, for the prosperity of fools destroys them by hardening them in sin. How light these prospering sinners make of God and religion; as if because they have so much of this world, they had no need to look after another. The world is the portion they have chosen, and take up with, and think themselves happy in, while they believe they can live without God.

"Who is the Almighty, that we should serve Him?" How slightly they speak of God, as if He were a mere name. How hardly they speak of religion. They call it a service that they look on as a task and drudgery. They will not believe it is in their interest to be religious. It was not their might or the power of their hand that got them this wealth, and therefore they ought to remember God, who gave it to them. Nor can they keep it without God, and therefore they are very unwise to lose their interest in Him and bid Him to depart from them.

"Therefore," says Job, "the counsel of the wicked is far from me. Far be it from me that I should be of their mind, say as they say, do as they do, and take my measures from them. I know better things than to walk in their counsel."

Prayer and Meditation

Give ear to my words, O LORD,
consider my meditation.
Give heed to the voice of my cry,
my King and my God,
for to You I will pray.
PSALM 5:1–2

In these verses David prays to God as a prayer-hearing God. Such He has always been, ever since men began to call upon the name of the Lord, and yet is still as ready to hear prayer as ever. David here calls Him "O Lord, Jehovah," a self-existent, self-sufficient Being whom we are bound to adore, and, "my King and my God, to whom I have sworn allegiance, and under whose protection I have put myself as my King." We believe that the God we pray to is a King and a God. The most powerful plea in prayer is to look upon Him as *our* King and *our* God.

What David prays for here, which may encourage our faith and hopes in all our addresses to God, is: "Give ear to my words, O Lord." Men perhaps will not or cannot hear us; our enemies are so haughty that they will not; our friends are at such a distance that they cannot. But God, though high, though in heaven, can and will. "Consider my meditation." David's prayers were not his words only, but his meditations. Meditation and prayer should go together. David promises that he will pray. The assurances God has given us of His readiness to hear prayer should confirm our resolution to live and die praying.

Prayer and Oppression

"But I say to you, love your enemies,
bless those who curse you,
do good to those who hate you,
and pray for those who spitefully
use you and persecute you."
MATTHEW 5:44

Though men are ever so bad themselves and carry it ever so basely toward us, yet that does not discharge us from the great debt we owe them of love to our kind, love to our kin. It is the great duty of Christians to love their enemies. While we cannot have complacency in one who is openly wicked and profane, yet we must take notice, with pleasure, of that even in our enemies which is amiable and commendable, and love that, though they are our enemies. We must have compassion for them and goodwill toward them.

We must pray for them who despitefully use us and persecute us. Christ Himself was so treated. When at any time we meet with such usage, we have an opportunity of showing our conformity both to the precept and to the example of Christ by praying for them who thus abuse us. We must pray that God will forgive them, that they may never fare the worse for anything they have done against us, and that He would make them to be at peace with us. This is heaping coals of fire on their heads.

Prayers as Praise and Thanksgiving

"In this manner, therefore, pray:
Our Father in heaven,
hallowed be Your name."
MATTHEW 6:9

Because we know not what to pray for, Jesus helps our infirmities by putting words into our mouths. Not that we are tied to the use of this form only, as if this were necessary to the consecrating of our other prayers. We are told to pray in this manner, with these words, or to this effect. Yet, without doubt, it is very good to use it as a form, and it is a pledge of the communion of saints, having been used by the church in all ages. It is used acceptably when it is used with understanding and without vain repetition.

Prayer is a form of praise and thanksgiving. The best pleading with God is praise. Praise is the way to obtain mercy, since it qualifies us to receive it. We praise God and give Him glory, not because He needs it—He is praised by a world of angels—but because He deserves it. Praise is the work and happiness of heaven, and all who would go to heaven must begin their heaven now. It becomes us to be copious in praising God. A true saint never thinks he can speak honorably enough of God.

The Spirit and Our Prayers

For we do not know what we should pray for as we ought,
but the Spirit Himself makes intercession for us
with groanings which cannot be uttered.
ROMANS 8:26

The Spirit helps our infirmities, especially our praying infirmities. The Spirit in the word helps. The Spirit in the heart helps. For this end the Holy Ghost was poured out. He helps, heaves with us, over against us, helps as we help one who would lift up a burden by lifting with him at the other end. We must not sit still and expect that the Spirit will do it all; when the Spirit goes before us, we must bestir ourselves. We cannot without God, and He will not without us. The Spirit itself makes intercession for us. Christ intercedes for us in heaven, and the Spirit intercedes for us in our hearts. So graciously has God provided for the encouragement of the praying remnant.

Now this intercession that the Spirit makes is with groanings that cannot be uttered. There may be praying in the Spirit when there is not a word spoken. It is not the rhetoric and eloquence, but the faith and fervency of our prayers that the Spirit works in us. We know not what to say or how to express ourselves. When we can only cry, "Abba, Father," with a holy, humble boldness, this is the work of the Spirit. The Spirit interceding in us evermore melts our wills into the will of God.

Prayers for All

Therefore I exhort first of all that supplications,
prayers, intercessions,
and giving of thanks be made for all men.
1 TIMOTHY 2:1

This is Paul's charge to Christians to pray for all men in general and particularly for all in authority. Paul does not send Timothy any prescribed form of prayer. Paul thought it enough to give them general heads; they, having the Scripture to direct them in prayer poured out on them, needed no further directions. The disciples of Christ must be praying people. There must be prayers for ourselves in the first place. This is implied here. We must also pray for all men. Though the kings at this time were heathens, yet they must pray for them. We must give thanks for them, pray for their welfare and for the welfare of their kingdoms, that in the peace thereof we may have peace. The summit of the ambition of good Christians is to lead a quiet and peaceable life. We cannot expect to be kept quiet and peaceable unless we keep in all godliness and honesty. Here we have our duty as Christians summed up in two words: godliness, that is, the right worshiping of God; and honesty, that is, good conduct toward all men. These two must go together. Christians are to be men much given to prayer. In our prayers we are to have a generous concern for others, as well as for ourselves; we are to pray for all men and to give thanks for all men.

Solomon's Prayer

*"Yet regard the prayer of Your servant and his supplication,
O LORD my God, and listen to the cry and the prayer
which Your servant is praying before You today."*
1 KINGS 8:28

Solomon first made a general surrender of the temple to God, which God had signified His acceptance of by taking possession. Next followed Solomon's prayer, his request that this temple may be deemed and taken not only for a house of sacrifice, but a house of prayer for all people. In this way it was a type of the gospel church.

First, Solomon prays in general that God would graciously hear and answer the prayer he was now praying. It was a humble prayer, an earnest prayer, a prayer made in faith. "Lord, hearken to it, have respect for it, not as the prayer of Israel's king but as the prayer of thy servant." Next, he prayed that God would in like manner hear and answer all the prayers that should, at any time hereafter, be made in or toward this house that he has now built. "Hear it in heaven, that is indeed your dwelling place, and, when you hear, forgive." None but priests could enter into that most holy place, but when anyone worshiped in the courts of the temple, it must be with an eye toward it, as an instituted medium of their worship, helping the weakness of their faith and typifying the mediation of Jesus Christ, who is the true temple.

An Answer to Each Prayer

He shall regard the prayer of the destitute,
and shall not despise their prayer.

PSALM 102:17

The prayers of God's people now seem to be slighted and no notice taken of them, but they will be reviewed and greatly encouraged. He will regard the prayer of the destitute. They are destitute. It is an elegant word that is used here, which signifies the heath in the wilderness, a low shrub or bush like the hyssop of the wall. They are in a low and broken state, enriched with spiritual blessings but destitute of temporal good things. When we consider our own poverty, our darkness and deadness, and the manifold defects in our prayers, we have cause to suspect that our prayers will be received with disdain in heaven. But we are assured here of the contrary, for we have an advocate with the Father and are under grace, not under the law. This shall be written for the generation to come, that none may despair, though they be destitute or think their prayers are forgotten because they are not answered immediately. Many who are now unborn shall, by reading the history of the church, praise the Lord for His answers to prayer.

God takes notice not only of the prayers of His afflicted people, which are the language of grace, but even of their groans, which are the language of nature.

The Minister's Priorities

"But we will give ourselves continually to prayer and to the ministry of the word."
ACTS 6:4

Preaching the gospel is the best work in which a minister can be employed. He must not entangle himself in the affairs of this life, no, not in the outward business of the house of God.

The apostles want to devote themselves wholly to their work as ministers, if they can be relieved of their charitable duties. "We will give ourselves continually to prayer and to the ministry of the Word." See here the two great gospel ordinances—the *Word* and *prayer.* By these two, the kingdom of Christ must be advanced and additions made to it. What is the great business of gospel ministers? To give themselves totally to prayer and to the ministry of the Word. They must be God's mouth to the people in the ministry of the Word and the people's mouth to God in prayer.

In order to secure the conviction and conversion of sinners and the edification and consolation of saints, we must not only offer up our prayers for them, but we must minister the Word to them. Nor must we only minister the Word to them, but we must pray for them. God's grace can do all without our preaching, but our preaching can do nothing without God's grace. Ministers who give themselves continually to prayer and the ministry of the Word are truly the successors of the apostles.

Let Your Requests Be Made Known

Be anxious for nothing,
but in everything by prayer and supplication,
with thanksgiving, let your requests be made known to God;
and the peace of God, which surpasses all understanding,
will guard your hearts and minds through Christ Jesus.

PHILIPPIANS 4:6–7

A caution against disquieting, perplexing care: "Be anxious for nothing." Avoid anxious care and distracting thought in the wants and difficulties of life. It is the duty and interest of Christians to live without care. There is a care of diligence that is our duty, but there is a care of distrust that is our sin and folly.

The author recommends constant prayer. "In everything by prayer and supplication, with thanksgiving, let your requests be made known to God." We must pray for every emergency, "in everything by prayer." When anything burdens our spirits, we must ease our minds by prayer; when our affairs are perplexed or distressed, we must seek direction and support. We must join thanksgiving with our prayers and supplications. We must not only seek supplies of good, but have receipts of mercy. Prayer is the offering up of our desires to God. Not that God needs to be told either our wants or desires, but He would like to hear of them from us. The effect of this will be the peace of God. The peace of God is a greater good than can be sufficiently valued or duly expressed. This peace will keep our hearts and minds through Jesus Christ. It will keep us from sinning under our troubles and from sinking under them.

Believe in Your Prayer

"Therefore I say to you,
whatever things you ask when you pray,
believe that you receive them,
and you will have them."
MARK 11:24

Christ taught the apostles to pray in faith, to have faith in God. They admired the power of Christ's word of command. "Why," said Christ, "a lively active faith would put as great a power into your prayers. Whoever shall say to this mountain, 'Be removed, and be cast into the sea'; and if he shall not doubt in his heart but shall believe that those things which he saith shall come to pass, he shall have whatsoever he saith." Through the strength and power of God in Christ, the greatest difficulty shall be got over, and the thing shall be effected. And "Therefore I say to you, whatever things you ask when you pray, believe that you receive them, and you will have them."

Now this is to be applied to that faith of miracles that the apostles and first preachers of the gospel were endued with. It may be applied to that miracle of faith that all true Christians are endued with. It justifies us and so removes mountains of guilt and casts them into the depths of the sea. It purifies the heart and so removes mountains of corruption. It is by faith that the world is conquered, Satan's fiery darts are quenched, and a soul is crucified with Christ and yet lives.

Teach Us to Pray

Now it came to pass, as He was praying in a certain place,
when He ceased, that one of His disciples said to Him,
"Lord, teach us to pray, as John also taught his disciples."

LUKE 11:1

Prayer is one of the great laws of natural religion. One great design of Christianity is to assist us in prayer, enforce the duty upon us, to instruct us in it, and to encourage us to expect advantage by it.

We find Christ Himself praying in a certain place. His disciples approached Him for direction in prayer. They came to Him with this request when He ceased praying, for they would not disturb Him when He was at prayer. One of His disciples said, "Lord, teach us." It becomes the disciples of Christ to apply themselves to Him for instruction in prayer. "Lord, teach us to pray" is itself a good prayer and a very needful one, for it is a hard thing to pray well, and it is only Jesus Christ who can teach us, by His Word and Spirit, how to pray.

Their plea was, "As John also taught his disciples. He took care to instruct his disciples in this necessary duty, and we would be taught as they were." While the Jews' prayers were generally adorations, praises of God, and doxologies, John taught his disciples prayers filled with petitions and requests. Christ taught His disciples a prayer consisting wholly of petitions, even omitting the doxology and the Amen.

Christ gave them direction, just the same as He had given them before in His Sermon on the Mount. They would find all their requests couched in these few words and would be able to explain and enlarge on them in their own words.

Joint Prayer

So, when he had considered this,
he came to the house of Mary,
the mother of John whose surname was Mark,
where many were gathered together praying.
ACTS 12:12

Peter considered how imminent his danger was, how great his deliverance, and what he had to do now. God's providence leaves room for the use of our prudence and, though He has undertaken to perform and perfect what He has begun, yet He expects we should consider the circumstances. Peter went directly to a friend's house, the house of Mary, a sister of Barnabas and the mother of John Mark. A church in the house makes it a little sanctuary.

There he found many who were gathered together praying in the dead of the night for him. They continued in prayer in token of the importunity. As long as we are kept waiting for a mercy, we must continue praying for it. It might seem that now when the affair came near to a crisis, they were more fervent in prayer than before, and this was a good sign that God intended to deliver Peter. They knew what an encouragement Christ gave to joint prayer. It was always the practice of God's praying people to unite their forces in prayer. Many had gotten together for this work. No doubt there were many private Christians who knew how to pray and to pray pertinently and to continue long in prayer. Peter came to them when they were thus employed. It was as if God were saying, "You are praying that Peter may be restored to you. Now here he is."

Pray Exceedingly

For what thanks can we render to God for you,
for all the joy with which we rejoice for your sake
before our God, night and day praying exceedingly
that we may see your face and perfect
what is lacking in your faith?

1 THESSALONIANS 3:9–10

When we are most cheerful, we should be most thankful. Paul speaks as if he could not tell how to express his thankfulness to God or his joy and rejoicing for their sakes. His heart was enlarged with love for them and with thanksgiving to God. He prayed for them night and day. In the midst of the business of the day or slumber of the night, he lifted up his heart to God in prayer. When we are most thankful, we should always give ourselves to prayer. There was something still lacking in their faith; Paul desired that this might be perfected and wanted to see their faces in order to accomplish that. He desired to be instrumental in the further benefit of the Thessalonians, and the only way to do this while at a distance was by prayer for them, together with his writing or sending to them.

He prays to God and Christ. Prayer is not only to be offered in the name of Christ, but offered up to Christ Himself, as our Lord and our Savior. Paul prays that their way might be shown to them. The taking of a journey to this or that place, one would think, depends on one's own will and lies in his own power. But the apostle knew that God our Father directs and orders His children where to go and what to do. Let us acknowledge God in all our ways, and He will direct our paths.

Prayer Opens Heaven

When all the people were baptized,
it came to pass that Jesus also was baptized;
and while He prayed, the heaven was opened.
And the Holy Spirit descended in bodily form like a dove
upon Him, and a voice came from heaven which said,
"You are My beloved Son; in You I am well pleased."
LUKE 3:21–22

When all the people were baptized, then Jesus was baptized. Christ would be baptized last, among the common people and after them. He saw what multitudes were hereby prepared to receive Him, and then He appeared.

Notice is here taken of Christ's praying when He was baptized, which was not in Matthew: being baptized and praying. He prayed as others did, for this is the way He would keep communion with His Father. He prayed for the discovery of His Father's favor to Him and the descent of the Spirit. What was promised to Christ, He needed to obtain by prayer: "Ask of me and I will give thee. . . ."

When He prayed, heaven was opened. Sin had shut up heaven, but Christ's prayer opened it again. Prayer is an ordinance that opens heaven: "Knock, and it shall be opened unto you."

The Holy Ghost descended in a bodily shape like a dove upon Him. When He begins to preach, the Spirit of the Lord is upon Him. This is expressed as sensible evidence for His encouragement in His work and for the satisfaction of John the Baptist, who was told before that by this sign he would be notified who was the Christ.

Then, there came a voice from heaven, "You are My beloved Son."

Answered Prayer

And she said, "O my lord!
As your soul lives, my lord,
I am the woman who stood by you here,
praying to the LORD. For this child I prayed,
and the LORD has granted me my petition
which I asked of Him.
Therefore I also have lent him to the LORD."

1 SAMUEL 1:26–28

These verses are about the solemn entering of Samuel into the service of the sanctuary. Some think it was as soon as he was weaned from the breast, which, the Jews say, was not until he was three years old. Others think it was not until he was weaned from childish things at eight or ten years old. It is said, "The child was young" (v. 24). Observe how his mother presented her child with a sacrifice of no less than three bullocks, with a meat offering for each. A bullock, perhaps, for each year of the child's life, or one for a burnt offering, another for a sin offering, and the third for a peace offering. She sacrificed with a grateful acknowledgment of God's goodness in answer to prayer. This she makes to Eli, because he had encouraged her to hope for an answer of peace. "For this child I prayed." She made a full surrender of all her interest in this child unto the Lord. "For this child I prayed." Whatever we give to God, it is what we have first asked and received from Him. "Of thy own, Lord, have we given thee." Whatever we give to God may upon this account be said to be lent to Him. When by baptism we dedicate our children to God, let us remember that they were His before by sovereign right and that they are ours still so much the more to our comfort.

Public Prayer

"And when you pray,
you shall not be like the hypocrites.
For they love to pray standing in the synagogues
and on the corners of the streets,
that they may be seen by men."
MATTHEW 6:5

It is taken for granted that all the disciples of Christ pray. You may as soon find a living man who does not breathe as a living Christian who does not pray. If prayerless, then graceless.

Now there were two great faults hypocrites were guilty of in prayer: vainglory and vain repetitions. We must not be proud and vainglorious in prayer, nor aim at the praise of men. And here observe the way and practice of the hypocrites: In all their exercises of devotion, it was plain that the chief thing they aimed at was to be commended by their neighbors. When they seemed to soar upwards in prayer, their eye was downwards upon this as their prey. Observe the places they chose for their devotion. They prayed in the synagogues, which were indeed proper places for public prayer, but not for personal prayer. They prayed on the corners of the streets, the broad streets that were most frequented. It was to cause themselves to be taken notice of.

Their pride in choosing those public places is expressed this way: They love to pray there. They did not love prayer for its own sake, but they loved it when it gave them an opportunity of making themselves noticed. It is that they may be seen of men, not that God might accept them, but that men might admire and applaud them.

The Prayers of the Saints

Then another angel, having a golden censer,
came and stood at the altar.
He was given much incense,
that he should offer it with the prayers
of all the saints upon the golden altar
which was before the throne.

REVELATION 8:3

The opening of the last seal. This was to introduce a new set of events. There was a profound silence in heaven for the space of half an hour, a silence of expectation. Great things were upon the wheel of providence, and the church of God, both in heaven and on earth, stood silent to see what God was doing.

The trumpets were delivered to the angels who were to sound them.

To prepare for this, another angel must first offer incense. This incense he was to offer up, with the prayers of all the saints, upon the golden altar. All the saints are a praying people; none of the children of God are born dumb. Times of danger should be praying times, and so should times of great expectation. Both our fears and our hopes should lead us to prayer. The prayers of the saints themselves need the incense and intercession of Christ to make them acceptable and effectual. No prayer thus recommended was ever denied audience or acceptance. These prayers that were thus accepted in heaven produced great changes upon earth. The same angel took of the fire from the altar in the same censer and cast it to the earth, and this presently caused strange commotions: noises, and thunderings, and lightnings, and an earthquake. And now, all things being prepared, the angels discharge their duty.

Continuing in Prayer

Now it came to pass in those days that
He went out to the mountain to pray,
and continued all night in prayer to God.
LUKE 6:12

In this verse, we have our Lord Jesus in secret.

In secret, we have Him praying to God. This evangelist takes frequent notice of Christ's retirements, to give us an example of secret prayer, without which it is impossible that the soul should prosper. In those days when His enemies were filled with madness against Him, He went out to pray. He was alone with God; He went out to a mountain to pray, where He might have no disturbance or interruption. He was alone with God for a long time: He "continued all night in prayer." We think one half hour a great deal, but Christ continued a whole night in meditation and secret prayer. We have a great deal of business at the throne of grace, and we should take great delight in communion with God, and by both of these, we may be kept sometimes long in prayer.

After He had continued all night in prayer, one would think that when day came, He would have rested. But as soon as anybody was stirring, He called them to Him. In serving God, our great care should be not to lose time but to make the end of one good duty the beginning of another.

The Upper Room

*These all continued with one accord
in prayer and supplication,
with the women and Mary the mother of Jesus,
and with His brothers.*

ACTS 1:14

Who were the disciples who stayed together? The eleven apostles are named (v. 13), as is Mary, the mother of our Lord. This is the last time that any mention is made of her. There were others: the brothers of our Lord, and to make up the hundred and twenty spoken of (v. 15), we may suppose that all or most of the seventy disciples were with them.

"These all continued with one accord in prayer and supplication." All God's people are praying people. It was now a time of trouble and anger, and, "Is any afflicted? Let him pray." They had new work before them, and before they entered upon it, they were instant in prayer to God. Before they were first sent forth, Christ spent time in prayer for them, and now they spent time in prayer for themselves. Those are in the best frame of mind to receive spiritual blessing who are in a praying frame of mind. God will be asked for promised mercies, and the nearer the answer seems to be, the more earnest we should be in prayer for it. They continued in prayer. Praise for the promise is a decent way of begging for the performance, and praise for former mercy is a good way of begging further mercy. Those who pray with one accord keep the unity of the Spirit in the bond of peace and are best prepared to receive the comforts of the Holy Ghost.

The Value of Scripture Study

All Scripture is given by inspiration of God,
and is profitable for doctrine, for reproof,
for correction, for instruction in righteousness,
that the man of God may be complete,
thoroughly equipped for every good work.
2 TIMOTHY 3:16–17

Those who would acquaint themselves with the things of God must know the Holy Scriptures. They must not be neglected by us and seldom or never studied. The prophets and apostles did not speak independently; what they received of the Lord, they delivered to us.

What use will Scripture be to us? It is able to make us wise to salvation. Those are wise indeed who are wise to salvation. The Scriptures will make us wise to salvation if they are mixed with faith. But if we do not believe their truth and goodness, they will do us no good. Scripture is profitable to us for all the purposes of the Christian life. It instructs us in that which is true, reproves us for that which is wrong, and directs us in that which is good. That which equips a man of God in this world is the Scripture. By it we are thoroughly furnished for every good work. Scripture has various uses and answers different ends and purposes. Scripture is a perfect rule of faith and practice. If we consult the Scripture and follow its directions, we shall be made men of God, perfected and thoroughly furnished to do every good work. Oh that we may love our Bibles more and keep them closer than ever!

The Power of Scripture

For the word of God is living and powerful,
and sharper than any two-edged sword. . .
and is a discerner of the thoughts and intents of the heart.

HEBREWS 4:12

The Word of God gives us great help in attaining the peace we need. It is living, very lively and active in seizing the conscience of the sinner, in cutting him to the heart, and in comforting him and binding up the wounds of the soul. It is powerful. It convinces powerfully, converts powerfully, and comforts powerfully. It is powerful enough to batter down Satan's kingdom and set up the kingdom of Christ upon the ruins. It is sharper than any two-edged sword. It will enter where no other sword can and make a more critical dissection. It pierces to the dividing asunder of the soul and the spirit, the soul and its habitual prevailing temper. It makes a soul that has been proud for a long time humble, a soul that has been perverse meek and obedient. This sword divides between the joints and the marrow. It can make men willing to undergo the sharpest operation for the mortifying of sin. It is a discerner of the thoughts and intents of the heart. The Word will turn the sinner inside out and let him see all that is in his heart.

God's Word Gives Light

The entrance of Your words gives light;
it gives understanding to the simple.
PSALM 119:130

The Word of God gives us admirable discoveries of God and Christ and another world, admirable proofs of divine love and grace. The majesty of the style, the purity of the matter, and the harmony of the parts are all wonderful. Its effects on the consciences of men for conviction and comfort are wonderful.

The great use for which the Word of God was intended is to give light, that is, to give understanding. Even the entrance of God's Word gives light. If we begin at the beginning and take it before us, we shall find that the very first verses of the Bible give us surprising and yet satisfying discoveries of the origin of the universe. We find we begin to see when we begin to study the Word of God. Some understand it as the New Testament, which is the opening or unfolding of the Old, which would give light concerning life and immortality. It shows us a way to heaven so plain that wayfaring men, though fools, shall not err therein.

God's Word Helps Us Grow

Therefore, laying aside all malice,
all deceit, hypocrisy, envy,
and all evil speaking, as newborn babes,
desire the pure milk of the word,
that you may grow thereby.
1 PETER 2:1–2

The best Christians need to be cautioned and warned against the worst sins. They are only sanctified in part and are still liable to temptations. Our best services toward God will neither please Him nor profit us if we are not conscientious in our duties to men. One sin not laid aside will hinder our spiritual profit and everlasting welfare.

The apostle, like a wise physician, goes on to direct us to wholesome food, that we may grow thereby. The duty exhorted to is a strong and constant desire for the Word of God. This milk of the Word must be sincere, not adulterated by the mixtures of men. A new life requires suitable food. Infants desire common milk, and their desires toward it are fervent and frequent. Such must Christians' desires be for the Word of God, that they may grow thereby. Strong desires and affections to the Word of God are a sure evidence of a person's being born again. Growth and improvement in wisdom and grace are the desire of every Christian. The Word of God does not leave a man as it finds him.

Doers of the Word

Therefore lay aside all filthiness and overflow of wickedness,
and receive with meekness the implanted word,
which is able to save your souls.
But be doers of the word,
and not hearers only, deceiving yourselves.
JAMES 1:21–22

We are required to prepare ourselves for the Word of God. In hearing the Word of God, we are to receive it as the stock does the graft, so that the fruit that is produced may be not according to the nature of the sour stock but according to the nature of the gospel that is engrafted into our souls. We must, therefore, yield ourselves to the Word of God and receive it with meekness, willing to hear of our faults and take it not only patiently, but thankfully. In all our hearing we should aim at the salvation of our souls. It is the design of the Word of God to make us wise to salvation.

Hearing is necessary for doing. The most attentive and frequent hearing of the Word of God will not avail us unless we are also doers of it. It is not enough to remember what we hear. Mere hearers are self-deceivers. As a looking glass shows us the spots and wrinkles on our faces, so the Word of God shows us our sins. It shows us what is wrong so it may be corrected. When we attend to the Word of God and see ourselves clearly, our true state and condition, and dress ourselves anew by the glass of God's Word, we make a proper use of God's Word.

Keep the Word Close

*"Therefore you shall lay up these words of mine
in your heart and in your soul."*

DEUTERONOMY 11:18

Moses repeats the directions he had given for the guidance and assistance of the people for their obedience. Let us all be directed by the three rules given here: (1) let our hearts be filled with the Word of God; (2) let our eyes be fixed upon the Word of God; bind these words for a sign upon your hand, which is always in view, and as frontlets between your eyes; and (3) let our tongues be employed in the Word of God; let it be the subject of our common discourse, wherever we are, especially with our children.

He repeats the assurances he had given them before in God's name, of prosperity and success if they were obedient. Nothing contributes more to the making of a strong nation, valuable to its friends and formidable to its enemies, than religion reigning in it, for who can be against those who are sincerely for God?

Day and Night

*"This Book of the Law shall not depart from your mouth,
but you shall meditate in it day and night."*
JOSHUA 1:8

Joshua was to conform himself in everything to the law of God and make this his rule. God puts the book of the law into Joshua's hand, and he is charged to meditate on it day and night. If ever any man's business might have excused him from meditation and other acts of devotion, one would think Joshua's might at this time. It was a great trust that was lodged in his hands; the care of it was enough to fill him, and yet he must find time and thoughts for meditation. He was not to let the Word depart out of his mouth; that is, all his orders to the people must be consistent with the law of God, and on all occasions he must speak according to this rule. There was no need to make new laws, but that good thing that was committed to him he must carefully and faithfully keep. He must observe to do this according to the law. Joshua was a man of great power and authority, yet he himself must be under command and do as he is bidden. No man's dignity or dominions sets him above the law of God.

Joshua must observe the checks of conscience, the hints of providence, and all the advantages of opportunity. He must not turn from the Word in his own practice or in any act of government. He must be strong and courageous. Finally, Joshua is assured that following this way will make him and those who follow him prosperous.

The Word and Our Purification

Having been born again,
not of corruptible seed but incorruptible,
through the word of God
which lives and abides forever.

1 PETER 1:23

Peter presupposes that the gospel had already produced at least an unfeigned love of the brethren in the newly converted. It is not to be doubted that every sincere Christian purifies his soul. The apostle takes this for granted. The Word of God is the great instrument of a sinner's purification. Many hear the truth but are never purified by it because they will not submit to it or obey it. The Spirit of God is the great agent in the purification of man's soul. The Spirit excites our endeavors and makes them successful. The aid of the Spirit does not supersede our own industry; these people purified their own souls, but it was through the Spirit. The souls of Christians must be purified before they can so much as honestly love one another.

He further impresses on Christians the duty of loving one another fervently with a pure heart from the consideration of their spiritual relation. All Christians are born again. They are brought into a new and dear relation to one another; they become brethren by their new birth. This new and second birth is much more desirable and excellent than the first. By the one, we become the children of men, but by the other, the sons and daughters of the Most High. Brethren by nature are bound to love one another, but the obligation is double where there is a spiritual relation.

Keeping the Word before You

"And these words which I command you today
shall be in your heart. You shall teach them diligently
to your children, and shall talk of them when you
sit in your house, when you walk by the way,
when you lie down, and when you rise up."

DEUTERONOMY 6:6–7

Means are prescribed here for the maintaining and keeping up of religion in our hearts and houses, that it might not wither and go to decay. They are these: (1) Meditation: "These words which I command you shall be in your heart"; (2) the religious education of children: "You shall teach them diligently to your children"; and by communicating your knowledge, you will increase it. Take all occasions to talk with those about you of divine things: not of unrevealed mysteries or matters of doubtful disputation, but of the plain truths and love of God and the things that belong to our peace. The more conversant we are with them, the more we shall admire them and be affected by them and may thereby be instrumental in communicating divine light and heat. God appointed them, at least for the present, to write some select sentences of the law that were most weighty and comprehensive upon the walls or in scrolls of parchment to be worn about their wrists; some think that the phylacteries so much used among the Jews took form from this. Christ blames the Pharisees not for wearing them but for affecting to have them broader than other people's. It was prudently and piously provided by the first reformers of the English church that then, when Bibles were scarce, some select portions of Scripture should be written on the walls and pillars of the churches, with which the people might become familiar.

You Are Mistaken

*"You are mistaken,
not knowing the Scriptures nor the power of God."*
MATTHEW 22:29

Those do greatly err, in the judgment of Christ, who deny the resurrection and a future life. Here Christ reproved with the meekness of wisdom and is not so sharp toward them (whatever the reason) as sometimes He was with the chief priests and elders. "You are mistaken, not knowing." Ignorance is the cause of error; those who are in the dark miss their way. Ignorance is the cause of error about the resurrection and the next life. What it is in particular instances, the wisest and best know not. It does not yet appear what we shall be; it is glory that is yet to be revealed. But it is a thing about which we are not left in the dark, blessed be God. They know not the power of God, which would lead men to infer that there may be a resurrection and a future life. The ignorance, disbelief, or weak belief in God's power is at the bottom of many errors, particularly for those who deny the resurrection. When we are told of the soul's existence and agency in a state of separation from the body, we are ready to say, "How can these things be?" If a man dies, shall he live again? Vain men, because they cannot comprehend the way of it, question the truth of it. This we must fasten upon in the first place: God is omnipotent and can do what He will. No room is left for doubting that He will do what He has promised. His power far exceeds the power of nature. The Scriptures decidedly affirm that there shall be a resurrection and a future state. The Scriptures speak plainly that the soul is immortal and there is another life after this. Christ rose again according to the Scriptures; and so shall we. Ignorance of the Scriptures is the rise of an abundance of mischief.

Opening Our Minds

And He opened their understanding,
that they might comprehend the Scriptures.
LUKE 24:45

Jesus gave the disciples insight into the Word of God. He refers them to the Word they had heard from him when he was with them (v. 44). " 'These are the words which I spoke to you while I was still with you.' " He refers them to the Word they had read in the Old Testament: " 'All things must be fulfilled which were written.' " Whatever they found written concerning the Messiah in the Old Testament must be fulfilled in Him, what was written concerning His sufferings as well as what was written concerning His kingdom. All things must be fulfilled. . . . Several parts of the Old Testament are mentioned here as containing things concerning Christ: the Law of Moses, the Prophets, the Psalms. . . . By an immediate and present work upon their minds, He gave them to comprehend the true intent and meaning of the Old Testament prophecies of Christ.

In His discourse with the two disciples, He took the veil off the text by opening the Scriptures; here He takes the veil off the heart by opening the mind. Jesus Christ. . .has access to our spirits and can immediately influence them. Even good men need to have their understandings opened. Though they are not darkness, yet in many things they are in the dark. Christ's way of working faith in the soul is by opening the understanding. Thus He comes into the soul by the door. The design of opening the understanding is that we may understand the Scriptures, not that we may be wise above what is written, but that we may be wiser in what is written.

That We Might Have Hope

*For whatever things were written before
were written for our learning,
that we through the patience and comfort
of the Scriptures might have hope.*

ROMANS 15:4

That which is written of Christ is written for our learning. He has left us an example. The example of Christ is recorded for our imitation. That which is written in the Scriptures of the Old Testament is written for our learning. What happened to the Old Testament saints happened to them as an example. They were written for our use and benefit. We must therefore labor not only to understand the literal meaning of the Scripture, but to learn out of it that which will do us good. Practical observations are more necessary than critical expositions. The Scripture was written that we might know what to hope for from God. Now, the way of attaining this hope is through the patience and comfort of the Scripture. Patience and comfort suppose trouble and sorrow; such is the lot of the saints in this world. But both these befriend that hope that is the life of our souls. Patience works experience, and experience, hope, which maketh not ashamed. The more patience we exercise under troubles, the more hopefully we may look through our troubles. Nothing is more destructive to hope than impatience. And the comfort of the Scriptures, that comfort that springs from the Word of God, is likewise a great stay to hope.

Prophets and the Word

"And if you say in your heart,
'How shall we know the word
which the LORD has not spoken?' "
DEUTERONOMY 18:21

The verses before this speak of the promise of the great prophet, with a command to receive and listen to him. Some think it is the promise of a succession of prophets who would continue for many ages in Israel. Besides the priests and Levites, whose office it was to teach Israel God's law, they should have prophets to reprove them for their faults, remind them of their duty, foretell things to come, and give judgments for warning and deliverances for their comfort.

Whether a succession of prophets is included in this promise or not, we can be sure that it is primarily intended as a promise of Christ and is the clearest promise of Him contained in the law of Moses. It is expressly applied to our Lord Jesus as the promised Messiah, and it was His Spirit that spoke through all the other prophets (1 Peter 1:10–12). It is also a charge and command given to all people to hear and believe, to hear and obey the great prophet promised here (v. 15). Whoever will not listen to him shall surely and severely be reckoned with for his contempt (v. 19).

Here is also a caution against false prophets. "How shall we know the word which the Lord has *not* spoken?" the people ask. The answer is that whatever is directly repugnant to sense, to the light and law of nature, and to the plain meaning of the written word, we may be sure did not come from the Lord. Neither did anything that tolerates sin and the encouragement to sin or has a manifest tendency to the destruction of piety or charity.

Respecting the Word

He who despises the word will be destroyed,
but he who fears the commandment will be rewarded.
The law of the wise is a fountain of life.
PROVERBS 13:13–14

Those who prefer the rules of policy before divine precepts, and the allurements of the world and the flesh before God's promises and comforts, despise His Word; but he who stands in awe of God, has reverence for His Word, and is afraid of displeasing God, shall be rewarded for his godly fear. By "the law of the wise," we may understand the principles and rules by which they govern themselves. They will be constant springs of comfort, as a fountain of life. The closer we keep to those rules, the more effectually we secure our own peace. Those who follow the dictates of this law will escape the snares of death that those who forsake the law of the wise run into.

Those who conduct themselves prudently and serve Christ are accepted by God and approved of. The way of sinners is rough and uneasy. It is hard on others, who complain of it, and hard on the sinner himself, who can have little enjoyment while doing what is disapproved of by all mankind.

It is wisdom to be cautious. Every prudent, discreet man acts with deliberation and is careful not to meddle with that with which he has no knowledge. It is folly to be rash, as the fool is who rushes into something he is no way fit for, and so makes himself ridiculous.

Dwelling Richly

Let the word of Christ dwell in you richly in all wisdom,
teaching and admonishing one another
in psalms and hymns and spiritual songs,
singing with grace in your hearts to the Lord.
COLOSSIANS 3:16

Let the Word of Christ dwell in you richly. It must dwell in us, or keep house, not as a servant but as a master. It must dwell in us, that is, always be ready and at hand for us in everything. It must dwell in us richly, not only keep house in our hearts, but keep a good house. Many have the Word of Christ dwelling in them, but it dwells in them poorly. The soul prospers when the Word of God dwells in us richly, in all wisdom.

The Word of Christ must dwell in us, not in all notion and speculation to make us doctors, but in all wisdom to make us good Christians. We sharpen ourselves by quickening others. We must admonish one another in psalms and hymns. Religious poetry seems countenanced by these expressions and is capable of great edification, but when we sing psalms, we make no melody unless we sing with grace in our hearts. And we are not only to quicken and encourage ourselves, but to teach and admonish one another. All must be done in the name of Christ. Those who do all things in Christ's name will always have words of thanksgiving to God.

Search the Scriptures

And so we have the prophetic word confirmed,
which you do well to heed as a light that shines in a dark place,
until the day dawns and the morning star rises in your hearts.
2 PETER 1:19

The Scriptures of the Old Testament are said to be made a more sure prophetical declaration of the power and coming of our Savior. But the New Testament is a history of that which in the Old Testament is a prophecy. Read the Old Testament as a prophecy of Christ, and with diligence and thankfulness, use the New as the best exposition of the Old. How firm and sure would our faith be if we had such a firm and sure Word to rest upon! All the prophecies of the Old Testament are more sure and certain to us who know the history of their accomplishment.

The apostle encourages us to search the Scriptures. We do well to heed them, apply our minds to understand their sense, and our hearts to believe the truth of this sure Word. If we thus apply ourselves to the Word of God, we certainly do. . .what is pleasing to God and profitable to ourselves. They must use the Scripture as a light God has sent into the world to dispel that darkness that is upon the face of the whole earth. They must acknowledge their own darkness. . . . If men are made wise to salvation, it is by the shining of the Word of God into their hearts. Natural notions of God are not sufficient for fallen man. When the light of the Scripture is darted into the dark understanding by the Holy Spirit of God, then the spiritual day dawns and the daystar arises in that soul. It is a growing knowledge. All who do good come to this light, while evildoers keep at a distance from it.

Every Word Is Pure

Every word of God is pure;
He is a shield to those who put their trust in Him.
Do not add to His words,
lest He rebuke you, and you be found a liar.
PROVERBS 30:5–6

The prophet Agur aims at three things:

1. To abase himself. Before he makes confession of his faith, he makes confession of his folly and the weakness and deficiency of reason, which make it so necessary that we be guided and governed by faith. Agur, when he was called wiser than most, acknowledged himself more foolish than any. Whatever high opinion others may have of us, it becomes us to have low thoughts of ourselves. He speaks of himself as wanting a revelation to guide him in the ways of truth and wisdom. The natural man, the natural powers perceive not the things of the Spirit of God.

2. He aims to advance Jesus Christ and the Father in Him.

3. He wants to assure us of the truth of the Word of God and to recommend it to us. Agur's pupils expected to be instructed in the things of God. "Alas!" he said. "I cannot undertake to instruct you. Go to the Word of God. Every word of God is pure; there is not the least mixture of falsehood and corruption in it." God in His Word, God in His promise is a shield, a sure protection for all those who put their trust in Him. It is sufficient, and therefore we must not add to it. We must be content with what God has thought fit to make known to us of His mind and not covet to be wise above what is written.

Scripture Stands Forever

"The grass withers, the flower fades,
but the word of our God stands forever."
ISAIAH 40:8

The time to favor Zion having come, the people of God must be prepared by repentance and faith. We have here the voice of one crying in the wilderness, which must be applied to John the Baptist; for though God was the speaker, he was the voice of one crying in the wilderness to prepare the way of the Lord, to dispose men's minds for the reception of the gospel of Christ.

By this accomplishment of the prophecies and promises of salvation, it appears that the Word of the Lord is sure. The power of man, when it does appear against the deliverance, is not to be feared, for it shall be as grass before the Word of the Lord: It will wither and be trodden down. The insulting Babylonians are as grass. The power of man, even when it would seem to be for deliverance, is not to be trusted, for it is only grass. When God is about to work salvation for His people, He will lead them away from depending on creatures and looking for it from hills and mountains. The Word of our God, that glory of the Lord that is now to be revealed, the gospel, and that grace that is brought with it to use and wrought by it in us, shall stand forever.

To prepare the way of the Lord, we must be convinced that all flesh is grass, weak and withering. We cannot save ourselves. All the beauty of the creature is but as the flower or grass. We must be convinced that the Word of the Lord will furnish us with a happiness that will run parallel with the duration of our souls, which will live forever.

God Will Provide

But Jesus answered him, saying,
"It is written, 'Man shall not live by bread alone,
but by every word of God.' "
LUKE 4:4

In this story of Christ's temptation, notice how He was prepared and fitted out for it. He was full of the Holy Ghost, who had descended on Him like a dove. Those are well armed against the strongest temptations who are full of the Holy Ghost.

Jesus continued fasting. As by retiring into the wilderness, He showed Himself perfectly indifferent to the world, so by His fasting, He showed Himself perfectly indifferent to the body. Satan cannot easily take hold of those who are thus loosened from and dead to the world and the flesh.

He would not do anything that looked like distrust of his Father. He would, like the other children of God, live in dependence on divine Providence and promise. He returned a Scripture answer to temptation: "It is written." These are the first words recorded as spoken by Christ after His installment in His prophetical office, and it is a quotation out of the Old Testament. The Word of God is our sword, and faith in that Word is our shield. We should therefore be mighty in the Scriptures. The Scripture He makes use of is quoted from Deuteronomy 8:3: " 'Man shall not live by bread alone.' I need not turn the stone into bread; man can live by every word of God, by whatever God will appoint that he shall live by." God has many means of subsistence and is not at any time to be distrusted, but at all times to be depended upon in the way of duty.

A Noble and Good Heart

"Now the parable is this: The seed is the word of God. . . .
But the ones that fell on the good ground are those who,
having heard the word with a noble and good heart,
keep it and bear fruit with patience."

LUKE 8:11, 15

The heart of man is like soil to the seed of God's Word. It is capable of receiving it and bringing forth the fruits of it, but unless the seed is sown in it, it will bring forth nothing valuable. The success of the seeding is very much according to the nature and temper of the soil.

The devil is a subtle and spiteful enemy. He takes the Word out of the hearts of careless hearers, lest they should believe and be saved (v. 12). This is added here to teach us that we cannot be saved unless we believe. Therefore the devil does all he can to keep us from believing. . . . Or, if we remember it, he creates prejudices in our minds against it or diverts our minds from it to something else.

The good ground that brings forth good fruit is an honest and good heart. A heart firmly fixed for God and duty, an upright heart, a tender heart is an honest and good heart, which having heard the Word, understands it, receives it, and keeps it as the soil not only receives but keeps the seed.

Where the Word is well kept, there is fruit brought forth with patience—patience to continue to the end in well doing.

In consideration of this, we ought to take heed how we hear, take heed of those things that will hinder our profiting by the Word we heard, take heed lest we hear carelessly and slightly, and take heed after we have heard the Word, lest we lose what we have gained.

Welcome the Word

For this reason we also thank God without ceasing,
because when you received the word of God
which you heard from us,
you welcomed it not as the word of men,
but as it is in truth, the word of God,
which also effectively works in you who believe.

1 THESSALONIANS 2:13

This verse concerns the success of the ministry to the Thessalonians. The Word of the gospel is preached by men like ourselves, men of like passions and infirmities with others. However, it is in truth the Word of God. Such was the Word the apostles preached by divine inspiration, and such is that which is left on record, and such is the Word that is preached in our day. Those are greatly to blame who give out their own fancies or injunctions for the Word of God. Those are also to blame who, in hearing the Word, look no further than to the ministry of men or the words of men. We should receive the Word of God as the Word of God. The words of men are frail and perishing, like themselves, and sometimes false, foolish, and fickle, but God's Word is holy, wise, just, and faithful and abides forever.

The Word they received effectually works in those who believe. Such as have this inward testimony of the truth of Scriptures have the best evidence of their divine original, though this is not sufficient to convince others who are strangers. The good effects that his successful preaching had upon himself and his fellow laborers was a constant cause of thankfulness. He never could be sufficiently thankful that God had counted him faithful and made his ministrations successful.

True Wisdom

The wisdom that is from above is first pure,
then peaceable, gentle, willing to yield,
full of mercy and good fruits,
without partiality and without hypocrisy.

JAMES 3:17

True wisdom is God's gift. It comes from above. It is pure, without a mixture of maxims or aims that would debase it, studious of holiness both in heart and life. The wisdom that is from above is peaceable. Those who are truly wise do what they can to preserve peace, that it may not be broken, and to make peace, that where it is lost it may be restored. Heavenly wisdom makes men peaceable. It is gentle, not being rude and overbearing in conversation or harsh and cruel in temper. Heavenly wisdom is easy to be entreated; it is very persuadable, either to what is good or from what is evil. There is an easiness that is weak and faulty, but it is not a blamable easiness to yield ourselves to the persuasions of God's Word and to all just requests of our fellow creatures. Heavenly wisdom is full of mercy and good fruits, both to relieve those who want and to forgive those who offend. Heavenly wisdom is without partiality. The wisest men are least apt to be censurers. That wisdom, which is from above, is without hypocrisy. It has no disguises or deceits. It is sincere and open, steady and uniform, and consistent with itself. True wisdom will go on to sow the fruits of righteousness in peace and thus make peace in the world (v. 18). And that which is sown in peace will produce a harvest of joys.

Ministry and Wisdom

"Rebuke a wise man, and he will love you.
Give instruction to a wise man, and he will be still wiser;
teach a just man, and he will increase in learning."
PROVERBS 9:8–9

Wisdom gives instruction to ministers and others who in their work are endeavoring to serve her designs. Their work must be not only to tell in general what preparation is made for souls, but also address themselves to particular persons, tell them of their faults, reprove, rebuke. They must instruct them how to change. . . . The Word of God is intended. . .for reproof, for correction, and for instruction in righteousness. They will meet with some scorners and wicked men who would mock the messengers of the Lord and misuse them. And, though they are not forbidden to invite those simple ones to Wisdom's house, yet they are advised not to pursue the invitation by reproving and rebuking them. Thus Christ said of the Pharisees, "Let them alone" (Matthew 15:14). They would meet with others who are wise and good and just. . . . All are not scorners. We meet with some who are so wise as to be willing and glad to be taught. If there is an occasion, we must reprove them, for wise men are not so perfectly wise but there is that in them which needs a reproof. . . . With our reproofs we must give them instruction and must teach them. It is as great an indication of wisdom to take a reproof well as to give it well. A wise man will be made wiser by the reproofs; he will increase in learning. . .and so grow in grace.

Let them know what the advantages of this wisdom will be: "By me your days shall be multiplied. It will contribute to the health of your body, and so the years of your life on earth shall be increased. It will bring you to heaven, and there the years of your life shall be increased without end" (v. 11).

Keep the Things That Are Written

*Blessed is he who reads and those who hear
the words of this prophecy, and keep those things
which are written in it; for the time is near.*

REVELATION 1:3

This chapter is a general preface to the whole book of Revelation, the revelation of Jesus Christ. As the prophet of the church, He has made known to us the things that are to come. It is a revelation that God gave to Christ; it is to Christ that we owe the knowledge we have of what we are to expect from God and what He expects of us. Christ employed an angel to communicate it to the churches. The angels. . .signified it to the apostle John, who was chosen for this service. Some think he was the only surviving disciple, the rest having sealed their testimony with their blood. John was to deliver this revelation to the church, to all his servants, who all have a right to the oracles of God.

The subject matter of this revelation are the things that must shortly come to pass. We have in this revelation a general idea of the methods of divine providence. These events were to come to pass not only surely, but shortly.

John bore record of the Word of God in general, and of the testimony of Jesus in particular, and of all the things he saw. He was an eyewitness, and he concealed nothing that he saw. . . .

Verse 1:3 is an apostolic benediction on those who give due respect to this divine revelation. . .to all who either read or hear the words of the prophecy. It is a blessed privilege to enjoy the oracles of God. It is a blessed thing to study the Scriptures. It is a privilege not only to read the Scriptures ourselves, but to hear them read by others. It is not sufficient to our blessedness that we read and hear the Scriptures, but we must keep the things that are written.

Light and Law

For the commandment is a lamp,
and the law a light;
reproofs of instruction are the way of life.
PROVERBS 6:23

This chapter is a general exhortation to faithfully adhere to the
Word of God and to take it for our guide in all our actions. We
must look upon the Word of God both as a light and as a law. It
is a light that our understandings must subscribe to; it is a lamp
to our eyes for discovery and so to our feet for direction. The
Word of God reveals to us truths of eternal certainty. Scripture
light is the sure light. It is a law that our wills must submit to.

We must receive it as our father's commandment and the
law of our mother (v. 20). It is God's commandment and His
law. Our parents directed us to it, trained us up in the knowledge
and observance of it. We believe because we have tried it ourselves and find it to be of God; but we were beholden to them
for recommending it to us. The cautions, counsels, and commands that our parents gave us agree with the Word of God.

We must retain the Word of God and the good instructions our parents gave us out of it.

We should tie them around our neck as an ornament,
about our throat as a guard that no forbidden fruit may be allowed to go in or any evil word allowed to go out through the
throat. If we bind it continually upon our hearts, we must follow its direction. "It will say unto thee, when thou art ready
to turn aside, This is the way; walk in it. Let it be thy rule,
and then thou shalt be led by the Spirit; he will be thy mon-
itor and support."

Epistles of Christ

You are our epistle written in our hearts,
known and read by all men;
clearly you are an epistle of Christ, ministered by us,
written not with ink but by the Spirit of the living God,
not on tablets of stone but on tablets of flesh,
that is, of the heart.

2 CORINTHIANS 3:2–3

In verse 1, the apostle makes an apology for seeming to commend himself. He neither needed nor desired any verbal commendation to them, no testimonial letters from them, as some others did, meaning the false apostles or teachers. The Corinthians themselves were his real commendation. . . .

The apostle is careful to ascribe all the praise to God. He says they were the epistle of Christ, while the apostle and others were but instruments. This epistle was not written with ink, but with the Spirit of the living God. Nor was it written on tablets of stone, but on the heart, upon the fleshy tablets of the heart, hearts that are softened by divine grace. He utterly disclaims the taking of any praise to themselves and ascribes all the glory to God. All the sufficiency is of God; to Him therefore are owed all the praise and glory of that good which is done. The best are no more than what the grace of God makes them.

The apostle goes on to make a comparison between the Old Testament and the New and values himself and his fellow laborers by this, that they were able ministers of the New Testament, that God had made them so (v. 6). He distinguishes between the letter and the Spirit of the New Testament. They were ministers not merely of the letter, but they were ministers of the Spirit, too, and the Spirit of the gospel gives life eternal.

Understanding the Scriptures

So Philip ran to him,
and heard him reading the prophet Isaiah, and said,
"Do you understand what you are reading?"
ACTS 8:30

We have here the story of the conversion of an Ethiopian eunuch to the faith of Christ. Philip found him reading in his Bible as he sat in his chariot (v. 28). He not only relieved the tediousness of the journey but redeemed time by reading the Scriptures, the book of Isaiah. . . . Persons of quality should abound more than others in the exercises of piety, because their example will influence many. It is wisdom for men of business to redeem time for holy duties, to fill up every minute with something that will be profitable to them. Those who are diligent in searching the Scriptures are in a fair way to improve in knowledge.

Philip asks a fair question: "Do you understand what you are reading?" When we read and hear the Word of God, we should often ask ourselves if we truly understand it. We cannot profit by the Scriptures unless we, in some measure, understand them.

The eunuch replies (v. 31), "How can I understand, unless someone guides me?" Those who would learn must see their need to be taught. He speaks as one very desirous to be taught. Though there are many things in the Scriptures that are hard to understand, we must not give up. Knowledge and grace grow gradually. In order to understand the Scripture, we should have someone to guide us: some good books, some good men, but above all, the Spirit of grace to lead us into all truth.

The Gift of Ministry

Till I come, give attention to reading,
to exhortation, to doctrine.
Do not neglect the gift that is in you,
which was given to you by prophecy
with the laying on of the hands of the eldership.

1 TIMOTHY 4:13–14

Paul charges Timothy to study hard. Though Timothy has extraordinary gifts, he must still use ordinary means. Or this may refer to the public reading of the Scriptures: He must read and exhort. He must teach them both what to do and what to believe. The best way for ministers to avoid being despised is to teach and practice the things that are delegated to them. Those ministers who are the best accomplished in their work must mind their studies and their work.

He charges Timothy to beware of negligence. The gifts of God will wither if they are neglected. Ordination was by prophecy and the laying on of the hands of the eldership (v. 14). The office of the ministry is a gift, the gift of Christ, and this was a very kind gift to His church. Ministers ought not to neglect the gift bestowed upon them, whether the office of the ministry or the qualifications for that office.

Having this work committed to him, Timothy must give himself wholly to it. Ministers are to be much in meditation. They are to meditate on the great trust committed to them. By this means, their profiting will appear in all things.

Paul presses upon Timothy the need to be very cautious. This will be the way to save himself and those who hear him. "Save yourself in the first place, so shall you be instrumental to save those who hear you" (v. 16). The best way to answer both these ends is to take heed to ourselves.

Divine Prophecy

No prophecy of Scripture is of any private interpretation,
for prophecy never came by the will of man,
but holy men of God spoke
as they were moved by the Holy Spirit.
2 PETER 1:20–21

All prophecy is of divine origin. No Scripture prophecy is of private interpretation, but the revelation of the mind of God. This was the difference between the prophets of the Lord and the false prophets. The prophets of the Lord did not speak or do anything of their own mind. The prophets and penmen of the Scripture spoke and wrote the mind of God. Every private man ought to search it and come to understand the sense and meaning thereof. This important truth of the divine origin of the Scriptures is to be known and owned by all who will give heed to the sure word of prophecy. As a man not barely believes, but knows assuredly that that very person is his particular friend in whom he sees all the distinguishing marks and characters of his friend, so the Christian knows that book to be the Word of God in which he sees all the proper marks and characters of a divinely inspired book. The divinity of the Scriptures must be known and acknowledged before men can give good heed to them.

The apostle tells us how the Old Testament came to be compiled: (1) all the penmen of the Scriptures were holy men of God; (2) the Holy Ghost is the supreme agent, and holy men are but instruments. The Holy Ghost inspired and dictated to them what they were to deliver of the mind of God. He effectually engaged them to speak and write what He had put into their mouths. Mix faith therefore with what you find in the Scriptures; esteem and reverence your Bible as a book written by holy men inspired, influenced, and assisted by the Holy Ghost.

Contempt

*"And whoever will not receive you
nor hear your words,
when you depart from that house or city,
shake off the dust from your feet."*

MATTHEW 10:14

Here Jesus instructs the disciples how to treat those who would not receive them or hear their words. There would be those who would slight them and put contempt on them and their message. The best and most powerful preachers of the gospel must expect to meet with some who will not so much as give them a hearing or show them any token of respect. Many turn a deaf ear, even to the joyful sound. Contempt of the gospel and contempt of gospel ministers commonly go together, and either of them will be construed into a contempt of Christ and will be reckoned with accordingly.

The directions given to the apostles were that they must depart out of that house or city. The gospel will not tarry long with those who put it away from them. At their departure, they must shake off the dust from their feet in detestation of those who will not hear. The apostles must not so much as carry away the dust of the city with them, as a denunciation of wrath against them. It was to signify that God would shake them off. They who despise God and His gospel shall be lightly esteemed.

The Law of the Prophets

"Do not think that I came to destroy the Law or the Prophets.
I did not come to destroy but to fulfill.
For assuredly, I say to you, till heaven and earth pass away,
one jot or one tittle will by no means
pass from the law till all is fulfilled."

MATTHEW 5:17–18

The rule that Christ came to establish agreed exactly with the Scriptures of the Old Testament, here called "the law and the prophets." Jesus protests against the thought of canceling and weakening the Old Testament. The Savior of souls is the destroyer of nothing that comes from God, much less those excellent dictates of Moses and the prophets. No, He came to fulfill them; that is: (1) to obey the commands of the law. He in all respects yielded obedience to the law and never broke the law in anything; (2) to make good the promises of the law and the predictions of the prophets; (3) to answer the types of law; (4) to fill up the defects of it, and so to complete and perfect it. As a picture that is first drawn roughly displays only some outlines of the intended piece, which are afterward filled in, so Christ made an improvement of the law and the prophets by His additions and explications; and (5) to carry on the same design. The gospel is the time of reformation—not the repeal of the law, but the amendment of it and, consequently, its establishment.

He asserts the perpetuity of it: "For assuredly, I say to you, till heaven and earth pass away, one jot or one tittle will by no means pass from the law till all is fulfilled." The Word of the Lord endures forever. . . . The care of God concerning His law extends itself even to those things that seem to be of least account, for whatever belongs to God and bears His stamp, no matter how little, shall be preserved.

Our Duty to God and Our Neighbor

"And now, Israel,
what does the LORD your God require of you,
but to fear the LORD your God,
to walk in all His ways and to love Him,
to serve the LORD your God
with all your heart and with all your soul,
and to keep the commandments of the LORD and
His statutes which I command you today for your good?"

DEUTERONOMY 10:12–13

We are here most plainly directed in our duty to God, to our neighbor, and to ourselves. We must fear the Lord our God. Fear Him as a great God and Lord and love Him as a good God and Father and benefactor. We must serve Him with all our heart and soul, and what we do for Him we must do cheerfully and with a good will. We must keep His commandments and His statutes.

We are also taught about our duty to our neighbor (v. 19): Love the stranger; and, if the stranger, much more our brethren, as ourselves. Two arguments are used here to enforce this duty: (1) God's common providence, which extends itself to all nations of men, they being made of one blood. God loves the stranger (v. 18), that is, He gives to all life, and breath, and all things, even to those who are Gentiles and strangers to the commonwealth of Israel and to Israel's God; and (2) the afflicted condition that the Israelites themselves had been in when they were strangers in Egypt. Those who have themselves been in distress and have found mercy with God should sympathize most feelingly with those who are in like distress and be ready to show kindness to them.

The Fruits of Obedience

" 'And it shall be that if you earnestly obey
My commandments which I command you today,
to love the LORD your God and serve Him with all your heart
and with all your soul,
then I will give you the rain for your land in its season,
the early rain and the latter rain,
that you may gather in your grain,
your new wine, and your oil.' "
DEUTERONOMY 11:13–14

Moses urges the Israelites, "If you will enter into Canaan and find it a good land indeed to you, keep the commandments. Keep all the commandments that I command you this day; love God, and serve Him with all your heart."

He does not go on to teach them the art of war, how to draw the bow and use the sword, and keep ranks, that they might be strong and go in and possess the land. No, but if they keep God's commandments and their religion, while they are true to it, it will be their strength and secure their success. Sin tends to shorten the days of a people's prosperity, but obedience will bring a lengthening of their tranquility. The better God has provided for our outward condition, for our ease and convenience, the more we should abound in His service. The less we have to do for our bodies, the more we should do for God and our souls. To awaken them to take heed, Moses tells them plainly that if they turn aside to other gods, they would provoke the wrath of God against them. Good things would be turned away from them; the heaven would withhold its rain, and then, of course, the earth would not yield its fruit.

Obedience and Love

"He who has My commandments and keeps them,
it is he who loves Me.
And he who loves Me will be loved by My Father,
and I will love him and manifest Myself to him."

JOHN 14:21

Christ will accept the love of those who have His commandments and keep them. The kind things He said here to His disciples were intended not for those who were now His followers, but for all who would believe in Him through their word. Having Christ's commandments, we must keep them. Having them in our heads, we must keep them in our hearts and lives. Those who do the duty of disciples are not those who have the greatest wit and know how to talk for Him or the greatest estate to lay out for Him, but those who keep His commandments. The surest evidence of our love for Christ is obedience to the laws of Christ.

What return will He make to them for their love? We could not love God if He did not first give us His grace to love Him. He loves them and lets them know that He loves them. God so loves the Son as to love all those who love Him. They shall have Christ's love. God will love Him as a Father, and I will love Him as a brother, an elder brother. In the nature of God, nothing shines more glorious than this, that He loved us. Christ was now leaving His disciples but promises to continue His love to them. He bears them on His heart and ever lives interceding for them. They will have the comfort of that love: "I will. . .manifest myself to him." Being promised to all who love Him and keep His commandments, it must be construed so as to extend to them.

Commitment and Deliverance

> "Our God whom we serve is able to deliver us from
> the burning fiery furnace. . . . But if not, let it be known to
> you, O king, that we do not serve your gods,
> nor will we worship the gold image which you have set up."
> DANIEL 3:17–18

We call Shadrach, Meshach, and Abednego the three children (they were actually young men), but we should call them the three champions, the first three of the worthies of God's kingdom among men. They did not go out of their way to court martyrdom, but when they were duly called to the fiery trial, they acquitted themselves bravely.

They trusted in the living God and by that faith chose rather to suffer than to sin. "If we must be thrown into the fiery furnace unless we serve your gods, though we worship not your gods, we are not atheists. There is a God whom we call ours. We serve this God. We are well assured that this God is able to deliver us from the burning fiery furnace." Nebuchadnezzar could only torment and kill the body; after that, there was no more that he could do. God will deliver us, either from death or in death.

They were not required to deny their God or to renounce His worship. Only one single act was required of them, which could be done in a minute, and they might after declare their sorrow for it. They might be excused if they went down the stream when it was so strong. . . . If they would comply, they would save their lives. But God had said: "You shall not bow down to any images, or worship them" (Deuteronomy 5:9). They would rather suffer than sin, and truly, the saving of them from this sinful compliance was as great a miracle as the saving of them in the fiery furnace.

The Dangers of Devotion

Then Daniel said to the king, "O king, live forever!
My God sent His angel and shut the lions' mouths,
so that they have not hurt me,
because I was found innocent before Him;
and also, O king, I have done no wrong before you."

DANIEL 6:21–22

Darius himself, with the utmost reluctance and against his conscience, signed the warrant for Daniel's execution; and Daniel, that venerable, grave man who carried such a mixture of majesty and sweetness in his countenance, is thrown into the den of lions to be devoured for worshiping his God. Darius justifies Daniel from guilt, admitting that his crime is serving his God continually. He leaves it to God to free Daniel. . . .

Darius could not forgive himself for throwing Daniel into danger. He passed the night fasting and forbade any music to be played. Early the next morning, he hurried to the den of lions, crying in a lamentable voice, "Daniel, servant of the living God, has your God, whom you serve continually, been able to deliver you from the lions?" (v. 20).

Daniel is alive, safe, and well, unhurt in the lions' den. Daniel knew the king's voice and cries out, "O king, live forever!" He does not reproach him but has heartily forgiven him. . . . God has preserved his life by a miracle. "He is my God, whom I own, and who owns me, for He has sent His angel." See the care God takes of His faithful worshipers. He does in effect shut the lions' mouths so they cannot hurt him. Daniel was represented to the king as disaffected with him and his government. We do not find that he said anything in his own vindication, but left it to God to establish his integrity, and God did so by working a miracle for Daniel's preservation.

Hear and Do

"Therefore whoever hears these sayings of Mine,
and does them, I will liken him to a wise man who built his
house on the rock: and the rain descended, the floods came,
and the winds blew and beat on that house;
and it did not fall, for it was founded on the rock."
MATTHEW 7:24–25

Jesus shows by a parable that hearing the sayings of Christ will not make us happy if we do not make it a habit to do them. . . . The hearers of Christ's Word are divided into two sorts: some who hear and do what they hear, others who hear and do not.

Some hear His sayings and do them. Blessed be God that there are any such, though comparatively few. To hear Christ is not barely to give Him the hearing, but to obey Him. It is a mercy that we hear His sayings. But if we practice not what we hear, we receive that grace in vain. All the sayings of Christ, not only the laws He enacted but the truths He revealed, must be done by us. It is not enough to hear Christ's sayings and understand them, remember them, talk of them, repeat them, and dispute for them. We must hear and do them. . . .

There are others who hear Christ's sayings and do them not. Their religion rests in bare hearing and goes no further. The seed is sown, but it never comes up. Those who only hear Christ's sayings, and do them not, sit down in the road to heaven, and that will never bring them to their journey's end.

These two sorts of hearers are represented by two builders. One was wise and built on a rock, and his building stood in a storm. The other was foolish and built upon the sand; his building fell. The general scope of this parable teaches us that the only way to make sure work for our souls and eternity is to hear and do the sayings of the Lord Jesus.

The Law of Liberty

*But he who looks into the perfect law of liberty
and continues in it,
and is not a forgetful hearer but a doer of the work,
this one will be blessed in what he does.*

JAMES 1:25

What is the proper use of the Word of God? The use we are to make of God's Word may be learned from its being compared to a looking glass in which a man may see his natural face. As a looking glass shows us the spots and defilements on our faces, so the Word of God shows us our sins. It shows us what is wrong so that it may be changed. When we attend to the Word of God so as to see ourselves, our true state and condition, and dress ourselves anew by the glass of God's Word, this is to make a proper use of it.

We have here an account of those who do not use this glass of the Word as they ought. In vain do we hear God's Word, and look into the gospel glass, if we go away and forget our spots and their remedy. This is the case of those who do not hear the Word as they ought. Those also are described who hear correctly and use the glass of God's Word as they should. The gospel is a law of liberty or liberation. The ceremonial law was a yoke of bondage. The gospel of Christ is a law of liberty. It is a perfect law. In hearing the Word, we look into this perfect law. Then only do we look into the law of liberty as we should when we continue therein. Those who thus do and continue in the law and Word of God are, and shall be, blessed in their deeds. This blessedness does not lie in knowing, but in doing, the will of God. It is not talking, but walking, that will bring us to heaven.

Fruitful and Faithful Disciples

"If you keep My commandments,
you will abide in My love;
just as I have kept My Father's commandments
and abide in His love."
JOHN 15:10

Jesus tells His disciples that if they bring forth much fruit and continue in His love, He will continue to rejoice in them as He had done. Fruitful and faithful disciples are the joy of the Lord Jesus. It is the will of Christ that His disciples should constantly and continually rejoice in Him. The joy of those who abide in Christ's love is a continual feast.

They were to show their love of Him by keeping His commandments. "If you keep My commandments, you will abide in My love." The promise is that you shall live in the love of Jesus as in a dwelling place, at home in Christ's love; as in a resting place, at ease in Christ's love; as in a stronghold, safe in Christ's love. The condition of this promise is "if you keep My commandments." The disciples were to keep Christ's commandments not only by a constant conformity to them themselves, but by a faithful delivery of them to others; they were to keep them as trustees.

To induce them to keep His commandments, He urges His own example: "As I have kept My Father's commandments and abide in His love." In others words: You are My friends if you do whatever I command you. Only those who prove themselves His obedient servants will be Christ's faithful friends. Universal obedience to Christ is the only acceptable obedience.

Those Who Know Him

The LORD also will be a refuge for the oppressed,
a refuge in times of trouble.
And those who know Your name will put their trust in You;
for You, LORD, have not forsaken those who seek You.
PSALM 9:9–10

David comforts himself and others in God and pleases himself with thoughts of God: (1) with thoughts of His eternity. On this earth we see nothing durable. Even strong cities are buried in rubbish and forgotten, but the Lord will endure forever; (2) with thoughts of His sovereignty both in government and judgment. He has prepared His throne, has fixed it by His infinite wisdom, has fixed it by His immutable counsel; (3) with thoughts of His justice and righteousness in all the administration of His government. He shall judge the world, all persons and all controversies, shall minister judgment to the people in righteousness and in uprightness, and there will not be the least complaint against it; (4) with thoughts of that peculiar favor that God bears to His own people and the special protection He takes them under. He will be a refuge for the oppressed, a high place, a strong place for the oppressed in times of trouble; and (5) with thoughts of that sweet satisfaction and repose of mind which those have who made God their refuge. "Those who know Your name will put their trust in You, as I have done, and then they will find, as I have found, that You do not forsake those who seek You." The better God is known, the more He is trusted. Those who know Him to be a God of infinite wisdom will trust Him further than they can see Him. Those who know Him to be a God of almighty power will trust Him when creature confidences fail and they have nothing else to trust in. . . . Those who know Him to be the Father of spirits and an everlasting Father will trust Him with their souls to the end.

A Good Name

Commit your way to the LORD, trust also in Him,
and He shall bring it to pass.
He shall bring forth your righteousness as the light,
and your justice as the noonday.

PSALM 37:5–6

We must make God our heart's delight, and then we shall have our heart's delight. We were commanded to do good, and then follows this command to delight in God. . . . And this pleasant duty has a promise annexed to it: He will give you the desires of your heart. . . . What is the desire of the heart of a good man? It is to know, and love, and live for God, to please Him and be pleased in Him.

We must make God our guide and submit in everything to His guidance, and then all our affairs, even those that seem intricate and confusing, shall be made to turn out well. The duty is very easy, and if we do it right, it will make us at ease. "Commit your way to the Lord." Cast your burden on the Lord, the burden of your cares. Reveal your way to the Lord; that is, by prayer spread your case, and all your cares about it, before the Lord, and then trust Him to bring it to a good conclusion, with full satisfaction that all is well that God does. . . . The promise is very sweet: He shall bring that to pass, whatever it is that you have committed to Him, if not to your contrivance, yet to your contentment. He will find means to extricate you out of your problems, to prevent your fears, and bring about your purposes to your satisfaction. "He shall bring forth your righteousness as the light, and your justice as the noonday." That is, He shall make it to appear that you are an honest man, and that is honor enough. If we take care to keep a good conscience, we may leave it to God to take care of our good name.

God's Providence

*"He who is faithful in what is least is faithful also in much;
and he who is unjust in what is least is unjust also in much."*

LUKE 16:10

If we do not make right use of the gifts of God's providence, how can we expect the gifts of His spiritual grace? . . .

The riches of this world are the less; grace and glory are greater. Now if we are unfaithful in the less, it may justly be feared that we should be so in the gifts of God's grace, and therefore they will be denied us. He who serves God and does good with his money will serve God and do good with the more noble and valuable talents of wisdom and grace, but he who buries the one talent of this world's wealth will never improve the five talents of spiritual riches. The riches of this world are unrighteous mammon, which is hastening from us rapidly, and, if we would make any advantage of it, we must bestir ourselves quickly. If we do not, how can we expect to be entrusted with spiritual riches, which are the only true riches?

Those who are truly rich and very rich are rich in faith and rich towards God, rich in Christ, the kingdom of God, and the righteousness thereof. If other things are added to us, by using them well we may take the firmer grip on the true riches and may be qualified to receive yet more grace from God. The riches of this world are not our own; they are God's. We have them from others; we use them for others; and we must shortly leave them to others. But spiritual and eternal riches are our own. They are a good part that will never be taken away from us. If we make Christ our own and the promises our own and heaven our own, we have that which we may truly call our own. But how can we expect God to enrich us with these if we do not serve Him with our worldly possessions, of which we are but stewards?

Do Not Waver

*He did not waver at the promise of God through unbelief,
but was strengthened in faith. . .and being fully convinced
that what He had promised He was also able to perform.*
ROMANS 4:20–21

Abraham did not waver at the promise of God through unbelief.
It was unlikely that Abraham could beget children at his age,
but. . .his faith thought of nothing but the faithfulness of
the promise, and this kept up his faith. . . . Abraham did not
argue; he did not hold any self-consultation about it, but by a
resolute act of his soul, with a holy boldness, ventured all on the
promise. He took it not for a point that would admit of argument or debate.

Unbelief is at the bottom of all our waverings at God's
promises. It is not the promise that fails, but our faith that
fails when we waver. Though weak faith shall not be rejected,
strong faith shall be commended and honored. The strength
of his faith appeared in the victory it won over his fears. Abraham's faith gave God the glory. . . . We never hear our Lord
Jesus commending anything as much as great faith.

Abraham saw the storms of doubts, fears, and temptations
likely to rise against the promise, but having taken God for his
pilot and the promise for his compass, like a bold adventurer he
sets up all his sails, regards neither winds nor clouds, but trusts
to the wisdom and faithfulness of his pilot, bravely heads for the
harbor, and comes home an unspeakable gainer. God was able.
Our waverings rise mainly from our distrust of the divine power.
It is necessary that we believe not only that He is faithful, but
that He is able. Faith is said to be the prime condition of our
justification, because it is a grace that above all others gives glory
to God.

The Devotion of Deacons

> For those who have served well as deacons
> obtain for themselves a good standing and
> great boldness in the faith which is in Christ Jesus.
>
> 1 TIMOTHY 3:13

Deacons must be grave. Seriousness becomes all Christians, but especially those who are in church office. They must not be double-tongued, for a double tongue comes from a double heart; flatterers and slanderers are double-tongued. They must not be given to much wine, for this opens the door to many temptations. They must not be greedy of filthy lucre: This would be especially bad in deacons who were entrusted with the church's money. If we keep a pure conscience, this will preserve in our souls the mystery of faith. The soundness of their judgments, their zeal for Christ, and the blamelessness of their conversation must be proved. Their wives, likewise, must have a good character. All who are related to ministers must double their care to walk as becomes the gospel of Christ, lest the ministry be blamed. As he said before of bishops or ministers, so here of the deacons: They must be the husband of one wife; they must rule their children and their own houses well. The families of deacons should be examples to other families.

In the primitive church there were only two orders of ministers or officers: bishops and deacons. The design of the deacon's office was to mind the temporal concerns of the church, such as the salaries of the ministers and providing for the poor. Integrity and uprightness in an inferior office are the way to be preferred to a higher station in the church. This will also give a man great boldness in the faith, whereas a want of integrity and uprightness will make a man timorous.

Rich in the Faith

Listen, my beloved brethren:
Has God not chosen the poor of this world
to be rich in faith and heirs of the kingdom
which He promised to those who love Him?
JAMES 2:5

God has made those heirs of a kingdom whom you make of no reputation. Many of the poor of this world are the chosen of God. Their being God's chosen does not prevent their being poor; their being poor does not at all prejudice the evidence of their being chosen. God designed to recommend His holy religion not by the external advantages of gaiety and pomp, but by its intrinsic worth, and therefore He chose the poor of this world.

Many poor of the world are rich in faith; thus the poorest may become rich. It is expected from those who have wealth that they be rich in good works, but it is expected from the poor of the world that they be rich in faith. Believing Christians are heirs of a kingdom, though they may be very poor as to present possessions. Where any are rich in faith, there will divine love also be. We read of the crown promised to those who love God. We find there is a kingdom, too. And as the crown is a crown of life, so the kingdom will be an everlasting kingdom. After such considerations as these, the charge is cutting indeed. Respecting persons on account of their riches or outward figure is shown to be a very great sin because of the mischiefs that are owning to worldly wealth and greatness. This will make your sin appear exceedingly wrong and foolish, in setting up that which tends to pull you down and to dishonor that worthy name by which you are called.

Ministry to the Saints

*For God is not unjust to forget your work
and labor of love which you have shown toward His name,
in that you have ministered to the saints, and do minister.*

HEBREWS 6:10

There are things that accompany salvation, things that are never separated from salvation. Ministers must sometimes speak by way of caution to those of whose salvation they have good hopes. And those who have in themselves good hopes should consider seriously how fatal a disappointment it would be if they should fall short. Thus, they are to work out their salvation with fear and trembling.

God had wrought a principle of holy love and charity in them. Good works and labor proceeding from love of God are commendable, and what is done to any in the name of God shall not go unrewarded. Those who expect a gracious reward for their labor of love must continue in it as long as they have ability and opportunity. Those who persevere in a diligent discharge of their duty shall attain the full assurance of hope in the end. Full assurance is a higher degree of hope. They differ not in nature, but only in degree. Full assurance is attainable by great diligence and perseverance to the end.

They should not be slothful. They must not love their ease or lose their opportunities. They should follow the good examples of those who have gone before. There are some who from assurance have gone to inherit the promises. The way by which they came to the inheritance was that of faith and patience. We must follow them in the way of faith and patience.

Do You Believe I Can?

And when He had come into the house,
the blind men came to Him. And Jesus said to them,
"Do you believe that I am able to do this?"
They said to Him, "Yes, Lord." Then He touched their eyes,
saying, "According to your faith let it be to you."
MATTHEW 9:28–29

When two blind men came to Jesus for mercy, He asked them, "Do you believe that I am able to do this?" Faith is a great condition of Christ's favors. They who would receive the mercy of Christ must firmly believe the power of Christ. What we would have Him do for us, we must be fully assured that He is able to do. . . . They had intimated their faith in the office of Christ as Son of David and in His mercy; Christ demands a profession of faith in His power. This will amount to their belief of His being not only the Son of David, but the Son of God, for it is God's prerogative to open the eyes of the blind. . . . To believe the power of Christ is not only to assure ourselves of it, but to commit ourselves to it and encourage ourselves in it.

To this question they gave an immediate answer, without hesitation: "Yes, Lord." He touched their eyes. He put the cure upon their faith. . . . When they begged for a cure, He enquired into their faith. . . . It is a great comfort to true believers that Jesus Christ knows their faith and is well pleased with it. Though it is weak, though others do not discern it, though they themselves are ready to question it, it is known to Him. They who apply themselves to Jesus Christ shall be dealt with according to their faith, not according to their fancies, nor according to their profession. True believers may be sure to find all that favor which is offered in the gospel, and our comforts ebb or flow, according as our faith is stronger or weaker.

An Eye of Faith

*Trust in the LORD, and do good; dwell in the land,
and feed on His faithfulness. Delight yourself also in the LORD,
and He shall give you the desires of your heart.*

PSALM 37:3–4

We are cautioned against discontent at the prosperity and success of evildoers. We may suppose that David speaks this to himself first. That is preached best—and with the most probability of success—to others, which is first preached to ourselves. When we look around, we see the world full of evildoers and workers of iniquity who flourish and prosper. When we look within, we find ourselves tempted to fret at this and to be envious. We are apt to fret at God, as if He were unkind to the world and unkind to His church by permitting such men to live and prosper and prevail, as they do. We are apt to envy them the liberty they take in getting wealth. . .and to wish that we could shake off the restraints of conscience and do the same.

When we look forward with an eye of faith, we shall see no reason to envy wicked people their prosperity, for their ruin is at the door and they are ripening fast for it. They flourish, but as grass and the green herb, which nobody envies or frets about. They will soon wither of themselves. Outward prosperity is a fading thing, and so is the life to which it is confined.

We are counseled to live a life of confidence in God. . . . If we do well for our own souls, we shall see little reason to envy those who do so ill for theirs. We must make God our hope in the way of duty, and then we shall have a comfortable life in this world. We are not to think we can trust in God and then live as we choose; we are to trust in the Lord and do good. Then we will "feed on His faithfulness." It is good living, good feeding, upon the promises.

Commit Your Works to the Lord

Commit your works to the LORD,
and your thoughts will be established.
PROVERBS 16:3

In short, man purposes. He has the freedom of thought and the freedom of will given to him. Let him form his projects and plan his schemes as he thinks best, but after all, God disposes. Man cannot go on with his business without the assistance and blessing of God, who made man's mouth and teaches us what we shall say.

We are all apt to be partial in judging ourselves. The judgment of God concerning us is according to truth: He weighs the spirit in a just and unerring balance, knows what is in us, and passes judgment on us accordingly, and by His judgment we will stand or fall.

The only way to have our thoughts established is to commit our works to the Lord. The great concerns of our souls must be committed to the grace of God. All our outward concerns must be committed to the providence of God and to the sovereign, wise, and gracious disposal of that providence. Roll your works upon the Lord; roll the burden of your care from yourself onto God.

Laboring in Strength

And the things that you have heard from me
among many witnesses,
commit these to faithful men who
will be able to teach others also.

2 TIMOTHY 2:2

Paul encourages Timothy to constancy and perseverance in his work (v. 1). Those who have work to do for God must strengthen themselves for it. Where there is the truth of grace, there must be a laboring after the strength of grace. We need to grow stronger and stronger in that which is good—instead of trying to be strong in our own strength. "Be strong, not confiding in their own sufficiency, but in the grace that is in Jesus Christ." There is grace enough in Him for all of us. We must be strong in this grace, not in ourselves or in the grace we have already received, but in the grace that is in Him.

Timothy must count on suffering, even to death, and therefore he must train others to succeed him in the ministry of the gospel. He must lodge the gospel as a trust in their hands and commit to them the things that he had heard. Two things he must have an eye to in ordaining ministers: their fidelity or integrity and also their ministerial ability. They must not only be knowing, but able to teach.

He must also endure hardship (v. 3). All Christians, but especially ministers, are soldiers of Jesus Christ. The soldiers of Christ must prove themselves good soldiers, faithful to their captain, resolute in His cause. Those who would prove themselves good soldiers must endure hardship. We must count on it in this world and bear it patiently when it comes.

The Duties of a Servant

"For everyone to whom much is given,
from him much will be required;
and to whom much has been committed,
of him they will ask the more."
LUKE 12:48

The disciples were made rulers of God's household. Ministers derive authority from Christ. Their business is to give God's children and servants their portion of meat, that which is proper for them; convictions and comfort to those to whom they respectively belong; to give it to them in due season; a word in season to him who is weary. They must prove themselves faithful and wise—faithful to their Master and faithful to their fellow servants. Ministers must be both skillful and faithful.

What would be their happiness if they proved themselves faithful and wise? Blessed is that servant who is doing and is not idle; that is, doing as he should be by public preaching and personal application. His happiness is illustrated by the preferment of a steward who has proved himself in small things. He shall be promoted to higher duties. Ministers who obtain mercy from the Lord to be faithful shall obtain further mercy to be abundantly rewarded for the faithful in the day of the Lord.

The knowledge of our duty is an aggravation of our sin. A servant who knows his Lord's will shall be burdened with many stripes. God will justly inflict more upon him because it takes a great degree of willfulness and contempt to sin when we know better. There is a good reason for this to be added: "For everyone to whom much is given, from him much will be required." Those who have greater capacities of mind than others, more knowledge and learning, more acquaintance with the Scriptures, to them much is given and therefore much expected.

The Work of Our Hands

And let the beauty of the LORD our God be upon us,
and establish the work of our hands for us;
yes, establish the work of our hands.

PSALM 90:17

"Let Your work appear upon Your servants; let it appear that You have wrought upon us, to bring us home to Yourself and to fit us for Yourself. Let Your work appear, and in it Your glory will appear to us and those who shall come after us" (v. 16). Perhaps in this prayer the Israelites distinguish between themselves and their children, for so God distinguished in His late message to them (Numbers 14:31–32): "Your carcasses shall fall in this wilderness, but your little ones will I bring into Canaan."

"Lord," they say, "let Your work appear on us, to reform us, and bring us to a better temper, and then let Your glory appease to our children, in performing the promise to them which we have forfeited." Let it appear that God favors us. Let the grace of God in us and the light of our good works make our faces shine, and let divine consolations put gladness into our hearts, and a luster upon our countenances, and that also will be the beauty of the Lord upon us. "Establish the work of our hands for us." God's working upon us does not discharge us from using our utmost endeavors in serving Him and working out our salvation. But when we have done all, we must wait upon God for the success.

David's Resolutions

My eyes shall be on the faithful of the land,
that they may dwell with me;
he who walks in a perfect way, he shall serve me.
PSALM 101:6

David resolved not to practice evil himself (v. 3). He further resolved not to keep bad servants or employ those who were vicious. He will have nothing to do with spiteful, malicious people who care not what mischief they do to those they have a grudge against. "A perverse heart shall depart from me; I will not know wickedness" (v. 4). David will prevent preferment of those who hope to curry favor with him. He will have no patience with those who are grasping at all preferments, for it is certain they do not aim at doing good, but only at aggrandizing themselves and their families. God resists the proud, and so will David. He will make use of no such persons as agents for him.

He resolved to put those in trust under him who were honest and good. "My eyes shall be on the faithful of the land." The kingdom must be searched for honest men, and if one man is better than another, he must be preferred. Saul had chosen servants for their goodliness, but David for their goodness.

He resolved to extend his zeal to the reformation of the city and country, as well as of the court. He would be zealous in promoting the reformation of manners and suppression of vice. That which he aimed at was not only the securing of his own government and the peace of the country, but the honor of God in the purity of His church.

Inward Peace

The work of righteousness will be peace,
and the effect of righteousness, quietness and assurance forever.
ISAIAH 32:17

Inward peace follows the indwelling of righteousness. It is itself peace, and the effort of it is quietness and assurance forever, that is, a holy serenity and security of mind. Those are the quiet and peaceable lives that are spent in all godliness and honesty (1 Timothy 2:2). Even the work of righteousness shall be peace. . . . Though the work of righteousness may be toilsome and expose us to contempt, yet it is peace. The effect of righteousness shall be quietness and assurance, to the endless ages of eternity.

When the terror of Sennacherib's invasion was over, the people were more sensible than ever of the mercy of a quiet life not disturbed with the alarms of war. Let every family keep itself quiet from strife within the house and put itself under God's protection.

Even when it shall hail, and there shall be a violent battering storm coming down on the forest that lies bleak, then shall Jerusalem be a quiet resting place, for the city shall be low in a low place, under the wind, not exposed to the fury of the storm, but sheltered by the mountains that are round about Jerusalem. There shall be good crops gathered every year. God will give the increase, but the husbandman must be industrious and sow beside all waters. If he does this, the corn shall come up so thick that he shall turn in his cattle, even the ox and the ass, to eat the tops of it. Some think this points to the ministry of the apostles who, as husbandmen, went forth to sow their seed beside all waters (vv. 19–20). When God sends these happy times, blessed are those who improve them in doing good with what they have, who sow beside all waters.

All in Vain?

"Then I said, 'I have labored in vain,
I have spent my strength for nothing and in vain;
yet surely my just reward is with the LORD,
and my work with my God.' "
ISAIAH 49:4

Isaiah spoke of the discouragement he had met with at his first setting out. "Then I said, with a sad heart, I have labored in vain; those who were careless, and strangers to God, are so still. I have called, and they have refused; I have stretched out my hands to a gainsaying people." Jeremiah was tempted to stop his work for the same reasons. It is the complaint of many a faithful minister who has not loitered, but labored, not spared, but spent his strength, and himself with it. They will not repent and believe.

He comforts himself under this discouragement with this consideration, that it was the cause of God in which he was engaged: "Yet surely my judgment is with the Lord, who is the judge of all, and my work with my God, whose servant I am." His comfort may be the comfort of all faithful ministers when they see little success of their labors. They are with God and for God; they are on His side and work together with Him. "He knows the way that I take; my judgment is with the Lord, to determine whether I have not delivered my soul and left the blood of those who perish on their own heads." Though the labor is in vain, if he is faithful, the Lord will justify him and bear him out, though men condemn him. The work is with the Lord, to give them success according to His purpose, in His own way and time.

All the Good Pleasure

Therefore we also pray always for you that
our God would count you worthy of this calling,
and fulfill all the good pleasure of His goodness
and the work of faith with power.

2 THESSALONIANS 1:11

The apostle gave thanks for the Thessalonians' faith, love, and patience. Where there is the truth of grace, there will be an increase of it, and where there is the increase of grace, God must have all the glory of it. We may be tempted to think that though when we were bad, we could not make ourselves good, yet when we are good, we can easily make ourselves better. Their faith grew exceedingly, and the growth of their faith appeared by the works of faith. Their charity abounded. Their patience as well as faith increased in all their persecutions and tribulations. They endured all these by faith and endured them with patience arising from Christian principles.

The apostle prayed that God would begin His good work of grace in them. We are called to God's kingdom and glory. Now if this is our calling, our great concern should be to be worthy of it. We should pray that He would make us worthy. The good pleasure of God denotes His gracious purposes towards His people. There are various and manifold purposes of grace and goodwill in God toward His people, and the apostle prays that all of them may be fulfilled in the Thessalonians. In particular, he prays that God would fulfill in them the work of faith with power. Our good works should so shine before men that others may glorify God, that the Christ may be glorified in and by us, and then we shall be glorified in and with Him.

Charity

"For the poor will never cease from the land;
therefore I command you, saying,
'You shall open your hand wide to your brother,
to your poor and your needy, in your land.'"
DEUTERONOMY 15:11

Every seventh year was a year of release. Among other acts of grace, those who had borrowed money and had not been able to pay it back would this year be released from their debts. If they were able, they were afterward bound in conscience to repay it, yet the creditor could never recover it by law. Many good expositors think this only forbids the exacting of the debt in the year of release, but others think it was a release of the debt forever, and this seems more probable.

The reasons for this law were to put honor upon the sabbatical year, because it is called the Lord's release, and to prevent the falling of any Israelite into extreme poverty. God's security is given by a divine promise that whatever they lost from their poor debtors would be made up by God's blessing on all they had and did.

It is taken for granted that there would be poor among them who would have occasion to borrow and that there would never cease to be some such objects of charity. In such a case we are commanded to lend or give according to our ability and the necessity of the case. When we have an occasion of charitable lending, if we cannot trust the borrower, we must trust God and lend, hoping for nothing again in this world, but expecting it will be recompensed in the resurrection of the just.

Fulfilling Your Ministry

But you be watchful in all things, endure afflictions,
do the work of an evangelist, fulfill your ministry.
2 TIMOTHY 4:5

Paul reminded Timothy of his duty before God: (1) to preach the Word. This is ministers' business. It is not their own notions and fancies that they are to preach but the pure, plain Word of God; (2) to urge what he preached: "Be ready in season and out of season. Convince, rebuke, exhort, with all longsuffering and teaching"; (3) he must tell people of their faults and endeavor, by dealing plainly with them, to bring them to repentance; (4) he must direct, encourage, and quicken those who began well. He must do so very patiently. He must do it rationally, not with passion, but with doctrine. Teach them the truth as it is in Jesus, and this will be a means both to reclaim them from evil and bring them to good; (5) he must watch in all things. "Watch to your work; watch against the temptations of Satan; watch over the souls of those who are committed to your charge"; (6) he must count upon afflictions and endure them; (7) he must remember his office and discharge its duties. The office of the evangelist was, as the apostles' deputy, to water the churches the apostles planted; and (8) he must fulfill his ministry, performing all the parts of his office with diligence and care. The best way to make full proof of our ministry is to fulfill it, to fill it up in all its parts with proper work.

Trying Our Own Works

But let each one examine his own work,
and then he will have rejoicing in himself alone,
and not in another.
GALATIANS 6:4

We are advised that everyone should prove his own works. By our own work is chiefly meant our own actions or behavior. These the apostle directs us to prove, that is, to seriously examine them by the rule of God's Word. Instead of being forward to judge and censure others, it would much more become us to search and try our own ways; our business lies more at home than abroad, with ourselves than with other men. The best way to keep us from being proud of ourselves is to prove ourselves. The better we are acquainted with our own hearts and ways, the less liable we shall be to despise and the more disposed to compassion and help for others.

This is the way to have rejoicing in ourselves alone. If we set ourselves earnestly to prove our own work, this would be a much better ground of joy and satisfaction than to be able to rejoice in another, either in the good opinion which others may have of us or by comparing ourselves with others. The joy that results is nothing to that which arises from trial of ourselves by the rule of God's Word and our being able to approve ourselves to Him. Though we have nothing in ourselves to boast of, yet we may have the matter of rejoicing in ourselves. If our consciences can witness for us, we may upon good ground rejoice. The true way to have rejoicing in ourselves is to be much in proving our own works. If we have the testimony of our consciences that we are accepted by God, we need not much concern ourselves about what others think or say of us.

Suffering Work

Thus says the LORD:
"Refrain your voice from weeping,
and your eyes from tears;
for your work shall be rewarded, says the LORD."

JEREMIAH 31:16

The inhabitants of Ramah grieved for their sons and their daughters who were carried away (1 Samuel 30:6). The tender parents even refused to be comforted for their children, because they were not with them, but were in the hands of their enemies; they were never likely to see them again.

This is applied by the evangelists to the great mourning that was at Bethlehem for the murder of the infants there by Herod (Matthew 2:17–18), and this Scripture is said to be fulfilled. Though we mourn, we must not murmur. In order to repress inordinate grief, we must consider that there is hope in our end, hope that the trouble will not last always, that it will be a happy end—the end will be peace. Though one generation falls in the wilderness, the next shall enter Canaan. Our suffering work will be rewarded. God makes His people glad according to the days wherein He has afflicted them, and so there is a proportion between the joys and the sorrows, as between the reward and the work (Romans 8:18). There is hope concerning children removed by death that they shall return to their own border, to the happy lot assigned them in the resurrection, a lot in the heavenly Canaan, that border of His sanctuary.

Choose Whom You Will Serve

*"But as for me and my house,
we will serve the LORD."*
JOSHUA 24:15

Joshua asks the Israelites to embrace their religion rationally and intelligently, for it is a reasonable service. He proposed the candidates: the Lord Jehovah on one side and either the gods of their ancestors or the gods of their neighbors (which would insinuate themselves into the affections of those who were fond of good fellowship) on the other side. He supposes there were those to whom it would seem evil to serve the Lord. There are prejudices and objections that some people raise against religion. It seems evil to them, hard and unreasonable to mortify the flesh, take up their cross, and so on. He leaves the matter to them. "Choose who you will serve, and do it today. Now that the matter is laid plainly before you, speedily bring it to a head."

Joshua indicates that it is the will of God that we should each make religion a serious and deliberate choice. Religion has so much reason and righteousness on its side and its merits are so obvious that it may be safely referred to every man who allows himself free thought either to choose or refuse it, for the merits of the cause are so plain that no considerate man will refuse to choose it. He directs their choice in the matter by an open declaration of his own decision: "But as for me and my house, we will serve the Lord."

God's Glory and Faithfulness

Be still, and know that I am God;
I will be exalted among the nations,
I will be exalted in the earth!

PSALM 46:10

This verse gives glory to God both as King of nations and as King of saints. Since God is King of saints, we must admit that His works are great and marvelous (Revelation 15:3). He does and will do great things. Let His enemies be still and threaten no more, but know that He is God, one infinitely above them. Let them rage no more, for it is all in vain. He who sits in heaven laughs at them, and in spite of all their impotent malice, He will be exalted on the earth, not merely in the church. Men will set up themselves, but let them know that God will be exalted and will glorify His own name. When they deal proudly, He will be above them and make them know that He is in control.

Let His people be still and tremble no more, but know to their comfort that the Lord is God. When we pray, "Father, glorify Your name," we ought to exercise faith on the answer given to that prayer when Christ Himself prayed it: "I have both glorified it, and I will glorify it yet again." Let all believers triumph in this. They have the presence of a God of power: The Lord of hosts is with us. This sovereign Lord sides with us, acts with us, and has promised He will never leave us. Hosts may be against us, but we need not fear them if the Lord of hosts is with us. We are under the protection of God, who is not only able to help us but has promised in honor and faithfulness to help us.

He Waits to Be Gracious

"Behold, I stand at the door and knock.
If anyone hears My voice and opens the door,
I will come in to him and dine with him,
and he with Me."
REVELATION 3:20

This verse gives us great and gracious encouragement to accept the admonition that Christ has given us. "You may think I have given you hard words and severe reproofs; it is all out of love to your souls." Sinners ought to take the rebukes of God's Word as tokens of His goodwill to their souls. Better are the frowns and wounds of a friend than the flattering smiles of an enemy. If they would comply with His admonitions, He was ready to make them good to their souls. Christ is graciously pleased by His Word and Spirit to come to the door of the heart of sinners. He finds this door shut against Him; the heart of man is by nature shut up against Christ. When He finds the heart shut, He does not immediately withdraw, but He waits to be gracious. Those who open to Him will enjoy His presence. He will dine with them. He will accept what is good in them. He will bring the best part of the entertainment with Him.

It is possible that by the reproofs and counsels of Christ, believers might be inspired with fresh zeal and vigor. If they did so, they would have a great reward. Christ Himself had met with His temptations and conflicts. He overcame them all and was more than a conqueror. Those who are conformed to Christ in His trials and victories will be conformed to Him in His glory.

Spiritual Joys

"Therefore you now have sorrow;
but I will see you again and your heart will rejoice,
and your joy no one will take from you."
JOHN 16:22

Here Jesus tells the disciples of the sorrow they were soon to experience. "You now have sorrow, because I am leaving you." Christ's withdrawings are a just cause of grief to His disciples. When the sun sets, the sunflower will hang its head.

He, more largely than before, assures them of a return of joy. Three things recommend the joy. The cause of it is "I will see you again." Christ will graciously return to those who wait for Him. Men, when they are exalted, will scarcely look at their inferiors, but the exalted Jesus will visit His disciples. Christ's returns are returns of joy to all His disciples. The cordiality of His return is that "Your heart will rejoice." Joy in the heart is solid and not flashy. It is secret, it is sweet, it is sure and not easily broken in upon. The continuance of their joy: "Your joy no one will take from you." They would if they could, but they shall not prevail. Some understand Him to be speaking of the eternal joy of the glorified. We may be robbed of our joys on earth by a thousand accidents, but heavenly joys are everlasting. I rather understand Him to be speaking of the spiritual joys of those who are sanctified. They could not rob them of their joy because they could not separate them from the love of Christ, could not rob them of their God or of their treasure in heaven.

Assured Rest

*"Come to Me,
all you who labor and are heavy laden,
and I will give you rest."*
MATTHEW 11:28

We must come to Jesus Christ as our Rest and repose ourselves in Him. "Come to Me, all you who labor and are heavy laden." The type of person invited is all who labor and are heavy laden. This is a word in season to anyone who is weary. But this is rather to be understood as the burden of sin, both the guilt and the power of it, not necessarily physical labor. All those—and those only—are invited to rest in Christ who are sensible of sin as a burden and groan under it: only those who are convinced of the evil of sin, of their own sin, but are contrite in soul and are really sick of their sins. This is a necessary preparation for pardon and peace. The Comforter must first convince. The invitation itself is "Come to Me." He holds out the golden scepter so we may touch the top of it and live. It is the duty and interest of weary and heavy laden sinners to come to Jesus Christ. We must accept Him as our Physician and Advocate, being freely willing to be saved by Him in His own way and on His own terms. The blessing promised is good, especially to those who do come: "I will give you rest." Rest is good, especially to those who labor and are heavy laden. Jesus Christ will give assured rest to those weary souls who by a lively faith come to Him for it, a rest in God, in His love.

Our Source of Courage

Wait on the LORD; be of good courage,
and He shall strengthen your heart;
wait, I say, on the LORD!

PSALM 27:14

David expresses his dependence on God. "When I am helpless as every poor orphan who was left fatherless and motherless, then I know the Lord will take me up" (v. 10). He believed he would see the goodness of the Lord in the land of the living; and, if he had not done so, he would have fainted under his afflictions. Those who walk by faith in the goodness of the Lord shall in due time walk in the sight of that goodness. It is his comfort, not so much that he will see the land of the living as that he will see the goodness of God in it, for that is the comfort of all creature comforts to a gracious soul. Heaven is that land that may truly be called the land of the living. This earth is the land of the dying. There is nothing like the believing hope of eternal life to keep us from fainting under all the calamities of this present time. In the meantime David says to himself or to his friends, "He shall strengthen your heart," shall sustain the spirit. In that strength, wait on the Lord by faith, and prayer, and a humble resignation to His will. "Wait, I say, on the Lord!" Whatever you do, do not become remiss in your attendance upon God. Those who wait on the Lord have reason to be of good courage.

Christian Contentment

Let your conduct be without covetousness;
be content with such things as you have.
For He Himself has said,
"I will never leave you nor forsake you."
HEBREWS 13:5

The apostle calls the believing Hebrews to the performance of many duties, one of which is Christian contentment. Covetousness is contrary to his grace and duty. We must take care not only to keep this sin down, but to root it out of our souls. Being satisfied and pleased with such things as we have is the opposite of covetousness. What God gives us from day to day, we must be content with. We must bring our minds to our present condition. Those who cannot do it would not be contented even if God raised their condition to their minds, for the mind would rise with the condition. Paul, though abased and empty, had learned in every state, in any state, to be content. The reason Christians have to be contented with their lot is that this promise contains the sum and substance of all the promises. From this comprehensive promise they may assure themselves of help from God (v. 6). Men can do nothing against God, and God can make all that men do against His people to turn out to their good.

I Will Exalt You

O LORD, You are my God.
I will exalt You, I will praise Your name,
for You have done wonderful things;
Your counsels of old are faithfulness and truth.
ISAIAH 25:1

The prophet determines to praise God. When God is punishing the kings of the earth, a poor prophet can go to Him and, with humble boldness, say, "I will praise Your name." God has relieved His needy people, being a strength to the poor, a strength to the needy. He strengthens the weak who are humble and support themselves upon Him. He not only makes them strong but He is Himself their strength. He is a refuge from the storm of rain or hail and a shadow from the scorching heat of the sun in summer. The blast of the terrible ones is as a storm against the wall, which makes a great noise but cannot overthrow the wall. The enemies of God's poor are terrible. Their rage is like a blast of wind: loud, blustering, and furious; but like the wind, they are under a divine check, for God holds the winds in His fist.

He shall bring down the noise of strangers, abate and still it, as the heat in a dry place is abated and moderated by the shadow of a cloud passing overhead. The oppressors of God's people are called strangers, for they forget that those they oppress are of the same blood as them. They are called terrible ones; they would rather be feared than loved. The branches, even the top branches, of the terrible ones will be broken off. If the laborers in God's vineyard are called to bear the burden and heat of the day, He will refresh them, as with the shadow of a cloud.

Our Covenant

"For the mountains shall depart and the hills be removed,
but My kindness shall not depart from you,
nor shall My covenant of peace be removed,"
says the LORD, who has mercy on you.
ISAIAH 54:10

Looking forward to future dangers, and in defiance of them, God's favors appear constant and His kindness everlasting, for it is formed into a covenant of peace.

This is as firm as the waters of Noah, that is, as firm as that promise God made concerning the deluge, that there should never be the like again (see Genesis 8:21–22; 9:11). God has kept His word, though the world has been very provoking. And thus inviolable is the covenant of grace: "I have sworn that I would not be angry with you, as I have been, nor rebuke you, as I have done" (v. 9).

It is more firm than the strongest parts of the visible creation. "The mountains shall depart and the hills be removed." Mountains have sometimes been shaken by earthquakes and removed, but the promises of God were never broken by the shock of any event. When our friends fail us, our God does not, nor does His kindness depart. Do the kings of the earth and the rulers set themselves against the Lord? They shall depart and be removed. God's kindness shall never depart from His people, for whomever He loves, He loves to the end. Therefore, the covenant is immovable and inviolable, because it is built not on our merit but on God's mercy, which is from everlasting to everlasting.

Your Father's Good Pleasure

> *"Do not fear, little flock,*
> *for it is your Father's good pleasure*
> *to give you the kingdom."*
> LUKE 12:32

When we frighten ourselves with an apprehension of evil to come, we concern ourselves with how to avoid it, when, after all, perhaps it is only the creation of our own imagination. Therefore, "Do not fear, little flock, for it is your Father's good pleasure to give you the kingdom." This comfortable Word we did not have in Matthew. Christ's flock in this world is a little flock. The church is a vineyard, a garden, a small spot, compared to the wilderness of this world. Though it is a little flock, quite outnumbered by its enemies, yet it is the will of Christ that they should not be afraid. "Fear not, little flock, but see yourselves safe under the protection and conduct of the great and good Shepherd." God has a kingdom in store for all who belong to Christ's little flock, a crown of glory (1 Peter 5:4). The kingdom is given according to the good pleasure of the Father: "It is your Father's good pleasure"; it is given not as payment for a debt, but by grace. The believing hopes and prospects of the kingdom should silence and suppress the fears of Christ's little flock in this world. "Fear no trouble; for, though it should come, it shall not come between you and the kingdom." That is not an evil worth trembling at, the thought of which cannot separate us from the love of God.

Not a Timorous People

"For I, the LORD your God,
will hold your right hand,
saying to you, 'Fear not, I will help you.' "
ISAIAH 41:13

The scope of this verse is to silence the fears and encourage the faith of the servants of God in their distresses. Perhaps it was intended, in the first place, for the support of God's Israel in captivity, but all who faithfully serve God through patience and comfort of this Scripture may have hope. A word of caution, counsel, and comfort is often repeated: Fear not. It is contrary to the will of God that His people should be a timorous people.

They may depend on His presence with them as their God. "I will hold your right hand," go hand in hand with you as your guide. When we are weak, He will hold us up, will encourage us, and so hold us by the right hand (Psalm 73:23). He will silence fears, "saying to you, 'Fear not.' " He has said it again and again in His Word, but He will go further: He will, by His Spirit, say it to their hearts.

Though their enemies are very formidable, yet the day is coming when God will reckon with them. There are those who are incensed against God's people, that strive with them (v. 11), that war against them (v. 12), that hate them. But let God's people await God's time. They shall be convinced of the folly of striving with God's people. They shall be ashamed and confounded, which might bring them to repentance, but will rather fill them with rage. They shall be ruined and undone (v. 11). They shall be as nothing before the justice and power of God.

Sweet Sleep

When you lie down,
you will not be afraid;
yes, you will lie down
and your sleep will be sweet.

PROVERBS 3:24

The exhortation is to have religion's rules always in view and always at heart (v. 21). "My son, let them not depart from your eyes; let not your eyes ever depart from them to wander after vanity. Have them always in mind, and as long as you live, keep up and cultivate your acquaintance with them." Have them always at heart, for it is in that treasury, the hidden man of the heart, that we must keep sound wisdom and discretion.

The way of duty is the way of safety. "We are in danger of falling, but wisdom will keep you, that your foot shall not stumble at those things which overthrow many, but which you shall know how to get over." By night we lie exposed and are most subject to frights. "But keep up communion with God, and keep a good conscience, and then when you lie down, you shall not be afraid of fire, or thieves, or specters, or any of the terrors of darkness, knowing that when we and all our friends are asleep, yet He who keeps Israel neither slumbers nor sleeps." The way to have a good night is to keep a good conscience; and the sleep, as of the laboring man, so of the wise and godly man, is sweet. Integrity and uprightness will preserve us, so that we need not be afraid of sudden fear (v. 25). But let not the wise and good man fear the desolation of the wicked when it comes, that is, the desolation which the wicked ones make of religion and the religious.

Our Adoption

For you did not receive the spirit of bondage again to fear,
but you received the Spirit of adoption
by whom we cry out, "Abba, Father."
ROMANS 8:15

Those who are the sons of God have the Spirit to work in them the disposition of children. "For you did not receive the spirit of bondage again to fear." Understand it first as that spirit of bondage which the Old Testament church was under, by reason of the darkness of that dispensation. You are not under that dispensation; you have not received that spirit. Secondly, there is that spirit of bondage which many of the saints themselves were under at their conversion. Then the Spirit Himself was to the saints a spirit of bondage: "But," says the apostle, "with you this is over." For you have received the Spirit of adoption. It is God's prerogative, when He adopts, to give a spirit of adoption—the nature of children. A sanctified soul bears the image of God, as the child bears the image of the father, "by whom we cry out, 'Abba, Father.' " Praying is called crying here. Children who cannot speak vent their desires by crying. Now the Spirit teaches us in prayer to come to God as a Father. And why both words, "Abba" and "Father"? Because Christ said so in prayer (Mark 14:36). It denotes an affectionate, endearing importunity. Little children, begging of their parents, can say little but "Father, Father," and that is enough. It also denotes that the adoption is common both to Jews and Gentiles.

Remember Who Saves

"I, even I, am He who comforts you.
Who are you that you should be afraid of
a man who will die,
and of the son of a man who will be made like grass?"

ISAIAH 51:12

Isaiah comforts the timorous by chiding them: Why are you cast down and why disquieted? It is absurd to have such fear. It is a disparagement to us to give way to them. "Who are you that you should be afraid?" It is absurd to be in such dread of a dying man. What! Afraid of a man who shall die, who shall be made as grass, shall wither and be trodden down or eaten up? We ought to look on every man as a man who will die. Those we fear we must look upon as frail and mortal and consider what a foolish thing it is for the servants of the living God to be afraid of dying men who are here today and gone tomorrow. It is absurd to fear continually every day. Now and then a danger may be imminent and threatening, and it may be prudent to fear it, but to tremble at the shaking of every leaf is to make ourselves subject to bondage (Hebrews 2:15). What has become of all the furious oppressors of God's Israel, that were a terror to them? They passed away and were not, and so shall these.

Those fears are impious. Are you afraid of a man who shall die, forgetting the Lord your Maker, who is also the Maker of all the world? Our inordinate fear of man is forgetfulness of God. When we upset ourselves with the fear of man, we forget that there is a God above him. We forget the experiences we have had of His care and His interposition for our relief many a time when we thought the oppressor ready to destroy.

The Value of Christ's Peace

"Peace I leave with you,
My peace I give to you;
not as the world gives do I give to you.
Let not your heart be troubled, neither let it be afraid."
JOHN 14:27

When Christ was about to leave the world, He made His will. What should He leave to His poor disciples who had left all for Him? Silver and gold He had not, but He left them what was infinitely better--His peace. He did not part in anger but in love, for this was His farewell, "Peace I leave with you."

The legacy that is here bequeathed was peace. Peace is put for all good. Peace is put for reconciliation and love. The peace bequeathed is peace with God. Peace in our own hearts seems to be specially meant. It is the peace on which the angels congratulated men at His birth (Luke 2:14).

This legacy is left to His disciples and followers. This legacy was left to them and their successors, to them and all true Christians in all ages. It is left not as the world gives. It is not a mere formality, but a real blessing. The world's gifts concern only the body and time; Christ's gifts enrich the soul for eternity. The peace Christ gives is infinitely more valuable than that which the world gives. As is the difference between a killing lethargy and a reviving, refreshing sleep, such is the difference between Christ's peace and the world's.

What use should they make of this gift? "Let not your heart be troubled, neither let it be afraid."

Conquerors by Grace

For I am persuaded that neither death nor life, nor angels nor principalities nor powers, nor things present nor things to come, nor height nor depth, nor any other created thing, shall be able to separate us from the love of God which is in Christ Jesus our Lord.

ROMANS 8:38–39

We are conquerors, not in our own strength, but in the grace that is in Christ Jesus. We are conquerors by virtue of Christ's victory. We have nothing to do but to pursue the victory and to divide the spoils, and so are more than conquerors.

A direct and positive conclusion of the whole matter is, "For I am persuaded." Here he enumerates all those things that might separate Christ and believers and concludes that it could not be done. Neither death nor life, neither the fear of death nor the hope of life. We shall not be separated from that love either in death or in life. Nor angels, nor principalities, nor powers. The good angels will not, the bad shall not, and neither can. The good angels are engaged friends; the bad are restrained enemies. Nor things present, nor things to come—neither the sense of troubles present nor the fear of troubles to come. Time shall not separate us, eternity shall not, from the love of Christ, whose favor is twisted in with both present things and things to come. Nor height, nor depth—neither the height of prosperity nor the depth of adversity, nothing from heaven above, nothing on earth below. Nor any other creature—anything that can be named or thought of. It will not, it cannot, separate us from the love of God which is in Christ Jesus our Lord. Nothing does it, can do it, except sin. This is the ground of the steadfastness of the love, because Jesus Christ, in whom He loves us, is the same yesterday, today, and forever.

What Shall We Seek?

"Therefore do not worry, saying,
'What shall we eat?' or 'What shall we drink?'
or 'What shall we wear?' . . .
For your heavenly Father knows that
you need all these things."
MATTHEW 6:31–32

There is scarcely any one sin against which our Lord Jesus warns His disciples more than the sin of disquieting, distracting, distrustful cares about the things of life. "Your heavenly Father knows that you need all these things," these necessary things, such as food and clothing. He knows our wants better than we do ourselves, and He is your Father who loves you and pities you and is ready to help you. We should relieve ourselves of the burden of care by casting it on God because He cares for us. If He cares, why should we worry?

"Seek first the kingdom of God and His righteousness, and all these things shall be added to you" (v. 33). Take no thought for your life, the life of the body, for you have greater and better things to think about: the life of your soul, your eternal happiness. That is the one needful thing about which you should employ your thoughts.

Our duty is to seek. Though we have not attained, but in many things fail and come short, sincere seeking is accepted. We must seek the things of Christ more than our own things. "Seek these things first; first in your days: let the morning of youth be dedicated to God. Seek this first every day; let waking thoughts be of God." Let Him who is the First have the first. All these things, the necessary supports of life, shall be given to you in addition.

We Are Never Alone

Nevertheless I am continually with You; You hold me by my right hand. You will guide me with Your counsel, and afterward receive me to glory.

PSALM 73:23–24

The psalmist admits his dependence on the grace of God. "Nevertheless I am continually with You," and in Your favor "You hold me by my right hand." He had said, in the hour of temptation (v. 14), "All the day long I have been plagued," but here he corrects himself for that passionate complaint. "Though God has chastened me, He has not cast me off. Notwithstanding all the crosses of my life, I have been continually with You. Though God has sometimes written bitter things against me, yet He has still held me by my right hand to prevent my losing my way in the wildernesses through which I have walked." If He thus maintains the spiritual life, the promise of eternal life, we ought not to complain. "My feet were almost gone, and they would have quite gone, past recovery, but You held me by my right hand and so kept me from falling."

He encouraged himself to hope that the same God who had delivered him from this evil work would preserve him to his heavenly kingdom, as St. Paul does (2 Timothy 4:18): "I am now upheld by You, therefore You shall guide me with Your counsel, leading me, as You have done hitherto, and You shall afterward receive me to glory" (v. 24). The psalmist would have paid dearly for following his own counsel in this temptation and therefore resolves for the future to take God's advice. If God directs us in the way of our duty, He will afterward reconcile us to all the dark providences that now puzzle and perplex us and ease us of the pain we have been put into by some threatening temptations.

Songs of Deliverance

You are my hiding place;
You shall preserve me from trouble;
You shall surround me with songs of deliverance.
PSALM 32:7

Here David speaks to God and professes his confidence in Him and expectation of Him. "You are my hiding place." When by faith I have recourse to you, I shall see all the reason in the world to be easy and to think myself out of the reach of any real evil. "You shall preserve me from trouble," such trouble as I was in while I kept silent (v. 3). When God has pardoned our sins, if He leaves us to ourselves, we shall soon run as far into debt again as before, and therefore, when we have received the comfort of our remission, we must fly to the grace of God to be preserved from returning to folly again. You shall not only deliver me, but "surround me with songs of deliverance." As everyone who is godly shall pray with me, so they shall give thanks with me.

Spiritual Guidance

*I will instruct you and teach you
in the way you should go;
I will guide you with My eye.*
PSALM 32:8

Being himself converted, the psalmist does what he can to strengthen his brethren (Luke 22:32). "I will instruct you," whoever desires instruction, "and teach you in the way you should go." When David became a penitent, he immediately became a preacher. "I will guide you with My eye." Some apply this to God's conduct and direction, but it is rather to be taken as David's promise to those who sat under his instruction, his own children and family. "I will counsel thee; my eye shall be upon thee. I will give you the best advice I can and then observe whether you take it or not."

Spiritual guides must be overseers. Here is a word of caution to sinners not to be unruly and ungovernable: "Do not be like the horse or like the mule, which have no understanding" (v. 9). It is our honor and happiness that we have understanding, that we are capable of being governed by reason and of reasoning with ourselves. Where there is renewing grace, there is no need of the bit and bridle of restraining grace. The reason for this caution is because the way of sin will certainly end in sorrow (v. 10). Here is a word of comfort to the saints. They are assured that if they will but trust in the Lord and keep close to Him, mercy shall compass them about on every side.

The Shadow of Your Wings

For You are my hope, O Lord GOD;
You are my trust from my youth.
PSALM 71:5

David professes his confidence in God and repeats his profession of that confidence, still presenting the profession to God and pleading it with Him. We praise God by telling Him what confidence we have in Him (v. 1). In You, O Lord, and in You only, do I put my trust. Whatever others do, I choose the God of Jacob for my help. "You are my rock and my fortress" (v. 3). "You are my refuge, my strong refuge" (v. 7). That is, I fly to You and am sure to be safe in You, and under Your protection. If You secure me, none can hurt me. You are my hope and my trust.

His confidence in God is supported and encouraged by his experiences. "You are my trust from my youth." Ever since I was capable of discerning between my right hand and my left, I stayed myself on you, for by you have I been held up from the womb. He who was our help from our birth ought to be our hope from our youth. If we received so much mercy from God before we were capable of doing Him any service, we should lose no time when we are capable. You are He who took me into the arms of Your grace, under the shadow of Your wings, into the bond of Your covenant. I have reason to hope that You will protect me; You who have helped me up before will not let me fall now. You who helped me when I could not help myself will not abandon me now that I am as helpless as I was then. My praise shall therefore be continually of You.

The Joyful Sound

Blessed are the people who know the joyful sound!
They walk, O LORD, in the light of Your countenance.
In Your name they rejoice all day long,
and in Your righteousness they are exalted.

PSALM 89:15–16

Glorious discoveries are made to believers and glad tidings of good brought to them. They "know the joyful sound." This may allude to the shout of a victorious army. Israel had the tokens of God's presence with them in their wars. Or it may mean the sound that was made over the sacrifices and on the solemn feast days. This was the happiness of Israel, that they had among them free and open profession of God's holy religion. Or it may allude to the sound of the jubilee trumpet, a joyful sound to servants and debtors, to whom it proclaimed release. The gospel is indeed a joyful sound, a sound of victory, of liberty, of communion with God. Blessed are the people who hear it and know it and bid it welcome.

Special tokens of God's favor are granted them: "They walk, O Lord, in the light of Your countenance." They shall govern themselves by Your directions, shall be guided by Your eye; and they shall delight themselves in Your consolations.

They never lack reasons for joy. Those who rejoice in Christ Jesus have enough to counterbalance their grievances and silence their griefs, and therefore their joy is full.

Their relation to God is their honor and dignity. "In Your righteousness they are exalted," not in any righteousness of their own. In Your favor, which through Christ we hope for, our horn shall be exalted. The horn denotes beauty, plenty, and power.

Trust

I will both lie down in peace, and sleep;
for You alone, O LORD, make me dwell in safety.
PSALM 4:8

David and the pious few who adhered to him joined in this prayer: "Lord, lift up the light of Your countenance upon us." He and his friends agree in their choice of God's favor as their felicity. It is this which, in their account, is better than life and all the comforts of life. Though David speaks of only himself in the seventh and eighth verses, he speaks in this prayer for others also, as Christ taught us to pray the "Our Father." All the saints come to the throne of grace on the same errand, and in this they are one: They all desire God's favor as their chief good. We should beg it for others as well as for ourselves, for in God's favor there is enough for us all, and we shall have plenty for others sharing in what we have. This is what, above anything, they rejoice in. "You have put gladness in my heart" (v. 7); inward, solid, substantial joy. "I will both lie down in peace, and sleep; for You alone, O Lord, make me dwell in safety." When he comes to sleep the sleep of death, he will then, like good old Simeon, depart in peace (Luke 2:29), being assured that God will receive his soul. He commits all his affairs to God and contentedly leaves the issue of them with Him.

Tokens of His Love

"I will not leave you orphans;
I will come to you."

JOHN 14:18

When friends are parting, they make a common request of each other. "Let me hear from you as often as you can." This Christ promised to His disciples, that out of sight they should not be out of mind.

He promised that He would continue His care of them. "I will not leave you orphans (or fatherless); I will come to you." His departure from them was neither total nor final. "Though I leave you without My bodily presence, yet I do not leave you without comfort." The life of true believers, though sometimes sorrowful, is never comfortless, because they are never orphans. God is their Father. "I will come to you. I will come speedily to you at My resurrection." He had often said, "The third day I will rise again. I will be coming daily to you in My Spirit," and in the tokens of His love and visits of His grace, He is still coming. The consideration of Christ's coming to us saves us from being comfortless in His absence from us.

He promises that they would continue their acquaintance with Him (vv. 19–20). "Yet a little while, and the world sees me no more." The malignant world thought they had seen enough of Him and cried, "Away with Him, crucify Him." And so shall their doom be; they shall see Him no more. But His disciples have communion with Him in His absence.

They saw Him with their bodily eyes after His resurrection. They saw Him with an eye of faith after His ascension; saw that in Him which the world saw not.

Our Safety

"Then you shall call, and the LORD will answer;
you shall cry, and He will say, 'Here I am.' "
ISAIAH 58:9

Those who are cheerful in doing good, God will make cheerful in enjoying good. This is a special gift of God. Those who have helped others out of trouble will obtain help from God when it is their turn. Good works shall be recompensed with a good name.

Good people are safe on all sides. Their defense is their righteousness and the glory of the Lord. He is our reward, on whom alone we can depend for safety when our sins pursue us and are ready to take hold of us. "Then you shall call, and the Lord will answer." He will give you the things you call for. You shall cry when you are in any distress or sudden fright, and He shall say, "Here I am." Whenever we are praying, God is there next to us, listening.

The Lord will guide you continually. While we are here in the wilderness of this world, we have need of continual direction from heaven. To a good man, God gives not only wisdom and knowledge, but joy. He is satisfied in himself with the testimony of his conscience and the assurances of God's favor. As a spring that continually sends out its water but is always full, so the charitable man abounds in good as he abounds in doing good and is never the poorer for his generosity.

We Are Family

*"I will be a Father to you,
and you shall be My sons and daughters,
says the LORD Almighty."*

2 CORINTHIANS 6:18

It is wrong for good people to join with the wicked and pro-fane. There is more danger that the bad will damage the good than hope that the good will benefit the bad. We should not yoke ourselves in friendship with wicked men and unbeliev-ers. We should never choose them for our friends. Much less should we join in religious communion with them. It is a very great absurdity (vv. 14–15). Believers are righteous, but unbe-lievers are unrighteous. Believers are made light in the Lord, but unbelievers are in darkness. What comfortable commu-nion can these have together? Christ and Belial are contrary, one to the other. It is a dishonor to the Christian's profession, for Christians are temples of the living God. There is a great deal of danger in communicating with unbelievers, danger of being defiled and of being rejected; therefore, the exhortation is (v. 17) to come out from among them, to be separate, as one would avoid the society of those who have leprosy or the plague, and not to touch the unclean thing. We must take care not to defile ourselves by conversation with those who defile themselves with sin. It is base ingratitude to God for all the favors He has bestowed on believers and promised to them. God has promised to be a Father to them and that they shall all be His sons and His daughters. Is there a greater honor or happiness than this?

Eternal Care

"Even to your old age, I am He,
and even to gray hairs I will carry you! I have made,
and I will bear; even I will carry, and will deliver you."
ISAIAH 46:4

The true God will never fail His worshipers. He formed them into a people and gave them their constitution. Every good man is what God makes him. You have been "upheld by Me from birth" and "carried from the womb" (v. 3). Just as God began early to do them good, He has constantly continued to do them good: He has carried them from the womb to this day. We have been carried in the arms of His power and in the bosom of His love and pity. Our spiritual life is sustained by His grace, as necessarily and constantly as our natural life by His providence.

"You have been upheld by me from birth," nursed when you were children; and "even to your old age I am He, when, by reason of your infirmities, you will need help as much as in your infancy." Israel was now growing old, and they had hastened their old age, and the calamities of it, by their irregularities. But God is still their God, will still carry them in the same everlasting arms that were laid under them in Moses' time. "I will now bear them upon eagles' wings out of Babylon, as in their infancy I bore them out of Egypt." This promise to aged Israel is applicable to every aged Israelite. "Even to your old age, when you grow unfit for business, when you are overcome with infirmities, and perhaps your relatives begin to grow weary of you, yet I am He, the very same by whom you have been upheld from birth and carried from the womb. You change, but I am the same. I will carry you, will bear you up and bear you out, and will carry you home at last."

Everlasting Love

> *"Yes, I have loved you with an everlasting love;*
> *therefore with lovingkindness I have drawn you."*
>
> JEREMIAH 31:3

God assures His people that He will do for them, in bringing them out of Babylon, as He had done for their fathers when He delivered them out of Egypt (v. 2). They were then, as these were, a people who survived the sword, that sword of Pharaoh with which he cut off all the male children as soon as they were born. They were then in the wilderness, where they seemed to be lost and forgotten, as these were now in a strange land; and yet they found grace in God's sight, were owned and highly honored by Him, and He was at this time going to cause them to rest in Canaan. God is still the same.

They reminded him of what God had done for their fathers, hinting that they now saw no such signs and were ready to ask, as Gideon did: "Where are all the wonders that our fathers told us of? The years of ancient times were glorious years, but now it is otherwise. What good will it do us that He appeared of old to us when now He is a God who hides Himself from us?" To this He answers with an assurance of the constancy of His love: "Yes, I have loved you not only with an ancient love, but with an everlasting love, a love that shall never fail; however, the comforts of it may be for a time suspended." Nothing can separate them from that love. Those whom God loves with this love He will draw into covenant and communion with Himself, by the influences of His Spirit upon their souls.

Union with Christ

"And I have declared to them Your name,
and will declare it,
that the love with which You loved Me may be in them,
and I in them."
JOHN 17:26

What Christ did for His disciples: "I have declared to them Your name." Christ declared His Father's name to believers, that with that divine light in their minds, a divine love may be sent abroad in their hearts, that they may partake of a divine nature. When God's love to us comes to us, it draws out the soul toward God. Let them not only be interested in the love of God; let them have the comfort of that interest, that they may not only know God, but know that they know Him. It is the love of God thus shed abroad in the heart that fills it with joy. This we must press after. If we have it, we must thank Christ for it; if we want it, we may thank ourselves.

There is no getting into the love of God but through Christ, nor can we keep ourselves in that love but by abiding in Christ. It is Christ in us that is the only hope of glory that will not make us ashamed. All our communion with God passes through the hands of the Lord Jesus. Christ had said just a little before, "I in them," and here it is repeated, and the prayer closed with it, to show how much the heart of Christ was set upon it. "I in them. Let me have this, and I desire no more." Let us therefore make sure of our union with Christ and then take the comfort of His intercession.

Spiritual Kindred

"For whoever does the will of My Father in heaven is My brother and sister and mother."

MATTHEW 12:50

Our nearest relatives must be comparatively hated; that is, we must love them less than Christ, and our duty to God must take preference. We must not take it poorly of our friends, or add it to their score of wickedness, if they prefer the pleasing of God before the pleasing of us. No, we must deny ourselves and our own satisfaction rather than do that which may in any way divert our friends from, or distract them in, their duty to God.

Jesus preferred His disciples, who were His spiritual kindred, before His natural relatives. He would rather be profiting His disciples than pleasing His relatives.

Christ's disciples are those who do the will of His Father; the same is His brother, and sister, and mother. His disciples, who had left everything to follow Him and embraced His doctrine, were dearer to Him than any who were His kin according to the flesh. It was very endearing and very encouraging for Christ to say, "Behold My mother and My brethren," yet it was not their privilege alone. This honor all the saints have. All obedient believers are close kin to Jesus Christ. He loves them, converses freely with them as His relatives. He bids them welcome to His table, sees that they lack nothing fit for them, and will never be ashamed of His poor relatives, but will confess them before men, before the angels, and before His Father.

Whatever We Ask

*"Whatever you ask in My name, that I will do,
that the Father may be glorified in the Son."*
JOHN 14:13

How were the disciples to derive power from Jesus when He was gone to the Father? By prayer. When friends move away, they promise to write each other. Thus, when Christ was going to His Father, He tells His disciples how they might write to Him and send their letters by a safe and ready way of conveyance. "Let Me hear from you by prayer, and you shall hear from Me by the Spirit." Humility was prescribed: You shall *ask....* "Ask anything, anything that is good and proper for you; anything, provided you know what you ask."

How were they to present their petitions? "Ask in My name." They were to plead His merit and intercession and to depend on it. If we ask in our own name, we cannot expect success, for, being strangers, we have no name in heaven. Being sinners, we have a bad name there. But Christ's is a good name, well known in heaven.

Whatever you ask, "that I will do. You may be sure I will. Not only shall it be done, but *I* will do it." By faith in His name, we may have what we will for the asking.

These prayers would succeed so "that the Father may be glorified in the Son." "Hallowed be Thy name" is an answered prayer and is put first because, if the heart is sincere in this, it consecrates all the other petitions. This, Christ will aim at in granting, and for the sake of this will do what they ask. The wisdom, power, and goodness of God were magnified in the Redeemer when His apostles and ministers were enabled to do such great things, both in proof of their doctrine and in the success of it.

A New Heart

*"I will give you a new heart and put a new spirit within you;
I will take the heart of stone out of your flesh and give you a heart
of flesh. I will put My Spirit within you and cause you to walk in
My statutes, and you will keep My judgments and do them."*

EZEKIEL 36:26–27

The people of God might be discouraged by the knowledge of their unfitness, and that is answered in these verses, with a promise that God would by His grace prepare them for His mercy and then bestow it. This was in part fulfilled in that wonderful effect which the captivity in Babylon had upon the Jews there, that effectually cured them of their inclination to idolatry.

God promises that He will work a good work in them. God would cleanse them from the pollutions of sin. "I will sprinkle clean water upon you," which signifies both the blood of Christ sprinkled on the conscience to purify that and to take away the sense of guilt, and the grace of the Spirit sprinkled on the whole soul to purify it from all corrupt inclinations, as Naaman was cleansed from his leprosy by dipping in the Jordan.

"I will save you from all your uncleannesses." God would give them a new heart, a disposition of mind vastly different from what it was before. Instead of a "heart of stone," insensible and unable to receive divine impressions and return devout affections, God would give a "heart of flesh," a soft and tender heart complying in everything with the will of God.

Since, beside our inclination to sin, we complain of an inability to do our duty, God will "cause you to walk in His statutes" and thoroughly furnish them with wisdom and will, and active powers, for every good work.

Songs of Praise

Speaking to one another in
psalms and hymns and spiritual songs,
singing and making melody in your heart to the Lord.
EPHESIANS 5:19

The apostle warns against drunkenness. Instead of being filled with wine, he exhorts them to be filled with the Spirit, and those who are full of drink are not likely to be full of the Spirit. Men should labor for a plentiful measure of the graces of the Spirit that would fill their souls with great joy and courage. We ought not to be satisfied with a little of the Spirit, because by its means we shall come to understand what the will of the Lord is. The apostle encourages believers to sing unto the Lord. The joy of Christians should express itself in songs of praise to their God. In these they should speak to their assemblies. Though Christianity is an enemy to profane mirth, yet it encourages joy and gladness. God's people have reason to rejoice and to sing for joy. They are to sing and to make melody in their hearts, not only with their voices, but with inward affection, and then it will be done to the Lord. Thanksgiving is another duty. We should always be giving thanks, and we should give thanks for all things. It is our duty in everything to give thanks to God the Father.

Worship and Bow Down

Oh come, let us worship and bow down;
let us kneel before the LORD our Maker.

PSALM 95:6

When we praise God, our song must be a joyful noise. Spiritual joy is the heart and soul of thankful praise. With humble reverence and holy awe, "let us worship and bow down; let us kneel before the Lord our Maker." This becomes those who know what an infinite distance there is between us and God, how much we are in danger of His wrath and in need of His mercy. We must speak forth, sing forth His praises out of the abundance of a heart filled with love, joy, and thankfulness. We must praise God in concert, in the solemn assemblies; let us join in singing to the Lord.

Because He is our God, not only has He dominion over us, as He has over all the creatures, but stands in special relation to us. He is our Creator; we must kneel before the Lord our Creator. Idolaters kneel before gods they have made themselves; we kneel before a God who made us. He is our Savior and the author of our blessedness. We are therefore His. We must praise Him because He preserves and maintains us. The gospel church is His flock. Christ is the great and good shepherd of it, and therefore to Him must be glory in the churches throughout the ages.

Firstfruits

*"Then you shall set it before the LORD your God,
and worship before the LORD your God."*
DEUTERONOMY 26:10

Here a good work is ordered: the presenting of a basket of the
firstfruits to God every year. When a man went into the field
or vineyard at the time when the fruits were ripening, he was
to mark that which he observed most mature and excellent,
and lay it up for the firstfruit basket: wheat, barley, grapes,
figs, pomegranates, olives, and dates; some of each sort must
be put in the same basket, with leaves between them, and presented to God in the place which He should choose.

Now from this law we may learn to acknowledge God as
the giver of all those good things that are the support and
comfort of our natural life. We learn to deny ourselves. What
is first ripe, we are most fond of. They who are nice and curious expect to be served with each fruit at its first coming in.
This way we learn to give God the first and best we have.
Those who consecrate the days of their youth and the prime
of their time to the service and honor of God bring Him their
firstfruits.

The Wise Men

"Where is He who has been born King of the Jews?
For we have seen His star in the East
and have come to worship Him."

MATTHEW 2:2

The wise men came from the East to Jerusalem in quest of the King of the Jews. They might have said, "If such a prince has been born, we will hear of Him shortly in our own country, and it will be time enough then to pay our homage to Him." But so impatient were they to be better acquainted with Him that they took a long journey on purpose to inquire after Him. Those who truly desire to know Christ and find Him will not regard the pain or peril of seeking after Him.

Their question is, "Where is He who has been born King of the Jews?" They do not ask whether there was such a person born, but where He was born. Those who know something of Christ cannot but want to know more about Him.

To this question they expected to find a ready answer and to find all Jerusalem worshiping at the feet of this new king, but no man could give them any information. There is more gross ignorance in the world and in the church than we are aware of. Many who we think could direct us to Christ are themselves strangers to Him. Are the wise men asked, "Why do you ask this question?" It is because they have seen His star in the East. Are they asked, "What business do you have with Him? What have the men of the East to do with the King of the Jews?" The wise men have their answer ready: "We have come to worship Him." Those in whose hearts the daystar has risen, to give them anything of the knowledge of Christ, must make it their business to worship Him.

In Spirit and in Truth

"God is Spirit,
and those who worship Him
must worship in spirit and truth."
JOHN 4:24

True worshipers worship the Father in spirit and in truth. As creatures, we worship the Father of all; as Christians, we worship the Father of our Lord Jesus. The difference is in the nature of the worship. Christians worship God in spiritual ordinances, not in the ceremonial observances of the law of Moses. All should and will worship God in spirit and in truth. This is spoken of as their character and their duty.

We must depend upon God's Spirit for strength and assistance. We must worship Him with fixedness of thought and a flame of affection, with all that is within us, and in truth, that is, in sincerity. We must mind the power more than the form. God must be thus worshiped, because they only are accounted the true worshipers. The gospel erects a spiritual way of worship, so that the professors of the gospel do not live up to gospel light and laws if they do not worship God in spirit and in truth.

Such worshipers are very rare. The gate of spiritual worshiping is narrow. Such worship is necessary and what the God of heaven insists upon. God is greatly pleased with and graciously accepts such worship and such worshipers. His seeking such worshipers implies His making them such. God is a spirit. It is easier to say what God is not than what He is. The spirituality of the divine nature is a very good reason for the spirituality of divine worship. If we do not worship God, who is a spirit, in the spirit, we miss the aim of worship.

Deborah's Song

"Hear, O kings! Give ear, O princes!
I, even I, will sing to the LORD;
I will sing praise to the LORD God of Israel."
JUDGES 5:3

God is praised by a song, which is a very natural expression of rejoicing. Is any merry? Let him sing; and holy joy is the very soul and root of praise and thanksgiving. Song is a very proper expedient for perpetuating the remembrance of great events. Neighbors would learn this song from one another, and children from their parents, and one generation would thus praise God's works to another and declare His mighty acts.

It appears that Deborah herself penned this song. She used her gifts as a prophetess in composing the song, and the strain throughout is very fine and lofty; the images are lively, the expressions elegant, and it is an admirable mixture of sweetness and majesty. We may suppose she used her power as a prophetess in obliging the conquering army of Israel to learn and sing this song. She has been the first wheel in the action and now is so in the thanksgiving.

She begins with a general hallelujah: "Praise (or bless, for that is the word) the Lord." The design of the song is to give glory to God; this, therefore, is put first to explain and direct all that follows, like the first petition of the Lord's Prayer, "Hallowed be Thy name."

All the Earth Shall Worship

Say to God, "How awesome are Your works!
Through the greatness of Your power
Your enemies shall submit themselves to You.
All the earth shall worship You and sing praises to You;
they shall sing praises to Your name."
PSALM 66:3–4

In these verses the psalmist calls upon all people to praise God, "all the earth." This speaks of the glory of God, for He is good to all. The duty of man is that all are obliged to praise God; it is part of the law of creation and therefore is required of every creature. Next is a prediction of the conversion of the Gentiles to the faith of Christ; the time would come when all the earth would praise God. The psalmist will abound in it himself and wishes that God might have His tribute paid Him by all the nations of the earth, and not only by the land of Israel. We must be hearty and zealous, open and public, as those who are not ashamed of our Master. And both these are implied in making a noise, a joyful noise. In praising God, we must do it so as to glorify Him.

He had called upon all lands to praise God and foretells that they shall do so. They shall sing to God, that is, sing to His name, for it is only to His declarative glory, that by which He has made Himself known, not to His essential glory, that we can contribute anything by our praises.

Holy Joy and Praise

And they worshiped Him,
and returned to Jerusalem with great joy,
and were continually in the temple
praising and blessing God.

LUKE 24:52–53

Jesus' ascension is described here. He was parted from them. Those who love us and pray for us and instruct us must someday be parted from us. Those who knew Him in the flesh must now know Him no more in the flesh. He was carried up into heaven. There was no need for a chariot of fire or horses of fire; He knew the way.

How cheerfully His disciples continued their attendance on Him. They paid their homage to Him at His going away, they worshiped Him. He blessed them, in token of gratitude for which they worshiped Him. The cloud that received Him out of their sight did not cut them or their services out of His sight. They returned to Jerusalem with great joy. There they went, and there they stayed with great joy. This was a wonderful change. When Christ told them that He must leave them, sorrow filled their hearts; yet now that they see Him go, they are filled with joy.

They attended the temple service at the hours of prayer and were continually in the temple, as their Master was when He was in Jerusalem. They knew the temple sacrifices were superseded by Christ's sacrifice, but they joined in the temple songs. Nothing better prepares the mind for receiving the Holy Ghost than holy joy and praise. Fears are silenced, sorrows sweetened and allayed, and hopes kept up. Let Him be continually praised and blessed.

Praise in Concert

I will bless the LORD at all times;
His praise shall continually be in my mouth.
PSALM 34:1

David engages and encourages himself to praise God. "I will bless the Lord at all times; His praise shall continually be in my mouth." He will praise Him heartily: " 'My soul shall make its boast in the Lord,' in my relation to Him, my interest in Him, and my expectations from Him." He calls upon others to join with him in praising God; he expects they will. "The humble shall hear of it," both of my deliverance and of my thankfulness, "and be glad" (v. 2). We cannot make God greater or higher than He is, but if we adore Him as infinitely great and higher than the highest, He is pleased to reckon this magnifying and exalting Him. This we must do together. God's praises sound best in concert. David has found himself a prayer-hearing God. "I sought the Lord, in my distress, entreated His favor, begged His help, and He heard me, answered my request immediately, and delivered me from all my fears, both from the death I feared and from the disquietude and disturbance produced by my fear of it."

Better Than Life

Because Your lovingkindness is better than life,
my lips shall praise You.
Thus I will bless You while I live;
I will lift up my hands in Your name.

PSALM 63:3–4

How soon are David's complaints and prayers turned into praises and thanksgivings! David was now in the wilderness and yet had his heart much enlarged through blessing God. David praised God "because Your lovingkindness is better than life." It is our spiritual life, and it is better than temporal life. We have better provisions and better possessions than the wealth of this world can offer us, and in the service of God, in communion with Him, we have better employments and better enjoyments than we can have in the business and talk of this world.

How will he praise God and for how long? "Thus I will bless You, thus as I have now begun. The present devout affections shall not pass away like the morning cloud, but shine more and more, like the morning sun. I will bless You while I live." Praising God must be the work of our whole lives. "I will lift up my hands in Your name." In all our prayers and praises, we are taught to begin with "Hallowed be Thy name" and to conclude with "Thine is the glory."

Hannah's Prayer

"My heart rejoices in the LORD;
my horn is exalted in the LORD.
I smile at my enemies,
because I rejoice in Your salvation.
No one is holy like the LORD,
for there is none besides You,
nor is there any rock like our God."
1 SAMUEL 2:1–2

When Hannah had received mercy from God, she owned it, with thankfulness to His praise. Praise is our rent, our tribute. We are unjust if we do not pay it. The mercy she had received was an answer to prayer, and therefore she thought herself especially obliged to give thanks for it. Thanksgiving is an essential part of prayer. Her voice was not heard while she made her request, but in her thanksgiving she spoke so all might hear her. She made her supplication with groanings that could not be uttered, but now her lips were opened to show forth God's praise.

What great things she says of God. She takes little notice of the particular mercy she was now rejoicing in. She overlooks the gift and praises the giver, while most of us forget the giver and focus only on the gift. What we give God the glory of, we may take the comfort of. Hannah does so in holy joy, "My heart rejoices in the Lord," not so much in her son as in her God. "My horn is exalted"; not only is her reputation saved by having a son, but greatly raised by having such a son.

Ceremonial Worship

Oh, give thanks to the LORD!
Call upon His name;
make known His deeds among the peoples!
Sing to Him, sing psalms to Him;
talk of all His wondrous works!
1 CHRONICLES 16:8–9

The worship of God is not only to be the work of a solemn day now and then, brought in to grace a triumph, but it ought to be the work of every day. At Jerusalem, where the ark was, Asaph and his brethren were appointed to minister before the ark continually with songs of praise. No sacrifices were offered there or incense burned, but David's prayers were directed as incense and the lifting up of his hands as the evening sacrifice. Spiritual worship took the place of ceremonial.

Yet the ceremonial worship, being of divine institution, must by no means be omitted; therefore at Gibeon, there were altars where the priests sacrificed and burnt incense according to the law of Moses. These must be kept up because, however inferior they were to the moral services of prayer and praise, they had a great deal of honor, and the observance of them was of great consequence. At Gibeon, David also appointed singers to give thanks to the Lord, and the burden of all their songs must be "For His mercy endures forever." The people were satisfied and went home pleased. David returned to bless his house, resolving to keep up his family worship, which public worship must not supersede.

Sacrifices of Prayer and Praise

"Offer to God thanksgiving,
and pay your vows to the Most High."
PSALM 50:14

The psalmist speaks of the best sacrifices of prayer and praise as those which, under the law, were preferred before all burnt offerings and sacrifices—and on which then the greatest stress was laid—and which now, under the gospel, replace the carnal ordinances that were imposed until the time of reformation. He shows us here what is good and what the Lord our God requires of us and will accept when sacrifices are slighted and superseded.

We must make a penitent acknowledgment of our sins. A broken and contrite heart is a sacrifice God will not despise. If the sin was not abandoned, the sin offering was not accepted. We must give God thanks for His mercies to us. Offer God thanksgiving every day, often every day. This will please the Lord, if it comes from a humble, thankful heart, better than an ox or bullock that has horns and hoofs. We must faithfully perform our covenants with Him, forsaking our sins and doing our duty better.

Dr. Hammond applies this to the great gospel ordinance of the Eucharist, in which we are to give thanks to God for His great love in sending His Son to save us. Instead of all the Old Testament types of a Christ to come, we have that blessed memorial of a Christ already come.

Joyful Worshipers

Enter into His gates with thanksgiving,
and into His courts with praise.
Be thankful to Him,
and bless His name.
For the LORD is good;
His mercy is everlasting,
and His truth endures to all generations.

PSALM 100:4–5

In all acts of religious worship, whether in secret or in our families, we come into God's presence and serve Him, but it is in public worship especially that we enter into His gates and into His courts. By holy joy we really serve God. Gospel worshipers should be joyful worshipers. We must come before His presence with singing, not only songs of joy, but songs of praise. We must take it as a favor to be admitted into His service and that we have instituted ordinances and the opportunity of waiting upon God in those ordinances.

The matter of praise, and motives to it, are very important. Know what God is in Himself and what He is to you. Knowledge is the mother of devotion and all obedience; blind sacrifices will never please a seeing God. Let us know these things concerning the Lord, Jehovah: That the Lord, He is God, the only living and true God. He is an eternal Spirit, incomprehensible and independent, the first cause and last end. He is our Creator: It is He who has made us and not we ourselves. We did not, we could not, make ourselves; therefore we are not our own but His. He is our sovereign ruler; we are His people. He is our bountiful benefactor. We are the sheep of His pasture, who He takes care of, the flock of His feeding. He is a God of infinite mercy and goodness.

The Duty of Praise

Praise the LORD!
For it is good to sing praises to our God;
for it is pleasant, and praise is beautiful.
PSALM 147:1

The duty of praise is recommended to us. We are called to it again and again: "Praise the Lord!" and again, "Sing to the Lord with thanksgiving; sing praises on the harp to our God" (v. 7). (Let all our praises be directed to Him and center in Him), for it is good to do so; it is our duty, and therefore good in itself. In giving honor to God, we really do ourselves a great deal of honor.

God is the proper object of our praises. Is Jerusalem to be raised out of small beginnings? Is it to be recovered out of its ruins? In both cases, the Lord builds up Jerusalem. The gospel church, the Jerusalem that is from above, is of His building. Are any of His people outcasts? Have they made themselves so by their own folly? He gathers them by giving them repentance and bringing them again into the communion of saints. They are broken in heart, humbled, and troubled by sin, inwardly pained at the remembrance of it. Their very hearts are rent under the sense of the dishonor they have done to God and the injury they have done to themselves by sin. To those whom God heals with the consolations of His Spirit, He speaks peace.

Giving God Glory

All Your works shall praise You, O LORD,
and Your saints shall bless You.

PSALM 145:10

Who shall be employed in giving glory to God? Whatever others do, the psalmist will himself be much in praising God. It was his duty; it was his delight. He would give glory to God not only in his solemn devotions, but in his common conversation. He will be constant to this work: "Every day will I bless You." No day must pass, though ever so busy a day, though ever so sorrowful a day, without praising God. God is every day blessing us, doing well for us; there is, therefore, good reason that we should bless Him every day, speaking well of Him. He is sure others will join this work. David's zeal would provoke many, and it has done so. They shall keep it up in an uninterrupted succession: "One generation shall praise Thy works to another."

What we must give God the glory of are His greatness and His great works. We must declare, "Great is the Lord," and if great, then "greatly to be praised" with all that is within us, to the utmost of our power. His greatness indeed cannot be comprehended. When we cannot, by searching, find the bottom, we must sit down at the brink and adore the depth. We must see God acting and working in all the affairs of this lower world.

David Gives Thanks

The LORD is my strength and my shield;
my heart trusted in Him, and I am helped;
therefore my heart greatly rejoices,
and with my song I will praise Him.
PSALM 28:7

It was in faith that David prayed, "Hear the voice of my supplications," and by the same faith he gives thanks that God has heard the voice of his supplications. Those who pray in faith may rejoice in hope. What we win by prayer, we must wear with praise.

He encourages himself to hope in God for the perfecting of everything that concerned him. This is the method of attaining peace: Let us begin with praise, that it is attainable. His experience of the benefit of that dependence is, "My heart trusted in Him, and in His power and promise, and it has not been in vain to do so, for I am helped. I have been often helped; not only has God given to me, in His due time, the help I trusted to Him for, but my very trusting Him has helped me in the meantime and kept me from fainting. Therefore, my heart greatly rejoices."

He pleases himself with the interest which all good people, through Christ, have in God, "The Lord is their strength; not mine only, but the strength of every believer." This is our communion with all saints, that God is their strength and ours, Christ their Lord and ours.

Religious Assemblies

"And it shall come to pass that
from one New Moon to another,
and from one Sabbath to another,
all flesh shall come to worship before Me," says the LORD.
ISAIAH 66:23

The public worship of God in religious assemblies shall be attended by all who are thus brought as an offering to the Lord. This is described in expressions suited to the Old Testament dispensation, to show that though the ceremonial law would be abolished and the temple service would come to an end, yet God would still be regularly worshiped. Heretofore, only Jews went up to appear before God, and they were bound to attend only three times a year, and the males only. But now all flesh, Gentiles as well as Jews, women as well as men, shall come and worship before God in His presence, though not in His temple at Jerusalem but in assemblies dispersed all the world over, which shall be to them as the tabernacle of meeting was to the Jews. God will record His name in them, and though but two or three come together, He will be among them and bless them. There is no necessity of one certain place, as the temple was of old. Christ is our temple, in whom by faith all believers meet. But it is fit that there should be a certain time appointed, that the service may be done frequently, and a token thereby given of the spiritual communion which all Christian assemblies have with each other by faith, hope, and holy love. Where the Lord's Day is weekly sanctified and the Lord's Supper monthly celebrated, and both duly attended, there the Christian new moons and Sabbaths are observed.

God Hears

If I regard iniquity in my heart,
The Lord will not hear.
But certainly God has heard me;
He has attended to the voice of my prayer.
PSALM 66:18–19

"Now this is strange," said the poor blind man healed by Jesus, "that the miracle wrought upon me has not convinced you, that you should thus shut your eyes against the light." He argues strongly against them, proving not only that he was not a sinner but that he was of God. He argues with great knowledge, though he could not read a letter of the book. He argues with great zeal for the honor of Christ, with great boldness and courage. His argument is somewhat like that of David in Psalm 66:18–20: "If I regard iniquity in my heart, the Lord will not hear me. But certainly God has heard me; He has attended to the voice of my prayer. . . . Blessed be God." The formerly blind man speaks the undoubted truth that none but good men are the favorites of heaven, not sinners. God does not hear sinners. This should be no discouragement to repenting, returning sinners, but to those who continue in their trespasses. God will not hear them. But "if anyone is a worshiper of God and does His will, He hears them." A good man is one who worships God and does His will. The unspeakable comfort of such a man is that God hears His prayers and answers them.

Whom Do We Worship?

> " 'You shall not make idols for yourselves;
> neither a carved image nor a sacred pillar
> shall you rear up for yourselves;
> nor shall you set up an engraved stone in your land,
> to bow down to it;
> for I am the LORD your God.' "
>
> LEVITICUS 26:1

Here is the teaching of those precepts of the law which were of the greatest consequence and by which especially their obedience would be tried. They are the abstract of the second and fourth commandments. "Be sure you never worship images, nor ever make any sort of images or pictures for a religious use." Next to God's being, unity, and universal influence, it is necessary that we know and believe that He is an infinite Spirit, and therefore to represent Him by an image in the making of it, to confine Him to an image in the consecrating of it, and to worship Him by an image in bowing down to it, changes His truth into a lie and His glory into shame, as much as anything. "Be sure you keep up a great veneration for Sabbaths and religious assemblies." As nothing tends more to corrupt religion than the use of images in devotion, so nothing contributes more to the support of it than keeping the Sabbaths and reverencing the sanctuary. These make up very much of the instrumental part of religion, by which the essentials of it are kept up.

Great encouragement is given them to live in constant obedience to all God's commandments. Human governments enforce their laws with penalties, but God will be known as the rewarder of those who seek and serve Him.

"Look to Me"

"Look to Me, and be saved, all you ends of the earth!
For I am God, and there is no other.
I have sworn by Myself; the word has gone out of
My mouth in righteousness, and shall not return,
that to Me every knee shall bow,
every tongue shall take an oath."

ISAIAH 45:22–23

What is said here is intended for idolaters, to show them their folly in worshiping gods that cannot help them and neglecting a God who can. Let all the nations that have escaped—not only the Jews, but those of other nations who were released by Cyrus—hear what is to be said against the worshiping of idols. They set up the wood of their graven image. Though they overlay it with gold, deck it with ornaments, and make a god of it, yet still it is but wood. They pray to a god that cannot save. "There is no other God besides me." None besides is fit to rule. None besides is able to help. As He is a just God, He is the Savior.

For the comfort and encouragement of God's faithful worshipers, whoever they are, God says to all His people, though they seem to be lost and forgotten in their dispersion, "Let them but look to Me by faith and prayer, look above second causes, look up to Me, and they shall be saved." When Christ is lifted up from the earth, He shall draw the eyes of all men to Him. "I have sworn by Myself" (and God can swear by no greater); "the word has gone out of My mouth," that He who made all should be Lord of all, that, since all beings are derived from Him, they should all be devoted to Him. He has assured us that the kingdoms of the world shall become His kingdom.

Jesus, the Servant

That at the name of Jesus
every knee should bow,
of those in heaven,
and of those on earth,
and of those under the earth.
PHILIPPIANS 2:10

One would think that the Lord Jesus, if He would be a man, should have been a prince. But quite the contrary: He took upon Him the form of a servant. He was brought up poor, probably working with His earthly father at his trade. His whole life was a life of humiliation, culminating in His death on the cross. He not only suffered, but was voluntarily obedient in the face of a painful, humiliating death fit only for criminals and slaves, not for a free man. Because He humbled Himself, God exalted Him highly. He exalted His whole person, the human nature as well as the divine. His exaltation here is made to consist of honor and power. He had a name above every name: Every knee must bow to Him. The whole creation must be in subjection to Him: things in heaven, things on earth, and things under the earth, the inhabitants of heaven and earth, the living and the dead. At the name of Jesus, all should pay a solemn homage. Every tongue should confess that Jesus Christ is Lord. The kingdom of Christ reaches to heaven and earth, to all the creatures in each, and to the dead as well as the living—to the glory of God the Father. Whatever respect is paid to Christ redounds to the honor of the Father.

The New Temple

So they sang praises with gladness,
and they bowed their heads and worshiped.
2 CHRONICLES 29:30

As soon as Hezekiah heard that the temple was ready for him, he lost no time, but was ready for it. He rose early to go up to the house of the Lord, earlier on that day than on other days, to show that his heart was upon his work there. Atonement must be made for the sins of the last reign. They thought it not enough to lament and forsake those sins, but they brought a sin offering. Even our repentance and reformation will not obtain pardon but in and through Christ, who was made a sin offering for us. No peace but through His blood; no, not for penitents.

The law of Moses appointed sacrifices to make atonement for the sins of the whole congregation, that the national judgments which their national sins deserved might be turned away. For this purpose we must now look to Christ, the great propitiation, as well as for the remission and salvation of particular persons.

While the offerings were burning on the altar, the Levites sang the song of the Lord, the psalms composed by David and Asaph, accompanied by the musical instruments which God by His prophets had commanded the use of and which had been long neglected. The king and all the congregation testified their consent to and concurrence in all that was done by bowing their heads and worshiping.

Turn from Sin

*"Do not go after other gods to
serve them and worship them,
and do not provoke Me to anger
with the works of your hands;
and I will not harm you."*

JEREMIAH 25:6

This was a message from God concerning all the people of Judah, which Jeremiah sent to all the people. Besides him, God had sent them other prophets on the same errand. There were other of God's servants besides the prophets who preached awakening sermons, which were never published. They all told them of their faults, their evil ways, and the evil of their doings. Those were not of God's sending who flattered them as if there were nothing amiss. They all reproved them for their idolatry, their going after other gods to serve them and to worship them, and gods that were the work of their own hands. They all called on them to repent of their sins and to reform their lives. This was the burden of every song: Personal reformation must be insisted on as necessary to a national deliverance. Everyone must turn from his own evil way. The street will not be clean unless everyone sweeps in front of his own door. The mercies they enjoyed should be continued to them: "You shall dwell in the land, dwell in peace in this good land, which the Lord has given you and your fathers. Nothing but sin will turn you out of it, and that shall not if you turn from it."

Worship Despite Fear

In his upper room,
with his windows open toward Jerusalem,
he knelt down on his knees three times that day,
and prayed and gave thanks before his God,
as was his custom since early days.
DANIEL 6:10

Daniel prayed in his house, sometimes alone and sometimes with his family about him, and made a solemn business of it. Every house not only may be, but ought to be, a house of prayer. In every prayer he gave thanks. When he prayed and gave thanks, he kneeled upon his knees. Kneeling is a begging posture, and we come to God as beggars, beggars for our lives. He opened the windows of his chamber, that the sight of the visible heavens might affect his heart with awe. He opened them toward Jerusalem, the holy city, though now in ruins, to signify the affection he had for its very stones and dust. He did this three times a day. It is good to have our hours of prayer to remind our conscience. If we think our bodies need refreshment by food three times a day, can we think less will serve our souls? All who knew him knew this practice, and he was not ashamed of it.

Daniel constantly adhered to this practice, even when it was made a capital crime. When he knew that the law was signed, he continued to do as he did before. Many good men would have thought it prudent to omit their prayer for the next thirty days, but Daniel, who had so many eyes on him, acted with courage. And we must take heed lest, under the pretense of discretion, we be found guilty of cowardice in the cause of God.

The Beauty of His Holiness

Give unto the LORD the glory due to His name;
worship the LORD in the beauty of holiness.

PSALM 29:2

David interpreted every clap of thunder as a call to himself and other princes to give glory to the great God. "O you mighty," you sons of the mighty, who have power, "give unto the Lord," and again, and a third time, "give unto the Lord" your own selves in the first place, and then your services. Give unto the Lord glory and strength; acknowledge His glory and strength, and whatever glory or strength He has entrusted you with, offer it to Him, to be used for His honor, in His service. Give Him your crowns; let them be laid at His feet. Give Him your scepters, your swords, your keys. Put all into His hand that you, in the use of them, may be to Him for a name and a praise. What is here said to the mighty is said to all: Worship God. It is the sum and substance of the everlasting gospel.

Religious worship is giving to the Lord the glory due to His name. Worship the Lord in the beauty of holiness. Adore Him, not only as infinitely awful and therefore to be feared above all, but as infinitely amiable and therefore to be loved and delighted in above all. Especially we must have an eye to the beauty of His holiness. There is a beauty in holiness, and it is that which puts an acceptable beauty upon all the acts of worship.

Idolatry

*"And take heed, lest you lift your eyes to heaven,
and when you see the sun, the moon, and the stars,
all the host of heaven,
you feel driven to worship them and serve them,
which the LORD your God has given to all the peoples
under the whole heaven as a heritage."*
DEUTERONOMY 4:19

Moses charges the Israelites to take particular heed of the sin of idolatry. Two sorts of idolatry he cautions them against, the first being the worship of images; however, by them they might intend to worship the true God, as they had done in the golden calf, so changing the truth of God into a lie and His glory into shame. The worship of the sun, moon, and stars is another sort of idolatry that they are cautioned against. This was the most ancient species of idolatry and the most plausible. The plausibleness of it made it more dangerous. When you see the sun, moon, and stars, you will be strongly tempted to give that glory to them which is due to Him who made them. It seems there was need of a great deal of resolution to arm them against this temptation, so weak was their faith in an invisible God and a visible world. These pretended deities, the sun, moon, and stars, were only blessings that the Lord God had imparted to all nations. It is absurd to worship them, for they are man's servants, made and ordained to give light to the earth.

Holy Awe

> *Give to the LORD the glory due His name;*
> *bring an offering, and come into His courts.*
> *Oh, worship the LORD in the beauty of holiness!*
> PSALM 96:8–9

In every nation those who feared God and wrought righteousness were accepted by Him, yet instituted ordinances were the peculiarities of the Jewish religion. All the earth is here summoned to fear the Lord, to worship Him. The acts of devotion to God are described here. We must give unto the Lord. It is what must be paid, and if not will be recovered. Yet, if it comes from holy love, God is pleased to accept it as a gift. We must give unto the Lord the glory due His name. We must bring an offering into His courts. We must bring ourselves in the first place. We must worship Him in the beauty of holiness, with holy hearts, sanctified by the grace of God, devoted to the glory of God. All acts of worship must be performed with holy awe and reverence.

The new song proclaims God great as well as good. He is great in His sovereignty over all who pretend to be deities—all princes, who were often deified after their deaths. He is great in His right, even to the noblest part of the creation, for it is His own work and derives its being from Him. Splendor and majesty are before Him above, where the angels cover their faces, unable to bear the dazzling luster of His glory. Strength and beauty are in His sanctuary, both that above and this below. If we attend Him in His sanctuary, we shall behold His beauty, for God is love, and experience His strength, for He is our rock.

Our Manner of Worship

"But the hour is coming, and now is,
when the true worshipers will worship
the Father in spirit and truth;
for the Father is seeking such to worship Him."
JOHN 4:23

Those who by the Scriptures have obtained some knowledge of God may worship Him comfortably to themselves, and acceptably to Him, for they know who they worship. Worship may be true where yet it is not pure and entire. Our Lord Jesus was pleased to reckon Himself among the worshipers of God. Let not the greatest of men think the worship of God below them, when the Son of God Himself did not. Salvation is of the Jews; and therefore they know who they worship and what grounds they go upon in their worship. The author of eternal salvation comes from the Jews and is sent first to bless them. The means of eternal salvation are afforded to them. The word of salvation was of the Jews. Having shown that the place is indifferent, He comes to show what is necessary and essential—that we worship God in spirit and in truth. The stress is upon the state of mind in which we worship Him. It concerns us to be right, not only in the object of our worship, but in the manner of it; and it is this which Christ here instructs us in.

Public Worship and Understanding

I will pray with the spirit,
and I will also pray with the understanding.
I will sing with the spirit,
and I will also sing with the understanding.

1 CORINTHIANS 14:15

The apostle directs them how they should sing and pray in public. He would have them perform both so as to be understood by others, that others might join with them. Public worship should be performed so as to be understood. Otherwise, the unlearned could not say "Amen" to their prayers or thanksgivings, could not join in the worship, for they did not understand it. All should say "Amen" inwardly, and it is not improper to testify this inward concurrence in public prayers and devotions by an audible "Amen." Now, how should the people say "Amen" to what they did not understand? The intention of public devotions is therefore entirely destroyed if they are performed in an unknown tongue. Others are not, cannot be, edified by what they understand not.

Children are apt to be struck by novelty and strange appearances. Do not act like them and prefer noise and show to work and substance. Christians should have wisdom and knowledge that are ripe and mature.

Brotherly Love

Beloved, if God so loved us,
we also ought to love one another.
1 JOHN 4:11

The Spirit of truth is known by love. The apostle would unite them in His love, that He might unite them in love to each other. Divine love to the brethren should constrain ours. This should be an invincible argument. Shall we refuse to love those whom the eternal God has loved? We should be admirers of His love, and lovers of His love, and consequently lovers of those whom He loves.

Christian love is an assurance of divine inhabitation. The sacred lovers of the brethren are the temples of God; the divine majesty has a peculiar residence there. Divine love attains accomplishment in us. God's love is not perfected in Him, but in and with us. Faith is perfected by its works, and love has brought us to the love of God, and thereupon to the love of the brethren; for His sake it is therein perfected. How ambitious we should be of this love, when God reckons His own love to us perfected thereby.

One would think that to speak of God dwelling in us, and we in Him, were to use words too high for mortals, had not God gone before us therein. What it fully is must be left to the revelation of the blessed world. But this mutual inhabitation we know, says the apostle, because He has given us His Spirit.

The Least of These

"And the King will answer and say to them,
'Assuredly, I say to you,
inasmuch as you did it to one of
the least of these My brethren,
you did it to Me.'"

MATTHEW 25:40

Gracious souls are apt to think poorly of their own good deeds, especially as unworthy to be compared with the glory that shall be revealed. Saints in heaven will wonder what brought them there and that God should so regard them and their services. "We have seen the poor in distress many a time, but when did we see you?" Christ is more among us than we think He is.

"Inasmuch as you did it to one of the least of these My brethren, you did it to Me." The good works of the saints, when they are produced in the great day, shall all be remembered and not the smallest overlooked: no, not a cup of cold water. They shall be interpreted most to their advantage. As Christ makes the best of their infirmities, so He makes the most of their services.

But what will become of the godly poor, who had no money to help others? Must they be shut out? No, Christ will own them, even the least of them, as His brethren. He will not be ashamed or think it any disparagement to Him to call them brethren. In the height of His glory, He will not disown His poor relations. He will take the kindness done to them as done to Himself, which shows a respect of the poor who were relieved, as well as the rich who relieved them.

Suppress Anger

So then, my beloved brethren,
let every man be swift to hear,
slow to speak, slow to wrath;
for the wrath of man does not produce
the righteousness of God.
JAMES 1:19–20

Be ready to hear and consider what God's Word teaches. Instead of censuring God under our trials, let us open our ears and hearts to hear what He will say to us. This may be understood as referring to the disputes and differences that Christians were running into among themselves. We should be swift to hear reason and truth on all sides and be slow to speak. When we do speak, there should be no wrath. If men would govern their tongues, they must govern their passions. If we would be slow to speak, we must be slow to wrath.

A very good reason is given for suppressing anger. The worst thing we can bring to a religious controversy is anger. Wrath is a human thing, and the wrath of man stands opposed to the righteousness of God. Those who pretend to serve the cause of God hereby show that they are acquainted neither with God nor His cause.

We are called upon to suppress other corrupt affections, as well as rash anger. We are taught, as Christians, to watch against all the disorders of a corrupt heart, which would prejudice it against the Word and ways of God. There is an abundance of evil in us to be watched against. It is not enough to restrain evil affections, but they must be cast from us. This must extend not only to outward sins, but to all sin of thought and affection, as well as speech and practice.

The Grace of Gentleness

He who is slow to anger is better than the mighty,
and he who rules his spirit than he who takes a city.

PROVERBS 16:32

The grace of gentleness is to be slow to anger, not easily put into a passion, nor apt to resent provocation, so slow in our motions toward anger that we may be quickly stopped and pacified. It is to have the rule of our own spirits, particularly our passions. He who gets and keeps the mastery of his passions is better than the mighty. Behold, one greater than Alexander or Caesar is here. The conquest of our own unruly passions requires more true wisdom and a more steady management than the obtaining of a victory over an enemy. No lives or treasures are sacrificed to it. It is harder to quash an insurrection at home than to resist an invasion from abroad; such are the gains of gentleness that, by it, we are more than conquerors.

Nothing comes to pass by chance, nor is an event determined by a blind fortune, but everything by the will and counsel of God. All the disposals of Providence concerning our affairs we must look upon to be the directing of our lot, the determining of what we referred to God, and we must be reconciled to them accordingly.

Family Relationships

Fathers, do not provoke your children,
lest they become discouraged.
COLOSSIANS 3:21

God gives an explanation of family duties. Wives are to submit themselves to their husbands. This is agreeable to the order of nature and the reason of things, as well as the appointment and will of God. It is submission to a husband, to her own husband, who stands in the nearest relation and is under strict engagements to his own proper duty. This is fit in the Lord. Husbands must love their wives and not be bitter against them (v. 19). They must love them with tender and faithful affection, as Christ loved the church. And they must not be bitter against them, but be kind and obliging to them in all things.

Here are the duties of children and parents: "Children, obey your parents in all things, for this is well pleasing to the Lord" (v. 20). They must be willing to do all their lawful commands, as those who have a natural right and are fitter to direct them than themselves. This is well pleasing to God. Parents must be tender, as well as children obedient. "Fathers, do not provoke your children, lest they become discouraged." Let not your authority over them be exercised with rigor and severity, but with kindness and gentleness, lest you, by holding the reins too tightly, make them fly out with the greater fierceness.

Husbands and Wives

Husbands, likewise,
dwell with them with understanding,
giving honor to the wife,
as to the weaker vessel,
and as being heirs together of the grace of life,
that your prayers may not be hindered.

1 PETER 3:7

Lest the Christian matrons should imagine that their conversion to Christ exempted them from subjection to their pagan or Jewish husbands, the apostle here tells them what their duty consists of. The apostle enforces them by the example of the holy women of old, who trusted in God (v. 5): The duties imposed upon you are not new, but what have ever been practiced by the greatest and best women in the world. Sarah obeyed her husband and followed him (v. 6): Whose daughters you are if you imitate her in faith and good works. The subjection of wives to their husbands is a duty which has been practiced universally by holy women in all ages. Christians ought to do their duty to one another not out of fear, nor from force, but from a willing mind and in obedience to the command of God.

The husband's duty to the wife includes: (1) cohabitation, dwelling with the wife according to knowledge, as wise and sober men who know the Word of God and their own duty; and (2) giving honor to the wife—giving due respect to her and placing a due trust and confidence in her. The wife is, in other and higher respects, equal to her husband; they are heirs together of the grace of life, and therefore should live peaceably with one another. If they do not, their prayers one with another and one for another will be hindered.

Charity within the Family

*But if anyone does not provide for his own,
and especially for those of his household,
he has denied the faith and is worse than an unbeliever.*
1 TIMOTHY 5:8

The general rule is to honor widows, maintain them, and relieve them with respect and tenderness. The church should not be charged with the maintenance of those widows who had relations of their own who were able to maintain them (v. 4). The respect of children to their parents, with their care of them, is fitly called piety. Children can never sufficiently repay their parents for the care they have taken of them, but they must endeavor to do so. If they spend that upon their lusts which should maintain their families, they have denied the faith. There should be prudence in the choice of the objects of charity, that it may not be thrown away on those who are not properly so, that there may be more for those who are real objects of charity.

Directions concerning the character of the widows who were to receive the church's charity: Particular care ought to be taken to relieve those who, when they had wherewithal, were ready to do every good work. Those who would find mercy when they are in distress must show mercy when they are in prosperity.

Husband and Wife

So husbands ought to love their own wives
as their own bodies;
he who loves his wife loves himself.

EPHESIANS 5:28

The duty of husbands is to love their wives, for without this they would abuse their superiority, it being a special and peculiar affection that is required in her behalf. The love of Christ to the church is proposed as an example of this. This love of His is a constant affection, despite the imperfections and failures that she is guilty of. The greatness of His love to the church appeared in His giving Himself to death for her. The love that God requires from the husband in behalf of his wife will make amends for the subjections that he demands from her to her husband, and the prescribed subjection of the wife will be an abundant return for that love of the husband which God has made her due. The reason Christ gave Himself for the church was that He might sanctify and cleanse her, with the washing of water by the Word. That He might present her to Himself a glorious church, not having spot or wrinkle, or any such thing, holy and without blemish, free from the least remains of sin. The church, in general, and particular believers will not be without spot or wrinkle until they come to glory. Those, and those only, who are sanctified now will be glorified hereafter. "So husbands ought to love their own wives as their own bodies." The wife being one with her husband, this is an argument why he should love her with as ardent an affection as that with which he loves himself.

Mutual Love

Let all bitterness, wrath, anger, clamor,
and evil speaking be put away from you, with all malice.
And be kind to one another, tenderhearted,
forgiving one another,
even as God in Christ forgave you.

EPHESIANS 4:31–32

The Lord gives another caution against wrath and anger, with further advice to mutual love. By bitterness, wrath, and anger are meant violent inward resentment against others, and by clamor, intemperate speeches, by which bitterness, wrath, and anger vent themselves. Christians should not be clamorous with their tongues. Evil speaking signifies all railing against whomever we are angry with. Malice is that rooted anger which prompts men to design mischief to others. The contrary to all this follows: "Be kind to one another." This implies the principle of love in the heart and the outward expression of it. Tenderhearted is merciful, to be quickly moved to compassion and pity. Occasions of difference will happen among Christ's disciples, and they must be ready to forgive, therefore resembling God Himself, who for Christ's sake forgave them. Those who are forgiven by God should be of a forgiving spirit and should forgive, even as God forgives. He who does not conscientiously discharge these duties can never fear nor love God in truth and in sincerity, whatever he may pretend to.

Feed Your Enemy

"If your enemy is hungry, feed him;
if he is thirsty, give him a drink;
for in so doing you will heap coals of fire on his head."
Do not be overcome by evil,
but overcome evil with good.
ROMANS 12:20–21

If your enemy is hungry, be ready to show him any kindness, so you may thereby testify to the sincerity of your forgiveness of him. We must do good to our enemies. If he is hungry, do not say, "Now God is avenging me of him." Feed him. Feed him abundantly, as we do children and sick people, with much tenderness. Contrive to do it so as to express your love. If he is thirsty, give him a drink in token of reconciliation and friendship. Confirm your love to him. Why must we do this? "You will heap coals of fire on his head," that is, melt him into repentance and friendship. You will win a friend by it, and if your kindness does not have that effect, then it will make his malice against you the more inexcusable. Not that this must be our intention in showing him kindness, but such will be the effect. Those who revenge are the conquered, and those who forgive are the conquerors. "Do not be overcome by evil." Let not the evil of any provocation that is given you have such a power over you as to disturb your peace, to destroy your love, or to bring you to think of or attempt any revenge. He who cannot quietly bear an injury is conquered by it. Overcome evil with good, with the good of patience and forbearance, and of kindness and beneficence to those who wrong you. He who has this rule over his spirit is better than the mighty.

The Merciful Obtain Mercy

Blessed is he who considers the poor;
the LORD will deliver him in time of trouble.
PSALM 41:1

God promises succor and comfort to those who consider the poor. David makes mention of these with application to his friends, who were kind to him: Blessed is he who considers poor David. The provocations that his enemies gave him only endeared his friends so much the more to him. Or he was speaking of himself. He had considered the poor and had provided for their relief. Therefore, he was sure God would, according to His promise, strengthen and comfort him in his sickness. We must regard them more generally with application to ourselves. Blessed are the merciful, for they shall obtain mercy. The mercy required of us is to consider the poor or afflicted, whether in mind, body, or estate. We must take notice of their affliction and inquire into their state, must sympathize with them and judge charitably concerning them. He who considers the poor shall be blessed upon the earth. This branch of godliness, as much as any, has the promise of the life that now is, and is usually rewarded by temporal blessings. Those who thus distinguish themselves from those who have hard hearts God will distinguish from those who have hard usage. They shall be preserved and kept alive when the arrows of death fly thickly about them. The goodwill of a God who loves us is sufficient to secure us from the ill will of all who hate us, men and devils, and that goodwill we may promise ourselves if we have considered the poor and helped to relieve and rescue them.

How to Enjoy Riches

Command those who are rich in this present age
not to be haughty,
nor to trust in uncertain riches but in the living God,
who gives us richly all things to enjoy.

1 TIMOTHY 6:17

The apostle adds a lesson for rich people. Timothy must charge those who are rich to beware of the temptations and improve the opportunities of their prosperous state. He must caution them to take heed of pride. He must caution them against vain confidence in their wealth. Nothing is more uncertain than the wealth of this world; many have had much of it one day and been stripped of all the next. Those who are rich must see God giving them their riches and giving them to enjoy them richly. Many have riches but enjoy them poorly, not having the heart to use them. He must charge them to do good with what they have. Those are truly rich who are rich in good works. He must charge them to think of another world and prepare for that which is to come by works of charity.

Ministers must not be afraid of the rich. They must caution them against pride and vain confidence in their riches. A lesson for ministers in the charge given to Timothy: Keep that which is committed to your trust. Every minister is a trustee. The truths of God, the ordinances of God, keep these. Keep close to the written Word, for that is committed to our trust. Some who have been very proud of their learning have by that been drawn away from the faith of Christ, which is a good reason why we should keep to the plain word of the gospel.

Family Enrichment

Behold, children are a heritage from the LORD,
the fruit of the womb is a reward.
PSALM 127:3

The enriching of a family is a work of time and thought, but cannot be effected without the favor of Providence. It is vain for you to rise up early and sit up late, and so to deny yourselves your bodily refreshments in the eager pursuit of the wealth of the world. All this is to get money, and all in vain unless God prospers them, for riches are not always to men of understanding.

Those who love God and are beloved by Him have their minds easy and live very comfortably without this ado. God gives us sleep as He gives it to His beloved, when with it He gives us grace to lie down in His fear, and when are we are awake to be still with Him and to use the refreshment we have by sleep in His service. He gives quietness and contentment of mind, a comfortable enjoyment of what is present, and a comfortable expectation of what is to come. Children are God's gift, and they are to us what He makes them, comforts or crosses. Children are a heritage and a reward and so are to be accounted blessings and not burdens, for He who sends mouths will send meat if we trust in Him. Children are a heritage for the Lord, as well as from Him. The family who has a large stock of children is like a quiver full of arrows of different sizes, all of use at one time or another, children of different capacities and inclinations.

Instruction

> *"Now therefore, listen to me, my children,*
> *for blessed are those who keep my ways.*
> *Hear instruction and be wise,*
> *and do not disdain it."*
>
> PROVERBS 8:32–33

An exhortation to hear and obey the voice of Wisdom, to discern the voice of Christ, as the sheep know the shepherd's voice. "Listen to Me, My children." Read the written Word, sit under the Word preached, bless God for both, and hear Him in both speaking to you. Let Wisdom's children justify Wisdom by hearkening to her. Hear Wisdom's words with a willing heart. "Hear instruction and be wise, and do not disdain it," either as that which you do not need or as that which you do not like. It is offered you as a kindness, and you refuse it at your peril. We must hear Wisdom so as to watch daily at her gates as beggars to receive alms, as clients and patients to receive advice, and as servants, with humility and patience at the posts of her doors. We must watch and wait, as Christ's hearers crowded close to hear Him early in the morning.

An assurance of happiness to all those who do hearken to Wisdom: They shall find what they seek. But will it make them amends if they do find it? Yes (v. 35): "Whoever finds me finds life," that is, all happiness, all that good which he needs or can desire. Christ is Wisdom, and he who finds Christ finds life, for Christ is life to all believers.

Reverence to Parents

The father of the righteous will greatly rejoice,
and he who begets a wise child will delight in him.
Let your father and your mother be glad,
and let her who bore you rejoice.
PROVERBS 23:24–25

Hearken to your father who begat you, and who therefore has authority over you and affection for you, and can have no other design than your own good. We ought to give reverence to the fathers of our flesh, who were the instruments of our being; much more ought we to obey and be in subjection to the Father of our spirits, who made us and is the author of our being. And since the mother, also, from a sense of duty to God and from love for her child gives him good instructions, let him not despise her or her advice.

"Buy the truth, and do not sell it" (v. 23). Truth is that by which the heart must be guided and governed, for without truth there is no goodness. We must buy it whatever it costs us; we shall not repent the bargain. Riches should be employed for the getting of knowledge, rather than knowledge for the getting of riches. When we are at pains in searching after truth, then we buy it. Heaven concedes everything to the laborious. We must not sell it. Do not part with it for pleasures, honors, riches, or anything in this world. God, in this exhortation, speaks to us as to children: "Son, Daughter, 'give Me your heart'" (v. 26). You shall love the Lord your God with all your heart. To this call we must readily answer, "My Father, take my heart, such as it is, and make it such as it should be; take possession of it, and set up Your throne in it."

Children of the Highest

"But love your enemies, do good, and lend,
hoping for nothing in return;
and your reward will be great,
and you will be sons of the Most High."

LUKE 6:35

Love your enemies and do them good. To recommend this difficult duty to us, it is represented as a generous thing and an attainment few arrive at. To love those who love us has nothing uncommon in it, nothing peculiar to Christ's disciples, for sinners will love those who love them. It is but following nature and puts no force at all upon us (v. 32): "And if you do good to those who do good to you, what credit is that to you?" What credit are you to the name of Christ, or what reputation do you bring to it, for sinners do the same? But it becomes you to do something more excellent and eminent, to do that which sinners will not do: You must render good for evil. Then we are to our God for a name and a praise, and He will have the thanks.

We must be kind to those from whom we expect no manner of advantage. "Lend, hoping for nothing in return." We must lend though we have reason to suspect that what we lend we lose, lend to those who are so poor that it is not probable they will be able to pay us again. Here are two motives to this generous charity: It will redound to our profit, for our reward shall be great, and what is lent and lost on earth from a true principle of charity will be made up to us. You shall not only be repaid, but rewarded, greatly rewarded; it will be said to you, "Come, you blessed, inherit the kingdom." It will redound to our honor, for we shall resemble God in His goodness, which is the greatest glory: "You shall be the children of the Most High."

God's Repayment

"Judge not, and you shall not be judged.
Condemn not, and you shall not be condemned.
Forgive, and you will be forgiven."
LUKE 6:37

We ought to be very careful in our censure of others, because we need grains of allowance ourselves. Therefore, judge not others, because then you yourselves shall not be judged. Therefore, condemn not others, because then you yourselves shall not be condemned. God will not judge and condemn you; men will not. They who are merciful to other people's names shall find others merciful to theirs.

If we are of a giving and a forgiving spirit, we shall ourselves reap the benefit of it: "Forgive, and you will be forgiven." If we forgive the injuries done to us by others, others will forgive our inadvertencies. If we forgive others' trespasses against us, God will forgive our trespasses against Him. And He will be no less mindful of the liberals who devise liberal things. "Give, and it will be given to you" (v. 38). Men shall return it to you, for God often makes use of men as instruments, not only of His avenging, but of His rewarding justice. God will incline the hearts of others to give to us when we need and to give liberally, "good measure, pressed down, shaken together" (v. 38). Whom God recompenses, He recompenses abundantly.

The Knowledge of God

" 'All your children shall be taught by the LORD,
and great shall be the peace of your children.' "

ISAIAH 54:13

Those things that shall be the beauty and honor of the church are knowledge, holiness, and love, the very image of God in which man was created, renewed, and restored. And these are the sapphires and carbuncles, the precious stones with which the gospel temple shall be beautified, built upon the foundation (1 Corinthians 3:12). The church is all glorious when it is full of the knowledge of God. "All your children shall be taught by the Lord." They shall be taught by those whom God will appoint and whose labors will be under His direction and blessing. It is a promise of the Spirit of illumination. Our Savior quotes it with application to gospel grace (John 6:45). When the members of it live in love and unity among themselves, "great shall be the peace of your children." All who are taught by God are taught to love one another. When holiness reigns—for that above anything is the beauty of the church—in righteousness shall you be established. The reformation of manners, the restoration of purity, the due administration of public justice, and the prevailing of honesty and fair dealing among men are the strength and stability of any church or state.

Gossip

> " 'You shall not go about as a talebearer among your people;
> nor shall you take a stand against the life of your neighbor.' "
> LEVITICUS 19:16

We are all forbidden to do anything injurious to our neighbor's good name in common conversation. "You shall not go about as a talebearer." The word used for a talebearer signifies a peddler or petty chapman, the interlopers of door-to-door trade who pick up ill-natured stories at one house and utter them at another, and commonly barter slanders by way of exchange. This sin is condemned in Proverbs 11:13; 20:19; Jeremiah 9:4–5; and Ezekiel 22:9.

Neither should we be talebearers in bearing witness: "Nor shall you take a stand against the life of your neighbor" if his blood is innocent. The Jews put this further sense on it: "He who can by his testimony clear one who is accused is obliged by this law to do it" (see Proverbs 24:11–12). We are commanded to rebuke our neighbor in love. Rather rebuke him than hate him for an injury. If we think that our neighbor has in any way wronged us, we must not hold a secret grudge against him and estrange ourselves from him. We must endeavor to convince our brother of the injury and reason the case fairly with him.

Watch Your Tongue

Keep your tongue from evil,
and your lips from speaking deceit.
PSALM 34:13

David undertakes to teach children here. It does not appear that he had any children of his own at this time; he is instructing the children of his people and therefore calls together a congregation of them. " 'Come, you children, listen to me' (v. 11). Leave your play, lay by your toys, and hear what I have to say to you; not only give me the hearing, but observe and obey me.' " He undertakes to teach them the fear of the Lord, including all the duties of religion.

He supposes that we all aim to be happy, then prescribes the true and only way to happiness, both in this world and that to come. We must learn to bridle our tongues and be careful what we say, that we never speak amiss to God's dishonor or our neighbor's prejudice. "Keep your tongue from evil, and your lips from speaking deceit." We must be upright and sincere in everything we say, not double-tongued. We must depart from evil—both evil works and evil workers (v. 14). It is not enough not to do harm in the world, but we must learn to be useful and live to some purpose. We must seek peace and pursue it: follow peace with all men, willing to deny ourselves a great deal, both in honor and interest, for peace's sake.

Peace and Quiet

Aspire to lead a quiet life,
to mind your own business,
and to work with your own hands,
as we commanded you,
that you may walk properly toward those who are outside,
and that you may lack nothing.

1 THESSALONIANS 4:11–12

The exhortation itself is to increase more and more in brotherly love (v. 10). They must be exhorted to pray for more and labor for more. There are none on this side of heaven who love perfectly.

He speaks of quietness and industry in their work. They should study to be quiet. It is the most desirable thing to have a calm and quiet temper and to be of peaceable, quiet behavior. Satan is very busy trying to disquiet us, and we have that in our own hearts that disposes us to be disquiet; therefore, let us study to be quiet. "Mind your own business." Those who are busybodies, meddling in other men's matters, generally have little quiet in their own minds and cause great disturbances among their neighbors. They seldom mind the exhortation to be diligent in their own work. Christianity does not discharge us from the work of our particular callings, but teaches us to be diligent therein. Thus we shall walk honestly, or decently and creditably, toward those who are without. This is to act as becomes the gospel and will gain a good report from those who are strangers or even enemies to it. Those who are diligent in their own business live comfortably and lack for nothing. They earn their own bread and have the greatest pleasure in so doing.

The New Man

Do not lie to one another,
since you have put off the old man with his deeds.

COLOSSIANS 3:9

We are to mortify inordinate passions (v. 8), putting off anger, wrath, and malice. Anger and wrath are bad, but malice is worse; it is anger heightened and settled. So we must also do to the product of them in the tongue, blasphemy, which seems here to mean not so much speaking ill of God as speaking ill of men—filthy language, all lewd and wanton discourse, which propagates the same defilements in the hearers. "Do not lie to one another" (lying makes us like the devil, who is the father of lies), "since you have put off the old man with his deeds, and have put on the new man" (v. 10). Those who have put off the old man have put it off with its deeds; and those who have put on the new man must put on all its deeds, renewed in knowledge, because an ignorant soul cannot be a good soul. Light is the first thing in the new creation, as it was in the first: after the image of Him who created him. It was the honor of man in innocence that he was made after the image of God. In the privilege of sanctification, there is neither Greek nor Jew, circumcised nor uncircumcised, barbarian, Scythian, slave nor free (v. 11). It is as much the duty of the one as of the other to be holy and as much the privilege of the one as of the other to receive from God the grace to be so. Christ is all in all. Christ is a Christian's all, all his hope and happiness.

Acting in Justice

Do not withhold good from those to whom it is due,
when it is in the power of your hand to do so.
PROVERBS 3:27

We must render to all their due, both in justice and charity, and not delay doing it. "Do not withhold good from those to whom it is due, when it is in the power of your hand to do so." It is a great fault to make yourself unable to do justly and show mercy because of your own extravagance. If you have enough today, do not say to your neighbor, "Go away and come back at a more convenient time. Tomorrow I will give" (v. 28). You are not even sure that you will be alive tomorrow or that tomorrow you shall have enough to give. Do not make excuses to shift off a duty that must be done or take pleasure in keeping your neighbor in pain and suspense, nor to show the power that the giver has over the beggar. Readily and cheerfully give good to those to whom it is due, to those who are entitled to it. This requires us to pay our debts without fraud or delay; to give wages to those who have earned them; to provide for our relations and those who are dependent on us; to render dues both to church and state, magistrates and ministers; to be ready for all acts of friendship and humanity, and in everything to be neighborly. These are things that are due by the law of doing as we would be done to—to be charitable to the poor and needy.

Business and Jubilee

> " 'And if you sell anything to your neighbor
> or buy from your neighbor's hand,
> you shall not oppress one another.' "
>
> LEVITICUS 25:14

Neither the buyer nor the seller must overreach. It must be settled what the clear yearly value of the land was and then how many years' purchase it was worth until the Year of Jubilee, when land reverted to the original owner. It is easy to see that the nearer the Jubilee was, the less the value of the land must be. "According to the fewer number of years you shall diminish its price" (v. 16).

Assurance is given them that they would not be losers but great gainers by observing these years of rest. It is promised that they would be safe. "You will dwell in the land in safety" (v. 18). The word signifies both outward safety and inward security and confidence of spirit. That they would be rich: "You will eat your fill" (v. 19). That they would not want food convenient that year in which they neither sowed nor reaped: "I will command My blessing in the sixth year, and it will bring forth produce enough for three years" (v. 21). It was intended for an encouragement to all God's people, in all ages, to trust Him in the way of duty and to cast their care upon Him.

Walking Righteously

He who walks righteously and speaks uprightly,
he who despises the gain of oppressions,
who gestures with his hands, refusing bribes,
who stops his ears from hearing of bloodshed,
and shuts his eyes from seeing evil:
he will dwell on high.

ISAIAH 33:15–16

The good man walks righteously. He acts by rules of equity, rendering to all their due—to God His due, to men, theirs. He speaks uprightly, with an honest intention. He thinks it a mean and sordid thing to enrich himself by any hardship put upon his neighbor. If he has a bribe thrust into his hands to prevent justice, he gestures with his hands, taking it as an affront. He stops his ears from hearing anything that tends to cruelty or any suggestions stirring him up to revenge. He shuts his eyes from seeing evil. He has such an abhorrence of sin that he cannot bear to see others commit it. Those who would preserve the purity of their souls must stop their ears to temptations and turn away their eyes from beholding vanity.

The good man shall be safe. "He will dwell on high" (v. 16). He shall not be really harmed by troubles. The floods of great waters shall not come near him, or if they do, his place of defense shall be God, the rock of ages. He shall want for nothing that is necessary for him. "Bread will be given him," even when the siege is hardest; and "his water will be sure" (v. 16). Those who fear the Lord shall not want for anything that is good for them.

What Does It Profit?

If a brother or sister is naked and destitute of daily food,
and one of you says to them,
"Depart in peace, be warmed and filled,"
but you do not give them the things
which are needed for the body,
what does it profit?"
JAMES 2:15–16

Faith without works will not profit us and cannot save us. "What does it profit, my brethren, if someone says he has faith but does not have works? Can faith save him?" (v. 14). Faith that does not save will not really profit us. All things should be accounted profitable or unprofitable to us as they tend to promote or hinder the salvation of our souls. For a man to actually have faith but to merely claim he has faith are two different things. Men may boast of their faith to others and be conceited of it in themselves when they are really destitute of faith.

As love or charity is an operative principle, so is faith. By seeing how it looks when a person pretends he is very charitable yet never does any works of charity, you may judge what sense there is in pretending to have faith without the fruits of it. What will such charity as this, that consists of bare words, avail either you or the poor? You might as well pretend that your love and charity will stand the test without acts of mercy, as think that a profession of faith will bear you out before God without works of piety and obedience. We are too apt to rest in a bare profession of faith and think that this will save us. Mock faith is as hateful as mock charity, and both show a heart dead to all real goodness.

Laboring to Support the Weak

"I have shown you in every way, by laboring like this, that you must support the weak. And remember the words of the Lord Jesus, that He said, 'It is more blessed to give than to receive.' "
ACTS 20:35

Paul, even when he worked for the supply of his own needs, spared something out of what he got for the relief of others. . . . "I have shown you in every way, by laboring like this, that you must support the weak." Understand it of their helping to support the sick, and the poor, and those who could not labor, because it agrees with Paul's exhortation, "Let him labor, working with his hands, that he may have to give to him who is in need." We must labor in honest employment not only so we may be able to live, but that we may be able to give.

This might seem a hard saying, and therefore Paul backs it with a saying of our Master. An excellent saying it is and has something of a paradox in it: "It is more blessed to give than to receive." It is more blessed to give to others than to receive from others; not only more blessed to be rich, and so on the giving hand, than to be poor, and so on the receiving hand, but more blessed to do good with what we have, much or little, than to invest it and make more. The sentiment of the children of this world is contrary to this; they are afraid of giving. They are in hope of getting. Clear gain is to them the most blessed thing that can be, but Christ tells us it is more blessed to give than to receive. It makes us more like God, who gives to all and receives from none, and to the Lord Jesus, who went about doing good. It is more blessed to give our pain than to receive pay for it. It is more pleasant to do good to the grateful, but it is more honorable to do good to the ungrateful, for then we have God as our paymaster.

Entertaining Strangers

Do not forget to entertain strangers,
for by so doing some have
unwittingly entertained angels.

HEBREWS 13:2

Concerning brotherly love, the spirit of Christianity is a spirit of love. Faith works by love. The true religion is the strongest bond of friendship. This brotherly love was in danger of being lost in a time of persecution, when it would be most necessary. Christians should always love and live as brethren, and the more they grow in devout affection to God their heavenly Father, the more they will grow in love to one another for His sake.

Concerning hospitality, we must add charity to brotherly kindness. The duty required is to entertain strangers. Seeing they are without any certain dwelling place, we should allow them room in our hearts and in our houses, as we have opportunity and ability. The motive is "for by doing so some have unwittingly entertained angels." God has often bestowed honors and favors on His hospitable servants beyond all their thoughts, unawares.

Concerning Christian sympathy, those who are at liberty must sympathize with those who are in bonds and adversity, as if they were bound with them in the same chain. The reason for this duty is "As being yourselves in the body"—not only in the natural body, but in the same mystical body. It would be un-natural for Christians not to bear each other's burdens.

Tender Mercies

Therefore, as the elect of God, holy and beloved,
put on tender mercies, kindness,
humility, meekness, longsuffering;
bearing with one another,
and forgiving one another.
COLOSSIANS 3:12–13

"Put on tender mercies." We must not only put off anger and wrath, but we must put on compassion and kindness, "as the elect of God, holy and beloved." Those who are the elect of God are beloved and ought to conduct themselves in everything as becomes them. We must put on: (1) Compassion toward the miserable: Those who owe so much to mercy ought to be merciful; (2) Kindness: The design of the gospel is not only to soften the minds of men, but to sweeten them and promote friendship among men as well as reconciliation with God; (3) Humility: There must not only be a humble demeanor, but a humble mind; (4) Meekness: We must prudently bridle our own anger and patiently bear the anger of others; (5) Longsuffering: Many can bear a short provocation but become weary of bearing when the time grows long; if God is longsuffering to us, we should exercise longsuffering to others; (6) Bearing with one another: We all have something that needs to be borne; we need the same good turn from others that we are bound to show them; and (7) Forgiving one another: Quarrels will sometimes happen, even among the elect of God, who are holy and beloved, but it is our duty to forgive one another in such cases. It is a branch of His example that we are obliged to follow if we ourselves would be forgiven.

True Wisdom

Who is wise and understanding among you?
Let him show by good conduct that his works are done
in the meekness of wisdom.

JAMES 3:13

The disciple explains the difference between those who pretend to be wise and those who really are so and between the wisdom that is from beneath and that which is from above.

We have some discussion here of true wisdom. A wise man will not value himself merely on knowing things, if he has not the wisdom to make a right application of that knowledge. These two things must be put together to make up the totality of true wisdom. If we are wiser than others, this should be evidenced by the goodness of our conduct. True wisdom may be known by its works. This refers not only to words, but to the whole of men's practice; therefore, it is said, "Let him show by good conduct that his works are done in the meekness of wisdom." He who thinks well or he who talks well is not allowed to consider himself wise if he does not live and act well. True wisdom may be known by the meekness of the spirit and temper. It is a great instance of wisdom to prudently bridle our own anger and patiently bear the anger of others. When we are mild and calm, we are best able to hear reason and best able to speak it. Wisdom produces meekness, and meekness increases wisdom.

Do Not Give Offence

It is good neither to eat meat nor drink wine
nor do anything by which your brother stumbles
or is offended or is made weak.
ROMANS 14:21

Consider the evil of giving offence. All things indeed are pure, but if we abuse this liberty, it turns into sin to us. Lawful things may be done unlawfully. It is observable that the apostle directs his reproof most against those who gave the offence. He directs his speech to the strong, because they were better able to bear the reproof and to begin the reformation. Take heed of doing anything that may give others occasion to speak evil of the Christian religion, in general, or of your Christian liberty, in particular. It is true we cannot hinder loose and ungoverned tongues from speaking evil of us and of the best things we have, but we must not (if we can help it) give them any occasion to do so. We must deny ourselves in many cases for the preservation of our credit and reputation, forbearing to do that which we rightly know we may lawfully do, when our doing it may be a prejudice to our good name.

The Fruits of the Spirit

*But the fruit of the Spirit is
love, joy, peace, longsuffering,
kindness, goodness, faithfulness,
gentleness, self-control.*
GALATIANS 5:22–23

Paul specifies the fruits of the Spirit that as Christians we are concerned to bring forth in ourselves. He particularly commends love and joy to us, by which we may understand constant delight in God; peace with God, or a peaceableness toward others; longsuffering; kindness, a sweetness of temper, easy to be entreated when any have wronged us; goodness, readiness to do good to all as we have opportunity; faith in what we profess and promise to others; gentleness, not to be easily provoked and, when we are provoked, easy to be pacified; and self-control.

Concerning those in whom these fruits are found, there is no law against them. They are not under law but under grace, for these fruits plainly show that such are led by the Spirit. This is the sincere care and endeavor of all real Christians. They are now sincerely endeavoring to die unto sin, as Christ had died for it. They have not yet obtained complete victory over it, but they are seeking the utter ruin and destruction of sin in their lives.

Commanded to Love

"A new commandment I give to you,
that you love one another;
as I have loved you, that you also love one another.
By this all will know that you are My disciples,
if you have love for one another."
JOHN 13:34–35

Jesus not only commends love, not only advises it, but commands it, and makes it one of the fundamental laws of His kingdom. This is a renewed commandment, like an old book in a new edition, corrected and enlarged. This commandment had been so corrupted that when Christ revised it, it might well have been called a new commandment. The law of brotherly love was forgotten as obsolete and out-of-date, so that as it came from Christ again, it was new to the people. It shall be new to eternity, when faith and hope are antiquated. Before it was "You shall love your neighbor." Now it is "You shall love one another."

The example of their Savior is another argument for brotherly love. "As I have loved you" is what makes it a new commandment. He had loved them, and thus they must love one another to the end. It may be understood of the special instance of love which He was now about to give in laying down His life for them. We must likewise love one another; we must set this before us as our goal because Christ has loved us.

Disciples of Love

He who loves his brother abides in the light,
and there is no cause for stumbling in him.
1 JOHN 2:10

We should see that the grace which was true in Christ is also true in us. The more our darkness is past and gospel light shines into us, the deeper our subjection to the commandments of our Lord should be, whether they are considered new or old. Before, this was to be proved by obedience to God; now, by Christian love. Some cannot be swayed by the sense of the love of Christ to their brethren and therefore remain in their dark state. He who is governed by such love proves his light to be good and genuine. He sees how appropriate it is that we should love those whom Christ has loved. Christian love teaches us to highly value our brother's soul and to dread everything that will be injurious to his innocence and peace. Hatred is a sign of spiritual darkness (v. 11). He who is possessed of hatred toward a Christian brother must be destitute of spiritual light; consequently, he walks in darkness and knows not where he goes, because darkness has blinded his eyes. It is the Lord Jesus who is the great Master of love: It is His school that is the school of love. His disciples are the disciples of love, and His family must be the family of love.

The Works of Love

My little children,
let us not love in word or in tongue,
but in deed and in truth.
1 JOHN 3:18

The example of God and Christ should inflame our hearts with holy love (v. 16). The great God has given His Son to death for us. Surely we should love those whom God has loved and loved so much.

The apostle proceeds to show us what should be the effect of our Christian love. It must be so fervent as to make us willing to suffer even to death for the safety and salvation of the dear brethren (v. 16). How mortified the Christian should be to this life and how well assured of a better! Christian love must be compassionate, generous, and communicative to the necessities of the brethren (v. 17). Those who have this world's goods must love a good God more, and their good brethren more, and be ready to distribute it for their sakes. This love to the brethren is love to God in them, and where there is none of this love to the brethren, there is no true love to God at all. There may be other fruits of this love. Compliments and flatteries do not become Christians, but the sincere expressions of sacred affection and the services or labors of love do.

This love will show our sincerity in religion and give us hope toward God (v. 19). It is a great happiness to be assured of our integrity in religion. The way to secure our inward peace is to abound in love and in the works of love.

Mutual Love

Be kindly affectionate to one another
with brotherly love,
in honor giving preference to one another.
ROMANS 12:10

There is a debt of mutual love that Christians owe and must pay, an affectionate love: "Be kindly affectionate to one another with brotherly love." This signifies not only love, but a readiness and inclination to love—kindness flowing out as from a spring. It properly denotes the love of parents to their children. Such must our love be to one another, and such it will be where there is a new nature and the law of love is written in the heart. This may recommend the grace of love to us: That as it is our duty to love others, so it is as much their duty to love us. And what can be sweeter on this side of heaven than to love and be loved?

It is a respectful love: "in honor giving preference to one another." Let us give others the preeminence. We should take notice of the gifts, graces, and performances of our brethren and value them accordingly, being more pleased to hear another praised than ourselves, leading one another in honor (so some read it), and not in taking honor but in giving it. Though we must prefer others as more capable and deserving than ourselves, yet we must not make that an excuse for doing nothing or, under the pretense of honoring others, indulging ourselves in ease and slothfulness.

The Joy of Salvation

Though now you do not see Him,
yet believing, you rejoice with joy inexpressible
and full of glory, receiving the end of your faith—
the salvation of your souls.
1 PETER 1:8–9

Two notable products or effects of faith are love and joy, and this joy is so great as to be above description. Where there are true faith and love to Christ, there is joy unspeakable and full of glory. It cannot be described by words; the best discovery is by an experimental taste of it. It is full of glory, full of heaven. There is much of heaven and the future glory in the present joys of improved Christians. Their faith removes the causes of sorrow and affords the best reasons for joy. Well might these early Christians rejoice with joy unspeakable, since they were every day receiving the end of their faith, the salvation of their souls. The salvation of the soul was the prize these Christians sought, the end they aimed at, which came nearer and more within their reach every day.

Every faithful Christian daily receives the salvation of his soul. These believers had the beginnings of heaven in the possession of holiness and a heavenly mind. They were on the losing side in the world, but the apostle reminds them of what they were receiving. If they lost an inferior good, they were all the while receiving the salvation of their souls. The glory of God and our own happiness are so connected that if we regularly seek the one, we must attain the other.

Holy Joy

I will greatly rejoice in the LORD,
my soul shall be joyful in my God;
for He has clothed me with
the garments of salvation.

ISAIAH 61:10

We are taught here to rejoice with holy joy to God's honor. In the beginning of this good work was the clothing of the church with righteousness and salvation. Upon this account, I will greatly rejoice in the Lord. The first gospel song begins like this, "My soul magnifies the Lord, and my spirit has rejoiced in God my Savior" (Luke 1:46–47). The salvation God wrought for the Jews and that reformation which appeared among them made them look as glorious as if they had been clothed in robes of state. Christ has clothed His church with an eternal salvation by clothing it with the righteousness both of justification and sanctification. Observe how the two are put together. Those, and only those, shall be clothed with the garments of salvation hereafter who are covered with the robe of righteousness now. Such is the beauty of God's grace in those who are clothed with the robe of righteousness.

Joy, Not Sorrow

"Go your way, eat the fat, drink the sweet,
and send portions to those for whom nothing is prepared;
for this day is holy to our LORD.
Do not sorrow, for the joy of the LORD is your strength."
NEHEMIAH 8:10

The people of Israel were wounded by the words of the law that were read to them. The law shows men their sins and their misery and danger because of sin. Therefore when they heard it, they all wept. It was a good sign that their hearts were tender, like Josiah's when he heard the words of the law. They wept to think how they had offended God.

They were healed and comforted by the words of peace that were spoken to them. It was one of the solemn feasts, on which it was their duty to rejoice, and even sorrow for sin must not hinder our joy in God but rather lead us to it. Ezra was pleased to see them so affected by the words, but Nehemiah observed that the day was holy and therefore was to be celebrated with joy and praise. They forbade the people to mourn and weep, instead commanding them to testify to their joy, to feast with charity to the poor: "Send portions to those for whom nothing is prepared," that your abundance may supply their want, that they may rejoice with you. It must be with piety and devotion: "The joy of the Lord is your strength." Holy joy will be oil to the wheels of our obedience.

Peace in Christ

> *"These things I have spoken to you,*
> *that in Me you may have peace.*
> *In the world you will have tribulation;*
> *but be of good cheer,*
> *I have overcome the world."*
>
> JOHN 16:33

Jesus comforts the disciples with a promise of peace in Him by virtue of His victory over the world, whatever troubles they might meet within it. "These things I have spoken to you that in Me you may have peace. In the world you will have tribulation. . .I have overcome the world."

His departure from them was really for the best. It is the will of Christ that His disciples should have peace within, whatever their troubles may be. Peace in Christ is the only true peace. Through Him we have peace with God, and so in Him we have peace in our own minds. The Word of Christ aims at this.

They were likely to meet with tribulation in the world. It has been the lot of Christ's disciples to have more or less tribulation in this world. Men persecute them because they are so good, and God corrects them because they are no better. Between both they shall have tribulation.

But be of good cheer, all shall be well. In the midst of the tribulations of this world, it is the duty and interest of Christ's disciples to be of good cheer; as sorrowful as the temper of the climate, yet always rejoicing, always cheerful, even in tribulation.

Peace with God

Therefore, having been justified by faith,
we have peace with God through our Lord Jesus Christ.
ROMANS 5:1

The precious benefits and privileges that flow from justification should quicken us all to give diligence to make it sure to ourselves. The fruits of this tree of life are exceedingly precious. We have peace with God. Sin breeds the quarrel between us and God; justification takes away the guilt. Immediately upon the removing of that obstacle, peace is made. By faith we lay hold of God's arm and of His strength and so are at peace. There is more in this peace than merely a cessation of enmity; there is friendship and lovingkindness, for God is either the worst enemy or the best friend. Christ has called His disciples friends, and surely a man needs no more to make him happy than to have God as his friend! But this is through our Lord Jesus Christ—through Him as the great Peacemaker, the mediator between God and man, not only the maker, but the matter and maintainer of our peace.

We have access by faith into this grace wherein we stand (v. 2). The saints' happy state is a state of grace, God's lovingkindness to us, and our conformity to God. We were not born in this state, but are brought into it. We could not have gotten into it by ourselves but are led into it as blind or lame or weak people are led. We have had access.

Gentleness

Brethren, if a man is overtaken in any trespass,
you who are spiritual restore such a one
in a spirit of gentleness,
considering yourself lest you also be tempted.

GALATIANS 6:1

We are taught to deal tenderly with those who are overtaken in a fault, brought to sin by the surprise of temptation. It is one thing to overtake a fault by contrivance and deliberation and another thing to be overtaken in a fault. Great tenderness should be used. Those who are spiritual must restore such a person with the spirit of gentleness. The original word signifies to "set in joint," as with a dislocated bone. We should endeavor to set them in joint again, comforting them in a sense of pardoning mercy, confirming our love to them. This is to be done with the spirit of gentleness, not in wrath and passion, as those who triumph in a brother's fall. Many necessary reproofs lose their efficacy by being given in wrath, but when they are managed with tenderness and from sincere concern for the welfare of those to whom they are given, they are likely to make an impression. This should be done with gentleness, "considering yourself lest you also be tempted." We ought to deal very gently with those who are overtaken in sin, because sometime it may be ourselves who need such help. This will dispose us to do to others as we desire to be done to in such a case.

Unity and Gentleness

*Endeavoring to keep the unity of the Spirit
in the bond of peace.*
EPHESIANS 4:3

This is an exhortation to mutual love. Love is the law of Christ's kingdom, the lesson of His school, the clothing of His family. The means of unity is lowliness and gentleness, longsuffering, and bearing with one another in love (v. 2). By lowliness, we are to understand humility as opposed to pride; by gentleness, that excellent disposition of soul that makes men unwilling to provoke others and not easily be provoked. Longsuffering implies a patient bearing of injuries without seeking revenge. The best Christians need to make the best of one another, to provoke one another's graces and not their passions. We find much in ourselves that is hard to forgive, so we must not think it much if we find that in others which we think hard to forgive, and yet we must forgive them. Without these things, unity cannot be preserved. The first step toward unity is humility. Pride and passion break the peace and make all the mischief. Humility and gentleness restore the peace: the more lowly mindedness, the more like-mindedness. The nature of that unity is the unity of the Spirit. The seat of Christianity is in the heart or spirit. It does not lie in one set of thoughts or in one form and mode of worship, but in one heart and one soul.

Longsuffering

Therefore be patient, brethren,
until the coming of the Lord.

JAMES 5:7

When we have done our work, we need patience to wait for our reward. This Christian patience is not a mere yielding to necessity, as the moral patience taught by some philosophers was, but a humble acquiescence in the wisdom and will of God. Because this is a lesson Christians must learn, though hard and difficult, it is repeated in verse 8: "Establish your hearts"; let your faith be firm, your practice of what is good constant and continued, and your resolutions for God and heaven fixed, in spite of all sufferings or temptations.

Consider what encouragement there is for Christians to be patient. Look to the example of the farmer: When he sows his corn in the ground, he waits many months for the rains and is willing to wait until the harvest for the fruit of his labor. Consider him who waits for a crop of corn; will you not wait for a crown of glory? If you should be called to wait a little longer than the farmer does, is it not something proportionally greater and infinitely more worth your waiting for? Think how short your waiting time may possibly be. Do not be impatient; do not quarrel with one another. The great Judge is at hand, as near as one who is just knocking at the door.

Patience in Suffering

For what credit is it if,
when you are beaten for your faults,
you take it patiently?
But when you do good and suffer,
if you take it patiently,
this is commendable before God.

1 PETER 2:20

If Christians were patient under their hardships while they suffered unjustly, this would be acceptable to God. There is no condition so poor but that a man may glorify God in it; the lowliest servant may do so. The most conscientious persons are very often the greatest sufferers. For conscience toward God, they suffer wrongfully; they do well and suffer for it. Sufferers of this sort are praiseworthy; they do honor to God and are accepted by Him.

There are more reasons to encourage Christian servants to patience under unjust sufferings (v. 21). From their Christian calling and the example of Christ, good Christians are a people called to be sufferers. Therefore they must expect it. They are bound to deny themselves and take up the cross. Jesus Christ suffered for us, in our stead and for our good (v. 24). The sufferings of Christ should quiet us under the most unjust and cruel sufferings we meet with in the world. Shall we sinners not submit to the light afflictions of this life, which work for us unspeakable advantages afterward?

Tiring in Goodness

And let us not grow weary while doing good,
for in due season we shall reap
if we do not lose heart.

GALATIANS 6:9

There is in all of us a proneness to tiring. We are very apt to flag and tire in duty. "In due season we shall reap if we do not lose heart." There is a recompense of reward in reserve for all who sincerely employ themselves in well doing. Though our reward may be delayed, it will surely come.

It is not enough that we be good ourselves, but we must do good to others. The objects of this duty are generally "all men." We are not to confine our charity and beneficence within too narrow bounds, but should be ready to extend it to all, as far as we are capable. We are to have a special regard to the household of faith. Though others are not to be excluded, yet these are to be preferred. The rule which we are to observe in doing good, as we have the opportunity, is that we should be sure to do it while we have the chance or while our life lasts. We must not, as too many do, neglect it during our lifetime and put it off until we are near death, under a pretense of doing something of this nature then, by leaving something behind for the good of others when we can no longer keep it ourselves. But we should take care to do good in our lifetime, indeed, to make this the business of our lives. We should be ready to improve every opportunity for it. Whenever God gives us a chance to be useful to others, He expects we should improve it according to our capacity and ability. None who stand in need of us are to be wholly overlooked, yet there is a difference to be made between some and others.

Tribulations and Hope

We also glory in tribulations,
knowing that tribulation produces perseverance;
and perseverance, character;
and character, hope.
ROMANS 5:3–4

We glory in tribulations, not only despite our tribulations but even *in* our tribulations. What a growing, increasing happiness the happiness of the saints is. We glory in tribulations, especially tribulations for righteousness' sake. This being the hardest point to understand, Paul shows the grounds and reasons of it. Tribulations, by a chain of causes, greatly befriend hope.

Tribulation produces patience, the powerful grace of God working in and with tribulation. It proves, and by proving improves, patience, as steel is hardened by the fire. Anything that brings patience is a matter of joy, for patience does us more good than tribulations can harm us. Tribulation in itself brings impatience, but as it is sanctified to the saints, it works patience. It brings an experience of God: The patient sufferers have the greatest experience of the divine consolations. It works an experience of ourselves. It is by tribulation that we make an experiment of our own sincerity. It works an approbation, as he is approved who has passed the test.

Kindness

We give no offense in anything,
that our ministry may not be blamed.
But in all things we commend ourselves
as ministers of God:
in much patience, in tribulations,
in needs, in distresses. . .
by purity, by knowledge,
by longsuffering, by kindness.

2 CORINTHIANS 6:3–4, 6

Paul's great desire was to be the servant of God and to prove himself so by much patience in afflictions. He was a great sufferer and met with many afflictions, but he exercised much patience in all. Those who would prove themselves to God must prove themselves faithful in trouble as well as in peace, not only in doing the work of God diligently, but also in bearing the will of God patiently. Paul proved himself by acting from good principles, which is pureness. There is no piety without purity. Knowledge was another principle, and zeal without this is but madness. He also acted with longsuffering and kindness, bearing with the hardness of men's hearts and hard treatment from their hands. He acted under the influence of the Holy Ghost, from the noble principle of unfeigned love, according to the rule of the Word of truth, under the power of God, having on the armor of righteousness, which is the best defense against the temptations of prosperity on the one hand and of adversity on the other.

Brotherly Kindness

Giving all diligence, add to your faith virtue,
to virtue knowledge, to knowledge self-control,
to self-control perseverance, to perseverance godliness,
to godliness brotherly kindness,
and to brotherly kindness love.
2 PETER 1:5–7

Those who want to make any progress in religion must be very industrious. Without giving all diligence, there is no gaining ground in the work of holiness. The believer must have virtue, and then knowledge, self-control, and patience follow. By virtue we mean strength and courage, without which the believer cannot stand up for good works. We need virtue while we live, and it will be of use when we come to die. The believer must add knowledge to his virtue, prudence to his courage. Christian prudence regards the persons we have to deal with and the place and company we are in. We must add self-control to our knowledge, be moderate in desiring and using the good things of natural life. Perseverance must have its perfect work. We are born to trouble and must pass through many tribulations to enter into the kingdom of heaven. To perseverance we must add godliness. When Christians bear afflictions with perseverance, they get an experimental knowledge of the lovingkindness of their heavenly Father. We must add brotherly kindness, a tender affection to all our fellow Christians, who are children of the same Father and therefore to be loved as those who are specially near and dear to us.

Love and Charity

Love suffers long and is kind;
love does not envy;
love does not parade itself,
is not puffed up.
1 CORINTHIANS 13:4

Love is longsuffering. It can endure evil and provocation without being filled with resentment or revenge. It will put up with many slights from the person it loves and wait long to see the kindly effect of such patience. It is kind. It seeks to be useful, and not only seizes on opportunities for doing good, but searches for them. It does not envy. It is not grieved at the good of others. Envy is the effect of ill will. The mind that is bent on doing good to all can never wish ill to any. It is not bloated with self-conceit. True love will give us esteem of our brethren, and this will limit our esteem of ourselves. True love stands in opposition to self-conceit. The Syriac renders it: "does not raise tumults and disturbances." Love calms the angry passions instead of raising them. Others render it: "does not act insidiously," does not seek to ensnare them. It is not apt to be cross and contradictory. Some understand it as dissembling and flattery. Love abhors such falsehood and flattery. It does nothing out of place or time, but behaves with courtesy and goodwill toward all.

Godliness

But reject profane and old wives' fables,
and exercise yourself toward godliness.
1 TIMOTHY 4:7

The apostles considered it a main part of their work to help their hearers remember certain things, for we are apt to forget, and slow to learn and remember, the things of God. The best way for ministers to grow in knowledge and faith is to remind the brethren: While we teach others, we teach ourselves. Godliness is here pressed upon Timothy and others. Those who would be godly must exercise themselves to godliness; it requires constant exercise. What will it avail us to mortify the body if we do not mortify sin? There is a great deal to be got by godliness. The promises made to godly people relate to the life that is now, but especially they relate to the life that is to come. If godly people have little of the good things of this life, it shall be made up to them in the good things of the life that is to come. It is not enough that we refuse profane and old wives' fables, but we must exercise ourselves to godliness.

The Work of the Minister

Be diligent to present yourself approved to God,
a worker who does not need to be ashamed,
rightly dividing the word of truth.

2 TIMOTHY 2:15

Paul directs Timothy in his work. He must make it his business to edify those who were under his charge. This is the work of ministers: not to tell people that which they never knew before, but to put them in mind of that which they do know, charging them not to argue about words. If people considered how little use most of the controversies in religion are, they would not be so zealous in their arguments over words. People are very prone to disagree about words, and such strifes never answer any other ends than to shake some and subvert others. "Be diligent to present yourself approved to God, a worker who does not need to be ashamed." Workmen who are unskillful, unfaithful, or lazy have reason to be ashamed, but those who mind their business and keep to their work are workmen who need not be ashamed. And what is their work? Not to invent a new gospel, but to rightly divide the gospel that is committed to their trust.

A Pattern of Good Works

*In all things showing yourself
to be a pattern of good works;
in doctrine showing integrity,
reverence, incorruptibility.*
TITUS 2:7

With these instructions to Titus, the apostle inserts some directions to himself. Without good works, Titus would pull down with one hand what he built with the other. Good doctrine and good life must go together. "In all things" some read as "above all things." Above all things, example, especially that of the teacher himself, is needed; hereby both light and influence are more likely to go together. Ministers must be examples to their flock, and the people followers of them, as they are of Christ. In their preaching therefore, the display of human learning or oratory is not to be affected. Sound speech must be used, which cannot be condemned; Scripture language in expressing Scripture truths is sound speech that cannot be condemned. Thus, be an example in word and in deeds, your life corresponding with your doctrine. The reason for the strictness of the minister's life and the gravity and soundness of his preaching is that adversaries would be seeking occasion to reflect and would do so, could they find anything amiss in doctrine or life. Faithful ministers will have enemies watching who will endeavor to find or pick holes in their teaching or behavior: the more need therefore for them to look to themselves.

Good Works and Enemies

Having your conduct honorable among the Gentiles,
that when they speak against you as evildoers,
they may, by your good works which they observe,
glorify God in the day of visitation.

1 PETER 2:12

This is a warning to beware of fleshly lusts. Knowing the difficulty and the importance of the duty, he uses his utmost interest in them: "Dearly beloved, I beseech you." The duty is to abstain from fleshly lusts that Christians should avoid, considering the respect they have for God. They are dearly beloved. Their condition in the world is that they are strangers and pilgrims and should not impede their passage by giving in to the lusts of the country through which they pass. The grand mischief that sin does to a man is this: It wars against the soul. Of all sorts of sin, none are more injurious to the soul than fleshly lusts.

He exhorts them further to an honest lifestyle. They lived among the Gentiles, who were inveterate enemies to them and constantly spoke of them as evildoers. A good life may not only stop their mouths, but may possibly be a means to bring them to glorify God and turn to you when they see you excel all others in good works. Vindicate yourselves by good works. This is the way to convince them. When the gospel shall come among them and take effect, a good life will encourage them in their own works, but an evil one will obstruct it.

Faithfulness

As you therefore have received Christ Jesus the Lord,
so walk in Him, rooted and built up in Him
and established in the faith,
as you have been taught,
abounding in it with thanksgiving.
COLOSSIANS 2:6–7

The apostle cautions the Colossians against deceivers. Satan spoils souls by beguiling them. He deceives them and by this means slays them. He could not ruin us if he did not cheat us, and he could not cheat us except through our own folly. Satan's agents beguile them with enticing words. How many are ruined by the flattery of those who lie in wait to deceive!

A sovereign antidote against seducers is "As you therefore have received Christ Jesus the Lord, so walk in Him, rooted and built up." All Christians have, at least in profession, received Jesus Christ the Lord, consented to Him, taken Him for theirs in every relation and every capacity. The great concern of those who have received Christ is to walk in Him. We must walk with Him in our daily course and keep up our communion with Him. The more closely we walk with Christ, the more we are rooted and established in the faith. The more firmly we are rooted in Him, the more closely we shall walk in Him: "Rooted and built up. . .as you have been taught." A good education has a good influence on our establishment. We must be established in the faith as we have been taught, abounding therein with thanksgiving.

Through Faith

That Christ may dwell in your hearts through faith;
that you, being rooted and grounded in love,
may be able to comprehend with all the saints
what is the width and length and depth and height—
to know the love of Christ.

EPHESIANS 3:17–19

Christ is an inhabitant of the soul of every good Christian. Where His Spirit dwells, there He dwells, and He dwells in the heart by faith. Faith opens the door of the soul to receive Christ; faith admits Him and submits to Him. By faith we are united to Christ. Many have some love for God and His servants, but it is a flash, like the cracking of thorns under a pot. It makes a great noise but is soon gone.

How desirable it is to have a settled, fixed sense of the love of God and Christ, so as to be able to say with the apostle, "He has loved me!" The best way to attain this is to be careful that we maintain a constant love of God in our souls. Christians should not aim to understand above all the saints; we should desire to understand with all the saints, to have as much knowledge as the saints are allowed to have in this world.

How magnificently the apostle speaks of the love of Christ. The dimensions of redeeming love are admirable: the width and length and depth and height. By enumerating these dimensions, the apostle signifies the greatness of the love of Christ, the unsearchable riches of His love. We should desire to understand this love.

Faithful until Death

"Be faithful until death,
and I will give you the crown of life."
REVELATION 2:10

Christ knows the future trials of His people and warns them of them. They had been impoverished by their tribulations before; now they must be imprisoned. Christ forearms them against these approaching troubles by His advice: Fear none of these things (v. 10). This is not only a word of command, but of efficacy. He shows them how their suffering would be alleviated and limited. The trials would not be universal; they would come to some of them, not all. These trials were not to be perpetual, but for a short time—ten days. They would come to try them, not to destroy them. He proposes a glorious reward for their fidelity: "Be faithful until death, and I will give you the crown of life." He who has said it is able to do it, and He has promised that He will do it. The suitableness of it is: a crown to reward their poverty, their fidelity, and their conflict, a crown of life to reward those who are faithful even until death.

The Testing of Faith

That the genuineness of your faith,
being much more precious than gold that perishes,
though it is tested by fire,
may be found to praise, honor,
and glory at the revelation of Jesus Christ.
1 PETER 1:7

The afflictions of serious Christians are designed for the trial of their faith. God's design in afflicting His people is their probation, not their destruction. This trial is principally about faith, because the trial of faith is, in effect, the trial of all that is good in us. Christ prays for this apostle that his faith might not fail. If it is supported, all the rest will stand firm. A tried faith is much more precious than tried gold.

Here is a double comparison of faith and gold. Gold is the most valuable and durable of all the metals. So is faith among the Christian virtues; it lasts until it brings the soul to heaven. The trial of faith is much more precious than the trial of gold. Gold does not increase through trial by fire; it grows less. But faith is established and multiplied by the afflictions it meets with. Gold must perish at last, but faith never will. If a tried faith be found to praise, honor, and glory, let this recommend faith to you as much more precious than gold, though assaulted and tried by afflictions. Jesus Christ will appear again in glory. The trial will soon be over, but the glory, honor, and praise will last to eternity.

Gentle to All

And a servant of the Lord must not quarrel
but be gentle to all, able to teach, patient.
2 TIMOTHY 2:24

Paul cautions Timothy against contention and against foolish
and unlearned questions, wars of words. Those who advanced
them thought themselves wise and learned, but Paul calls
them foolish and unlearned. They breed debates and quarrels
among Christians. Religion consists more in believing and
practicing what God requires than in subtle disputes. "A servant of the Lord must not quarrel." The servant of the Lord
must be gentle to all men and able to teach. Those who are
prone to argue are unable to teach. "In humility correcting"
(v. 25) not only those who subject themselves, but those who
oppose themselves. This is the way to convey truth in its light
and power and to overcome evil with good. That which ministers must look forward to in instructing those who oppose
them is their recovery. Repentance is God's gift. The same God
who gives us the discovery of the truth does by His grace bring
us to the acknowledging of it; otherwise, our hearts would continue in rebellion against it. And thus, sinners recover themselves out of the snare of the devil.

Christian Duties

*Remind them to be subject to
rulers and authorities, to obey,
to be ready for every good work,
to speak evil of no one,
to be peaceable, gentle,
showing all humility to all men.*
TITUS 3:1–2

Christians must be reminded to show themselves as examples of all due subjection and obedience to the government that is over them. They should be ready for every good work. Mere harmlessness—or good words and good meanings only—are not enough without good works. They should speak evil of no man. If no good can be spoken, rather than speak evil unnecessarily, say nothing. They must not go up and down as talebearers, carrying ill-natured stories. Since this evil is too common, it is of great harm. This is among the sins to be put off; for if indulged, it unfits for Christian communion here and the society of the blessed in heaven. They were not to be peaceable, either with hand or tongue. Contention and strife rise from men's lusts, which must be curbed, not indulged. They were to be gentle, equitable, and just, not taking words or action in the worst sense, and sometimes yielding for the sake of peace, even when strictly correct. They were to show humility to all men in their speech and conduct—humility in all instances and occasions, not only toward friends, but to all men.

Gentle Care

But we were gentle among you,
just as a nursing mother cherishes her own children.
1 THESSALONIANS 2:7

Paul showed the kindness and care of a mother who cherishes her children. This is the way to win people, rather than ruling with strictness. As a nursing mother bears with the demands of her child and condescends to simple duties for its good, cherishing it, so in like manner should the ministers of Christ behave toward their people. This gentleness the apostle expressed several ways: (1) By the most affectionate desire for their welfare, "So, affectionately longing for you" (v. 8). It was their spiritual and eternal welfare that he was earnestly desirous of; (2) By great readiness to do them good, willingly imparting to them "not only the gospel of God, but also our own lives." He was willing to spend and be spent in the service of men's souls; (3) By bodily labor, that his ministry might not be burdensome to them (v. 9). To the labor of the ministry, he added that of his calling as a tentmaker, that he might earn his own bread. He spent part of the night, as well as the day, in his work, that he might have an opportunity to do good to the souls of men in the daytime; (4) By the holiness of their lives, concerning which he appeals not only to them, but to God also (vv. 10–13). They were observers of their outward works in public, and God was witness not only of their behavior in secret, but of the inward principles from which they acted.

Gentle Salvation

*He will feed His flock like a shepherd;
He will gather the lambs with His arm,
and carry them in His bosom,
and gently lead those who are with young.*

ISAIAH 40:11

What the glory is that will be revealed: He will come with a strong hand, too strong to be obstructed, though it may be opposed. He shall recompense to all according to their works, as a righteous Judge. "His reward is with Him, and His work before Him" (v. 10). He Himself knows what He will do. God is the "Shepherd of Israel" (Psalm 80:1). Christ is the good shepherd (John 10:11). He shall feed His flock like a shepherd. His Word is food for His flock to feed on, and His ordinances are fields for them to feed in; His ministers are under-shepherds. He takes care of the lambs that are weak and cannot help themselves, and those who are with young. The good shepherd has a tender care for children, for young converts, and for weak believers and those who are of a sorrowful spirit. These are the lambs of His flock. He will gather them in when they wander, gather them up when they fall, gather them together when they are dispersed, and gather them home to Himself at last—all this with His own arm, out of which none shall be able to snatch them (John 10:28). He will gently lead them.

Worship

People shall worship Him,
each one from his place,
indeed all the shores of the nations.
ZEPHANIAH 2:11

The Moabites and Ammonites were both descended from Lot, and their countries adjoined. They are both charged with insulting the people of God and triumphing in their calamities. They spoke against the people of the Lord of hosts as a deserted, abandoned people. "But I have heard them" (says God) (v. 8). The Moabites and Ammonites are both laid under the same doom. They shall be as Sodom and Gomorrah, whose ruins in the Dead Sea lay near the countries of Moab and Ammon. They shall be laid waste, never again to be inhabited, or not for a long time (v. 9).

Other nations shall also be humbled. Heathen gods must be abolished. Their worshipers have gloried in them, but the Lord will famish all the gods of the earth, will starve them out of their strongholds. When the gospel gets around, by it men shall be brought to worship Him who lives forever, "each one from his place." They shall not need to go up to Jerusalem to worship the God of Israel, but wherever they are, they may have access to Him.

Attendance

Not forsaking the assembling of ourselves together,
as is the manner of some,
but exhorting one another.
HEBREWS 10:25

We have the means prescribed for the promotion or fidelity and perseverance. We should consider one another, provoke all to love and to good works. Christians ought to have a tender consideration and concern for one another. A good example given to others is the best and most effective provocation to love and good works. We are not to forsake the assembling of ourselves together. Even in those times, there were some who forsook these assemblies. The communion of saints is a great help and privilege and a good means of steadiness and perseverance. We are to exhort one another, to watch over one another, and to be jealous of ourselves and one another with a godly jealousy. This would be the best friendship. We should observe the approaching times of trial. Christians ought to observe the signs of the times, such as God has foretold. There is a trying day coming to us all, the day of our death, and we should observe all the signs of its approach and improve them to greater watchfulness and diligence in duty.

Come before Him

Give to the LORD the glory due His name;
bring an offering, and come before Him.
Oh, worship the LORD in the beauty of holiness!

1 CHRONICLES 16:29

This is a thanksgiving psalm that David, guided by the Spirit, composed to be sung upon the occasion of the public entry of the ark into the tent prepared for it. It is gathered out of several psalms, which some think warrants us to do likewise and make up hymns out of David's psalms, a part of one and a part of another, put together so as may be most proper to express and excite the devotion of Christians.

In the midst of our praises, we must not forget to pray for the succor and relief of those saints and servants of God who are in distress. When we are rejoicing in God's favors to us, we must remember our afflicted brethren and pray for their salvation and deliverance as our own. We are members one of another, and therefore when we mean, "Lord, save them," it is not improper to say, "Lord, save us." Let us make God the Alpha and the Omega of our praises. David begins with "Oh, give thanks to the Lord"; he concludes with "Blessed be the Lord."

Him Only You Shall Serve

" 'You shall worship the LORD your God,
and Him only you shall serve.' "

MATTHEW 4:10

What the devil said to Jesus during the temptation was, "All these things will I give You if You will fall down and worship me" (v. 9). Jesus rejected the proposal with abhorrence and detestation: "Away with you, Satan!" The offer appears abominable at first sight and therefore is immediately rejected. While Satan tempted Christ to harm Himself by throwing Himself down from the roof, though He did not yield, He heard it. But now that the temptation flies in the face of God, He cannot bear it. It is good to be peremptory in resisting temptation and to stop our ears to Satan's charms.

Jesus countered with an argument from Scripture. The argument is very suitable and exactly to the purpose, taken from Deuteronomy 6:13 and 10:20: "You shall worship the Lord your God, and Him only you shall serve." Our Savior has recourse to the fundamental law in this case, which is indispensable and universally obligatory. Religious worship is due to God only. Christ quotes this law concerning religious worship and applies it to Satan's temptation. He showed that in His estate of humiliation as a man, He still worshiped God, both publicly and privately. Thus, it became Him to fulfill all righteousness. Secondly, He showed that the law of religious worship is eternal obligation.

Gather in His Name

*"For where two or three are gathered together in My name,
I am there in the midst of them."*
MATTHEW 18:20

Assemblies of Christians for holy purposes are here appointed, directed, and encouraged. The church of Christ in the world exists most visibly in religious assemblies. It is the will of Christ that these should be set up and kept up. If there is no liberty and opportunity for large assemblies, then it is the will of God that two or three gather together. When we cannot do what we would in religion, we must do what we can, and God will accept us. They are directed to gather together in Christ's name. In the exercise of church discipline, they must come together in the name of Christ. In meeting for worship, we must have an eye to Christ and communion with all who call upon Him. When we come together to worship God in dependence on the Spirit and grace of Christ, then we are met together in His name. They are here encouraged with an assurance of the presence of Christ: "I am there in the midst of them."

Where His saints are, His sanctuary is, and there He will dwell. He is in the midst of them, in their hearts. It is a spiritual presence, the presence of Christ's Spirit with their spirits, that is intended here. Though only two or three meet together, Christ is among them. This is an encouragement to the meeting of a few.

The Head of the Church

And He is the head of the body, the church,
who is the beginning, the firstborn from the dead,
that in all things He may have the preeminence.

COLOSSIANS 1:18

Jesus is the end, as well as the cause of all things. He had a being before the world was made and therefore from all eternity. He not only had a being before He was born of the virgin, but He had a being before all time. The whole creation is kept together by the power of the Son of God and made to consist in its proper frame. He is the head of the body of the church. Not only a head of government and direction, but a head of vital influence, as the head of the natural body, for all grace and strength are derived from Him. He is the beginning, "the firstborn from the dead," the principle of our resurrection. He is the first and only one who rose by His own power and has given us evidence of our resurrection from the dead. He has preeminence in all things, preferred above angels and all the powers in heaven. Among men He should have preeminence. All fullness dwells in Him, and it pleased the Father it should do so (v. 19), not only a fullness of abundance for Himself but abundance for us.

The Body of Christ

And He put all things under His feet,
and gave Him to be head over all things to the church,
which is His body,
the fullness of Him who fills all in all.
EPHESIANS 1:22–23

The apostle digresses a little to make mention of the Lord Jesus and His exaltation. He sits at the Father's right hand in heavenly places (v. 20–21). The Father put all things under His feet. God "gave Him to be head over all things." It was a gift to Christ, and it was a gift to the church, to be provided with a head endued with so much power and authority. He gave Him all power, both in heaven and on earth. But what completes the comfort of this is that He is the head over all things to the church. The same power who supports the world supports the church, and we are sure He loves His church, for it is His body, and He will take care of it. It is "the fullness of Him who fills all in all." Jesus Christ fills all in all. Christ as Mediator would not be complete if He had no church. How could He be a king if He had no kingdom?

Humility

For I say, through the grace given to me,
to everyone who is among you,
not to think of himself more highly
than he ought to think, but to think soberly,
as God has dealt to each one a measure of faith.

ROMANS 12:3

Pride is a sin that is bred in the bone of all of us. "Not to think of himself more highly than he ought to think." We must take heed of having too great an opinion of ourselves. We must not be self-conceited or hold our own wisdom too highly. There is a high thought of ourselves that we may and must have to think ourselves too good to be the slaves of sin and drudges to this world. We should think soberly; that is, we must have a modest opinion of ourselves and our own abilities, according to what we have received from God, and not otherwise. The words will bear another interpretation: "Of himself" is not in the original; therefore it may be read, "That no man be wise above what he ought to be wise, but be wise unto sobriety." There is a knowledge that puffs up. We must take heed of this and labor after that knowledge that tends to sobriety. This refers also to that exhortation: "Be not wise in your own conceits." It is good to be wise, but it is bad to think ourselves so, for there is more hope of a fool than of him who is wise in his own eyes.

One Body in Christ

For as we have many members in one body,
but all the members do not have the same function,
so we, being many, are one body in Christ,
and individually members of one another.
ROMANS 12:4–5

God deals out His gifts according to the measure of faith. The measure of spiritual gifts, He calls the measure of faith, for this is the radical grace. What we have and do that is good is right and acceptable, as long as it is founded in faith. Christ had the Spirit given to Him without measure, but the saints have it by measure. Christ, who had gifts without measure, was meek and lowly. Shall we who are stunted be proud and self-conceited?

God has dealt out gifts to others as well as to us. Had we the monopoly of the Spirit, there might be some pretense for our conceitedness, but others have their share as well as we. Therefore, it ill becomes us to lift up ourselves and despise others, as if we were the only people in favor with heaven. This reasoning, He illustrates by a comparison taken from the members of the natural body. All the saints make up one body in Christ, who is the head of the body. Believers lie not in a confused, disorderly heap, but are organized and knit together. Particular believers are members of this body, receiving life and spirits from the head. Some members in the body are bigger and more useful than others, and each received according to his proportion.

Judgment Is His

> *But why do you judge your brother?*
> *Or why do you show contempt for your brother?*
> *For we shall all stand before the judgment seat of Christ.*
>
> ROMANS 14:10

Because all of us must shortly give an account, "Why do you judge your brother? Or why do you show contempt for your brother?" Why all this clashing, and contradicting, and censuring among Christians? "We shall all stand before the judgment seat of Christ." Christ will be the Judge, and before Him we shall stand as persons to be tried. To illustrate this, He quotes a passage out of the Old Testament that speaks of Christ's universal sovereignty and dominion, and that established with an oath: " 'As I live, says the Lord, every knee shall bow to Me' " (v. 11). It is a prophecy, in general, of Christ's Godhead. Divine honor is due to Him and must be paid. The bowing of the knee to Him and the confession made with the tongue are but outward expressions of inward adoration and praise, every knee and every tongue, either freely or by force.

All His friends do it freely. They bow to Him—the understanding bowed to His truths, the will to His laws, the whole man to His authority—and this expressed by the bowing of the knee, the posture of adoration and prayer. They confess to Him—acknowledging His glory, grace, and greatness—acknowledging their own meanness and vileness, confessing their sins to Him.

Living Sacrifices

I beseech you therefore, brethren,
by the mercies of God,
that you present your bodies a living sacrifice,
holy, acceptable to God,
which is your reasonable service.

ROMANS 12:1

Christ, who was once offered to bear the sins of many, is the only sacrifice of atonement, but our persons and performances tendered to God through Christ are sacrifices of acknowledgment to the honor of God. Presenting them denotes a voluntary act; it must be a freewill offering. The presenting of the body to God implies not only avoiding the sins that are committed with or against the body, but using the body as a servant of the soul in the service of God. It is to yield the members of our bodies as instruments of righteousness. Though bodily exercise alone profits little, yet it is a proof of the dedication of our souls to God. A body sincerely devoted to God is a living sacrifice. It is Christ living in the soul by faith that makes the body a living sacrifice. Holy love kindles the sacrifices, puts life into the duties. There must be that real holiness that consists in an entire rectitude of heart and life. Our bodies must not be made the instruments of sin and uncleanness, but set apart for God and put to holy uses. It is the soul that is the proper subject of holiness, but a sanctified soul communicates a holiness to the body. That is holy which is according to the will of God. When the bodily actions are holy, the body is holy.

Service

*For you, brethren,
have been called to liberty;
only do not use liberty as an opportunity for the flesh,
but through love serve one another.*

GALATIANS 5:13

The apostle exhorts Christians to serious practical godliness. They should not strive with one another but love one another. He tells them that they "have been called to liberty," but yet he would have them be very careful that they did not use this liberty improperly. On the contrary, he would have them serve one another through love. The liberty we enjoy as Christians is not a licentious liberty; though Christ has redeemed us from the curse of the law, He has not freed us from the obligation of it. Though we ought to stand fast in our Christian liberty, we should not insist upon it to the breach of Christian charity, but should always maintain such a temper toward each other as may dispose us by love to serve one another.

Love is the sum of the whole law. It will appear that we are the disciples of Christ when we have love one for another. If it does not wholly extinguish those unhappy discords that are among Christians, at least the fatal consequences of them will be prevented. Christian churches can only be ruined by their own hands. If Christians act like brute beasts, biting and devouring each other, what can be expected but that the God of love should deny His grace to them and the Spirit of love should depart from them?

Shepherding the Church

*"Therefore take heed to yourselves and to all the flock,
among which the Holy Spirit has made you overseers,
to shepherd the church of God which
He purchased with His own blood."*
ACTS 20:28

Paul commanded the church leaders to mind the work to which they were called. Dignity calls for duty; if the Holy Ghost has made them overseers of the flock, they must be true to their trust. They must take heed to themselves in the first place, must walk circumspectly. "You have many eyes upon you, some to take example by you, others to pick quarrels with you, and therefore you ought to take heed to yourselves." Those are not likely to be skillful or faithful keepers of the vineyards of others who do not keep their own. Ministers must not only take heed to their own souls, but must have a constant regard for the souls of those who are under their charge, that none of them wander from the fold or be seized by the beasts of prey, that none of them be missing.

They must feed the church of God, must lead the sheep of Christ into the green pastures, must lay meat before them, must feed them with wholesome doctrine, and must see that nothing is wanting that is necessary to their being nourished to eternal life. There is need of pastors, not only to gather the church of God, but to feed it by building up those within. They must watch as shepherds keep watch over their flocks by night: watch against everything that will be hurtful to the flock, and watch for everything that will be advantageous to it.

Preach the Word

Preach the word!
Be ready in season and out of season.
Convince, rebuke, exhort,
with all longsuffering and teaching.
2 TIMOTHY 4:2

The reason to enforce this charge is that errors and heresies were likely to creep into the church. "Improve the present time when they will endure it." They will grow weary of the old, plain gospel of Christ, and then they will be greedy for fables. False teachers were not of God's sending, but they chose them to please their itching ears. People do so when they will not endure sound doctrine: that preaching which is searching, plain, and to the purpose. There is a wide difference between the Word of God and the word of such teachers; the one is sound doctrine, the Word of truth, the other is only fables. Paul for his part had almost done his work, so the ministers needed to be prepared, "therefore there will be the more occasion for you." The fewer hands there are to work, the more industrious those hands must be that are at work. "I have done the work of my day and generation; do you in like manner the work of your day and generation."

Gifts

As each one has received a gift,
minister it to one another,
as good stewards of the manifold grace of God.
1 PETER 4:10

Whatever gift, whatever power of doing good is given to us, we should minister with the same to one another. In receiving and using the manifold gifts of God, we must look upon ourselves as stewards only.

The apostle exemplified his direction about gifts in two particulars: speaking and ministering. If any man speaks or teaches, he must do it as an oracle of God. It is the duty of Christians in private as well as ministers in public to speak to one another of the things of God. What they teach and speak must be the pure Word and oracles of God. It highly concerns all preachers of the gospel to keep close to the Word of God.

If any man ministers, let him do it according to the ability that God gives, that God in all things may be glorified through Jesus Christ. He is the only way to the Father, to be given praise and dominion forever. Whatever we are called to do for the honor of God and the good of others, we should do it with all our might. In all the duties and services of life, we should aim at the glory of God.

The Proper Use of Gifts

Even so you,
since you are zealous for spiritual gifts,
let it be for the edification of the church
that you seek to excel.

1 CORINTHIANS 14:12

Be chiefly desirous of those gifts that are most for the church's edification. "Covet those gifts most that will do the best service to men's souls." If they spoke a foreign language, they should beg of God the gift of interpreting it (v. 13). The church must understand if it is to be edified. The sum is that they should perform all religious exercises in their assemblies so that all might join in them and profit by them. He enforces this advice. His own mind might be devoutly engaged, but his understanding would be unfruitful (v. 14); he would not be understood, nor therefore would others join with him in his devotions. Language that is most obvious and easy to be understood is the most proper for public devotions.

Edification

How is it then, brethren?
Whenever you come together,
each of you has a psalm,
has a teaching, has a tongue,
has a revelation, has an interpretation.
Let all things be done for edification.

1 CORINTHIANS 14:26

Paul blames the Corinthians for the confusion they introduced into the assembly. "You are apt to confound the several parts of worship," or "You are apt to be confused if you do not stay for one another. Can this be edifying? Let all things be done for edification." The apostle gives the reasons for these regulations. They would be for the church's benefit, their instruction and consolation. Divine inspiration should by no means throw Christian assemblies into confusion. If they are managed in a tumultuous and confused manner, what notion must this give of the God who is worshiped! Does it look as if He were the God of peace and order and an enemy to confusion? Things were orderly managed in all the other churches, and it would be scandalous for them, who exceeded most churches in spiritual gifts, to be more disorderly than any in the exercise of them.

Offices of the Church

*Now you are the body of Christ,
and members individually.
And God has appointed these in the church:
first apostles, second prophets, third teachers,
after that miracles, then gifts of healings,
helps, administration, varieties of tongues.*

1 CORINTHIANS 12:27–28

The relation wherein Christians stand to Christ and one another is: "Now you are the body of Christ, and members individually." All have a common relation to one another.
Concerning the variety of offices instituted by Christ and gifts
or favors dispensed by Him, observe the plenteous variety of
these gifts and offices. He was no hoarder of His benefits and
favors. They had no lack of them, but a store of them—all
that was necessary, and even more. Observe the order of these
offices and gifts. Those of most value have the first place. God
does, and we should, value things according to their real
worth. What holds the last and lowest rank in this enumera-
tion is diversity of tongues. It is by itself the most useless and
insignificant of all these gifts. The Corinthians valued themselves exceedingly on this gift. How proper a method it is to
beat down pride, to let persons know the true value of that
which they pride themselves in! It is but too common a thing
for men to value themselves most on what has the least worth.

Use of Offices

And He Himself gave some to be apostles,
some prophets, some evangelists,
and some pastors and teachers,
for the equipping of the saints for the work of ministry,
for the edifying of the body of Christ.
EPHESIANS 4:11–12

The great gift that Christ gave to the church at His ascension was that of the ministry of peace and reconciliation. The gift of the ministry is the fruit of Christ's ascension. The officers who Christ gave to His church were of two sorts—extraordinary and ordinary. The extraordinary ones were apostles, prophets, and evangelists. The apostles were chief. They, having been the witnesses of His miracles and doctrine, He sent them forth to spread the gospel. The prophets seem to have been those who expounded the writings of the Old Testament. The evangelists were ordained persons whom the apostles took for their companions in travel. And then there are the ordinary ministers, such as pastors and teachers. Some take these two names to signify one office. Others think they designate two distinct offices, and pastors are fixed at the head of particular churches. They are frequently called bishops and elders. The teachers were those whose work it was to instruct the people by way of exhortation. How rich is the church that still has such a variety of gifts! How kind Christ is to His church!

Tithing

"Bring all the tithes into the storehouse,
that there may be food in My house."
MALACHI 3:10

Bring in the full tithes to the utmost that the law requires, that there may be meat in God's house for those who serve at the altar, whether there is meat in your houses or not. Let God be first served, and then " 'try Me now in this,' says the Lord of hosts, 'If I will not open for you the windows of heaven' " (v. 10). The expression is figurative; every good gift coming from above, God will plentifully pour out on them the bounties of His providence. Very sudden plenty is expressed by opening the windows of heaven. Here they are opened to pour down blessings to such a degree that there would not be room enough to receive them. God will not only be reconciled to sinners who repent and reform, but He will be a bountiful benefactor to them. God has blessings ready to bestow upon us, but, through the weakness of our faith and narrowness of our desires, we have no room to receive them. Whereas the fruits of their ground had been eaten up by locusts and caterpillars, God would now remove that judgment. Whereas they had lain under the reproach of famine, now all nations shall call them blessed.

Cheerful Givers

So let each one give as he purposes in his heart,
not grudgingly or of necessity;
for God loves a cheerful giver.
2 CORINTHIANS 9:7

Here we have proper directions to be observed about the right manner of bestowing charity. It should be bountifully. Men who expect a good return at harvest are not wont to pinch and spare in sowing their seed. Giving should be deliberate, "each one as he purposes in his heart." Works of charity, like other good works, should be done with thought and design. It should be freely given, "not grudgingly or of necessity," but cheerfully. Persons sometimes will give merely to satisfy the demands of those who ask their charity, and what they give is in a manner squeezed or forced from them, and this unwillingness spoils all they do.

We are given good encouragement to perform this work of charity. They themselves would not lose what they gave in charity. What is given to the poor is far from being lost, as the precious seed that is cast onto the ground is not lost, for it will spring up and bear fruit. The sower shall receive it again with increase. God loves a cheerful giver. Can a man be a loser by doing that with which God is pleased?

Giving in Secret

*"Take heed that you do not do
your charitable deeds before men,
to be seen by them."*

MATTHEW 6:1

We must watch against hypocrisy, which was the leaven of the Pharisees, as well as against their doctrine. Almsgiving, prayer, and fasting are three great Christian duties. Thus we must not only depart from evil but do good, and do it well, and so dwell forever.

We are cautioned against hypocrisy in giving alms. Take heed of it. It is a subtle sin; vainglory insinuates itself into what we do before we are aware. It is a sin we are in great danger of. Take heed of hypocrisy, for if it reigns in you, it will ruin you. It is the dead fly that spoils the whole box of precious ointment.

The giving of alms is a great duty, and a duty which all the disciples of Christ, according to their ability, must abound in. The Jews called the poor box "the box of righteousness." It is true that our alms do not deserve heaven, but it is just as true that we cannot go to heaven without them. Christ takes it for granted that His disciples give alms; He will not own those who do not. Giving alms is a duty that has a great reward attending it, which is lost if it is done in hypocrisy. It shall be repaid in the resurrection of the just, in eternal riches.

Sharing Abundances

For I do not mean that others should be
eased and you burdened;
but by an equality,
that now at this time your abundance may supply their lack,
that their abundance also may supply your lack.

2 CORINTHIANS 8:13–14

Good intentions are good things. They are like buds and blossoms, pleasant to behold, and they give hope of good fruit. But they are lost and signify nothing without performances acceptable to God. When men purpose that which is good and endeavor to perform also, God will accept what they can do and not reject them for what is not in their power to do. This Scripture will by no means justify those who think good intentions are enough.

Another argument is taken from the distribution of the things of this world and the mutability of human affairs (v. 13–15). Those who have a greater abundance may supply those who are in want, that there may be room for charity. It is the will of God that, by our mutually supplying one another, there should be some sort of equality. All should think themselves concerned to supply those who are in want. This is illustrated by the instance of gathering and distributing manna in the wilderness: He who had gathered much had nothing left over.

According to Ability

Then the disciples,
each according to his ability,
determined to send relief to
the brethren dwelling in Judea.
ACTS 11:29

Though we must, as we have opportunity, do good to all men, we must have special regard to the household of faith. No poor must be neglected, but God's poor should be most particularly regarded. But the communion of saints is here extended further, and provision is made by the church at Antioch for the relief of the poor in Judea, whom they call their brethren. Now we may suppose that the greatest part of those who turned Christian in that country were the poor. If a famine came, it would go very hard with them. If any of them perished from want, it would be a great reproach to the Christian profession. Therefore this early care was taken, to send them a stock beforehand, lest if it should be put off until the famine came, it would be too late. The agreement among the disciples was that every man should contribute according to his ability. Merchants find their profit in sending goods to countries that lie very remote, and so should we in giving alms to those afar off who need them, which we should do when we are called to it. What may be said to be according to our ability, we must judge for ourselves, but must be careful that we judge righteously.

Such as You Have

*"But rather give alms of such things as you have;
then indeed all things are clean to you."*
LUKE 11:41

To this, Luke adds a rule for making our creature comforts
clean to us. "Instead of washing your hands before you go to
meat, give alms of such things as you have"; let the poor have
their share out of them, and then "all things are clean to you,"
and you may use them comfortably. Here is a plain allusion
to the law of Moses, by which it was provided that certain
portions of the increase of their lands should be given to the
Levite, the stranger, the fatherless, and the widow. When
that was done, what was reserved for their own use was clean
to them (Deuteronomy 26:12–15). We can with comfort enjoy the gifts of God's bounty ourselves when we send portions
to them for whom nothing is prepared. What we have is not
our own unless God has His dues out of it, and it is by generosity to the poor that we clean up to ourselves our liberty to
make use of our creature comforts.

Tithing Abundantly

*As soon as the commandment was circulated,
the children of Israel brought in
abundance the firstfruits of grain and wine, oil and honey,
and of all the produce of the field;
and they brought in abundantly
the tithe of everything.*

2 CHRONICLES 31:5

The people brought in their tithes very readily. What the priests had need of for themselves and their families, they made use of, and the surplus was laid in heaps (v. 6). Hezekiah questioned the priests and Levites concerning them, asking why they did not use what was paid in but hoarded it up, to which they replied that they had made use of all they had need for, the maintenance of themselves and their families and for their winter store, and that this was left over. They did not hoard these heaps for covetnesses, but to show what plentiful provision God had made for them. See the acknowledgment which the king and princes made of it (v. 8). They gave thanks to God for His good providence, which gave them something to bring, and His good grace, which gave them hearts to bring it.

Wisdom and Knowledge

For God gives wisdom and knowledge and joy
to a man who is good in His sight.
ECCLESIASTES 2:26

Riches are a blessing or a curse to a man, accordingly as he has or has not a heart to make good use of them. God makes them a reward to a good man if with them He gives him wisdom and knowledge and joy to enjoy them cheerfully himself and to communicate them charitably to others. He makes them a punishment to a bad man if He denies him a heart to take the comfort of them, for they only tantalize him and tyrannize him. Godliness with contentment is great gain. Ungodliness is commonly punished with discontent and an insatiable covetousness, which are sins that are their own punishment.

The Tongue of the Learned

"The Lord GOD has given Me the tongue of the learned,
that I should know how to speak a word in season
to him who is weary."

ISAIAH 50:4

Our Lord Jesus, having proved Himself able to save, here shows Himself as willing as He is able. We suppose the prophet Isaiah to say something of himself in these verses, encouraging himself to go on in his work as a prophet, notwithstanding hardships, not doubting that God would strengthen him. Instead, like David, he speaks of himself as a type of Christ.

Isaiah, as a prophet, was qualified for the work to which he was called, but Christ was anointed with the Spirit above His fellows. To make the Man of God perfect, He has the tongue of the learned, to know how to give instruction, "how to speak a word in season to him who is weary." God gave Christ the tongue of the learned for the comfort of those who are weary and heavily laden under the burden of sin (Matthew 11:28). See what is the best learning of a minister: to know how to comfort troubled consciences and to speak properly and plainly to the various cases of poor souls. An ability to do this is God's gift.

Increase Learning

A wise man will hear and increase learning,
and a man of understanding will attain wise counsel.
PROVERBS 1:5

Solomon had an eye to posterity in writing this book, hoping by it to season the minds of the rising generation with the generous principles of wisdom and virtue. Those who are young and simple may by them be made wise and are not excluded from Solomon's school as they were from Plato's. Even wise men must hear and not think themselves too wise to learn. A wise man, by increasing in learning, is profitable to others as a counselor. A man of understanding in these precepts of wisdom will by degrees attain to wise counsel. He shall come to sit at the helm, as the word signifies. Those whom God has blessed with wisdom must study to do good with it. It is more dignity indeed to be a counselor for the prince, but it is more charity to be a counselor to the poor.

Wisdom

And find the knowledge of God.
For the LORD gives wisdom.
PROVERBS 2:5–6

God has wisdom to bestow. The Lord not only is wise Himself, but He gives wisdom. He has blessed the world with a revelation of His will. Out of His mouth, by the law and the prophets, by the written Word, and by His ministers, come knowledge and understanding, such a discovery of truth and good as will make us truly knowing and intelligent. He has particularly provided that good men who are sincerely disposed to do His will shall have that knowledge and that understanding (vv. 7–8). The righteous and those who walk uprightly are His saints, devoted to His honor and set apart for His service. The means of wisdom are given to all, but wisdom itself, sound wisdom, is laid up for the righteous, laid up in Christ their head. The same that is the Spirit of revelation in the Word is a Spirit of wisdom in the souls of those who are sanctified.

Withstand the Evil Day

Therefore take up the whole armor of God,
that you may be able to withstand in the evil day,
and having done all, to stand.
EPHESIANS 6:13

We must be spiritually well armed: "Take up the whole armor of God." Get and exercise all the Christian graces, the whole armor, that no part is naked and exposed to the enemy. Those who would have true grace must aim at all grace, the whole armor. We have no armor of our own that will be strong enough in a trying time. Nothing will stand us in stead but the armor of God.

Our enemies strive to prevent our ascent to heaven. They assault us in the things that belong to our souls. We have need of faith in our Christian warfare because we have spiritual enemies to grapple with, as well as of faith in our Christian work, because we have spiritual strength to call on.

Our duty is to then stand our ground and withstand our enemies. We must not yield to the devil's allurements and assaults but oppose them. If he stands up against us, we must stand against him. To stand against Satan is to struggle against sin, that you may be able to withstand in the day of temptation or any affliction. "And having done all, to stand." Resist him, and he will flee. If we move back, he will gain ground. Our present business is to withstand the assaults of the devil and to stand; then our warfare will be accomplished, and we shall finally be victorious.

Built on Rock

"And I also say to you that you are Peter,
and on this rock I will build My church,
and the gates of Hades shall not prevail against it."

MATTHEW 16:18

The church is built upon a rock, a firm, strong, and lasting foundation that time will not waste, nor will it sink under the weight of the building. Christ would not build His house on sand, for He knew that storms would arise. It is built upon this rock, "thou art Peter," which signifies a stone or rock. Christ gave him that name when He first called him, and here He confirms it. From the mention of this significant name, occasion is taken for the metaphor of building upon a rock.

Christ promises to preserve and secure His church. When it is built, the gates of hell will not prevail against it. This implies that the church has enemies who fight against it and endeavor to ruin and overthrow it, here represented by the gates of hell, that is, the city of hell (which is directly opposite to the heavenly city, the city of the living God), the devil's interest in the children of men. This assures us that the enemies of the church will not gain their point. While the world stands, Christ will have a church in it. Somewhere or other, the Christian religion will have a being, though not always in the same degree of purity and splendor, so it shall never be cut off in its entirety. The church may be foiled in particular encounters, but in the main battle, it will be more than a conqueror.

Choose Today

> *"See, I have set before you today*
> *life and good, death and evil."*
> DEUTERONOMY 30:15

Moses here concludes with a very bright light and a very strong fire that, if possible, what he had been preaching might find entrance into the understanding and affections of this unthinking people.

He states the case very fairly. Every man wants to obtain life and good and to escape death and evil; he desires happiness and dreads misery. "Well," says Moses, "I have shown you the way to obtain all the happiness you can desire and to avoid all misery. Be obedient, and all shall be well and nothing wrong." Every man is moved and governed in his actions by hope and fear, hope of good and fear of evil, real or apparent. "Now," says Moses, "I have tried both ways. If you will be either drawn to obedience by the certain prospect of advantage from it, or driven to obedience by the no less certain prospect of ruin in case you are disobedient; if you will be wrought upon either way, you will be kept close to God and your duty. But if you will not, you are utterly inexcusable."

Having stated his case, he fairly puts them to their choice, with a warning to choose well. In the last verse (v. 20), he shows them what their duty is: to love God and to love Him as the Lord, a Being most amiable, and as their God, a God in covenant with them. He is their life and the length of their days.

Not Fearing Death

Why should I fear in the days of evil,
when the iniquity at my heels surrounds me?
PSALM 49:5

All men may know, and therefore let all men consider, that their riches will not profit them in the day of death. Poor people are as much in danger from an inordinate desire toward the wealth of the world as rich people are from an inordinate delight in it. What the psalmist had to say is wisdom and understanding; it will make those wise and intelligent who receive it. It was what he himself had well digested.

He begins with the application of it to himself: "Why should I fear?" He means, Why should I fear their fear?—the fears of worldly people. Why should I fear in the days of evil, when the iniquity at my heels, or of my supplanters who endeavor to trip up my heels, surrounds me with their mischievous attempts? Why should I be afraid of those whose power lies in their wealth? I will not fear their power, for it cannot enable them to ruin me. The iniquity at my heels (our past sins) will surround us, will be set in order before us. In these days worldly, wicked people will be afraid. Nothing is more dreadful to those who have set their hearts on the world than to think of leaving it. But why should a good man who has God with him fear death?

The Souls of His Saints

You who love the LORD, hate evil!
He preserves the souls of His saints;
He delivers them out of the hand of the wicked.
PSALM 97:10

The exaltation of Christ and the advancement of God's glory among men are the rejoicing of all the saints. He preserves their lives as long as He has any work for them to do. But something more is meant than their lives, for those who will be His disciples must be willing to lay down their lives. It is the immortal soul that Christ preserves, the inward man, which may be renewed more and more when the outward man decays. "Light is sown for the righteous" (v. 11), that is, gladness for the upright in heart. The subjects of Christ's kingdom are told to expect tribulation in the world, yet He lets them know for their comfort that light is sown for them. What is sown will come up again in due time. Though, like winter seed, it may lie long under the earth, yet it will return in a rich and plentiful increase. Christ told His disciples at parting, "You will be sorrowful, but your sorrow will be turned into joy" (John 16:20).

Let it be pure and holy joy. You who love the Lord Jesus, who love His appearing and kingdom, who love His Word and His exaltation, see that you hate evil. A true love of God will show itself in a real hatred of all sin as that abominable thing that He hates. Let all joy terminate in God. All the lines of joy must meet in Him as in the center. Let it express itself in praise and thanksgiving.

Deliverance

For if God did not spare the angels who sinned,
but cast them down to hell and delivered them into
chains of darkness, to be reserved for judgment; . . .
then the Lord knows how to deliver the godly
out of temptations and to reserve the unjust
under punishment for the day of judgment.
2 PETER 2:4, 9

No station will exempt a sinner from punishment. God did not spare the angels who sinned. The greater the offender, the greater the punishment. Sin debases and degrades the persons who commit it. The angels of heaven are divested of all their glory upon their disobedience. Sin is the work of darkness, and darkness is the wages of sin. Those who will not walk according to the light and direction of God's law shall be deprived of the light of God's countenance.

But if there are a few righteous, they shall be preserved. God does not destroy the good with the bad. In wrath He remembers mercy. The cause of destruction was a world of ungodly men. Ungodliness puts men out of divine protection and exposes them to utter destruction.

The Lord knows those who are His. He has set apart the godly for Himself, and if there is only one in five cities, He knows him. The wisdom of God is never at a loss about ways and means to deliver His people. They are often utterly at a loss, but He can find and provide a way of escape. The deliverance of the godly is the work of God. The unjust have no share in the salvation God works out for the righteous. The wicked are reserved to the day of judgment.

Heal and Save

And when He had called His twelve disciples to Him,
He gave them power over unclean spirits, to cast them out,
and to heal all kinds of sickness and all kinds of disease.
MATTHEW 10:1

Jesus gave His disciples power over unclean spirits, to cast them out. The power that is committed to the ministers of Christ is directly leveled against the devil and his kingdom. Christ gave them power to cast him out of the bodies of people, but that was to signify the destruction of the devil's spiritual kingdom and all the works of the devil, for which purpose the Son of God was manifested.

He gave them power to heal all types of sickness. He authorized them to work miracles for the confirmation of their doctrine, to prove that it was of God; to prove that it is not only faithful, but well worthy of all acceptance; that the design of the gospel is to heal and save. The miracles Christ wrought and appointed His apostles to work showed Him to be not only the great Teacher and Ruler, but the Redeemer of the world. They were to heal all types of sickness and disease, without exception, including those who were thought incurable and the shame of physicians. In the grace of the gospel, there is a salve for every sore, a remedy for every malady. There is no spiritual disease so malignant that the power of Christ cannot cure it. Let none therefore say there is no hope or that the breach is wide as the sea and cannot be healed.

Gathering the Elect

"And He will send His angels with
a great sound of a trumpet,
and they will gather together
His elect from the four winds,
from one end of heaven to the other."

MATTHEW 24:31

The angels will be attendants to Christ at His second coming; they will be obliged to wait upon Him. They are now ministering Spirits sent forth by Him (Hebrews 1:14) and will be so then. Their ministration will be ushered in with a great sound of a trumpet. Very fitfully, then, shall there be the sound of a trumpet at the last day, when the saints shall enter upon their eternal jubilee.

"They will gather together His elect from the four winds." At the second coming of Jesus Christ, there will be a general meeting of all the saints. The gifts of love to eternity follow the thoughts of love from eternity, and the Lord knows those who are His. The angels shall be employed to bring them together as Christ's servants and as the saints' friends. "From one end of heaven to the other." The elect of God are scattered abroad (John 11:52), but when that great gathering day comes, not one of them will be missing. Distance of place shall keep none out of heaven, if distance of affection does not.

Authority over Unclean Spirits

Then they were all amazed and
spoke among themselves, saying,
"What a word this is!
For with authority and power
He commands the unclean spirits,
and they come out."

LUKE 4:36

In the breaking of Satan's power, the enemy that is conquered shows his malice, and Christ, the conqueror, shows His over-ruling grace. The devil showed what he would have done when he threw the man in their midst, as if he would have dashed him to pieces. Christ showed what a power He had over him, in that He not only forced him to leave the man, but to leave him without so much as hurting him. Whom Satan cannot destroy, he will hurt all he can, but this is a comfort: He can harm them no further than Christ permits. He shall not do them any real harm. He came out and hurt him not. Christ's power over devils was universally acknowledged and adored. They were all amazed, saying, "What a word this is!" Those who pretended to cast out devils did so with an abundance of charms and spells, but Christ commanded them with authority and power. This, as much as anything, gained Christ a reputation and spread His fame. This instance of His power magnified and was looked upon as greatly magnifying Him. On account of this, His fame went out more than ever, into every place in the country around about. Our Lord Jesus, when He set out in His public ministry, was greatly talked of, more than afterward, when people's admiration wore off along with the novelty of the thing.

Satan Falls as Lightning

"Behold, I give you the authority to
trample on serpents and scorpions,
and over all the power of the enemy,
and nothing shall by any means hurt you."

LUKE 10:19

All our victories over Satan are obtained by power derived from Jesus Christ. We must enter battle with our spiritual enemies in His name. If the work is done in His name, the honor is due to His name. The apostles spoke with an air of exultation. "Even the devils are subject to us." If devils are subject to us, what can stand before us?

Jesus confirmed that what they said agreed with His own observation (v. 18): "I saw Satan fall like lightning from heaven." Satan and his kingdom fell before the preaching of the gospel. He falls like lightning falls from heaven, so suddenly, so irrecoverably. Satan falls from heaven when he falls from the throne in men's hearts. And Christ foresaw that the preaching of the gospel would, wherever it went, pull down Satan's kingdom. Now is the prince of this world cast out.

Jesus repeated, ratified, and enlarged their commission: "Behold, I give you the authority to trample on serpents." They had employed their power vigorously against Satan, and now Christ entrusts them with greater power. He gave them an offensive power to tread on serpents and scorpions, devils and malignant spirits, the old serpent. As the devils have now been subject to you, so they shall still be. He gave them a defensive power: "Nothing shall by any means hurt you." If wicked men are as serpents to you, and you dwell among those scorpions, you may despise their rage and tread upon it. They may hiss, but they cannot hurt.

Knowing Whom to Fear

"But I will show you whom you should fear:
Fear Him who, after He has killed,
has power to cast into hell;
yes, I say to you, fear Him!"
LUKE 12:5

Jesus charged His disciples to be faithful to the trust reposed in them and not betray it through cowardice or base fear. "Whether men will hear, or whether they will forbear, tell them the truth, the whole truth, and nothing but the truth. What has been spoken to you privately, that do you preach publicly, whoever is offended." It was likely to be a suffering cause, though never a sinking one. Let them therefore arm themselves with courage. Diverse arguments are furnished to steel them with a holy resolution in their work.

"The power of your enemies is a limited power" (v. 4). "I say to you, My friends" (Christ's disciples are His friends; He calls them friends and gives them this friendly advice), "do not be afraid." Those whom Christ owns for His friends need not be afraid of any enemies. "Do not be afraid of those who kill the body, and after that have no more that they can do." Those can do Christ's disciples no real harm who can only kill the body, for they only send it to its rest and the soul to its joy a little sooner.

God is to be feared more than the most powerful men: "I will show you whom you should fear." By owning Christ, you may incur the wrath of men, but by denying Christ and disowning Him, you will incur the wrath of God, which has power to send you to hell. Therefore, fear Him. "It is true," said that blessed martyr Bishop Hooper, "life is sweet, and death bitter; but eternal life is more sweet, and eternal death more bitter."

Exceeding Greatness

Far above all principality and power
and might and dominion,
and every name that is named,
not only in this age but
also in that which is to come.

EPHESIANS 1:21

There is a present inheritance in the saints, for grace is glory begun, and holiness is happiness in the bud. There is a glory in this inheritance, and it is desirable to know this experimentally. It may be understood of the glorious inheritance in heaven, where God does, as it were, lay forth all His riches. Let us endeavor then, by reading, contemplation, and prayer, to know as much of heaven as we can, that we may be desiring and longing to be there.

It is a difficult thing to bring a soul to believe in Christ. Nothing less than an almighty power will work this in us. The apostle speaks as if he lacked words to express the exceeding greatness of God's almighty power, that power which God exerts toward His people and by which He raised Christ from the dead. That indeed was the great proof of the truth of the gospel to the world, but the transcript of that in ourselves is the great proof to us. Many understand the apostle here as speaking of that exceeding greatness of power that God will exert for raising believers to eternal life, even the same mighty power that He wrought in Christ when He raised Him. And how desirable a thing it must be to become at length acquainted with that power by being raised thereby to eternal life!

Fit for the Kingdom

He has delivered us from the power of darkness
and conveyed us into the kingdom of
the Son of His love.

COLOSSIANS 1:13

Those in whom the work of grace is wrought must give thanks to the Father. "He has delivered us from the power of darkness." He has saved us from the dominion of sin, which is darkness. He has "conveyed us into the kingdom of the Son of His love," made us members of the church of Christ, which is a state of light and purity. The conversion of a sinner is the conveyance of a soul into the kingdom of Christ out of the kingdom of the devil. It is the kingdom of His dear Son. He made us fit to partake of the inheritance of the saints in light. God gives grace and glory. Glory is the inheritance of the saints in light. It belongs to them as children and is an inheritance in light through communion with God, who is light. This grace is a fitness for the inheritance. All who are designed for heaven hereafter are prepared for heaven now. Those who are sanctified and renewed go out of the world with their heaven about them. Those who have the inheritance of sons have the education of sons. This fitness for heaven is the down payment of the Scripture in our hearts, which is part payment and assures the full payment.

The Lawless One

And then the lawless one will be revealed,
whom the Lord will consume with the breath of His mouth
and destroy with the brightness of His coming.

2 THESSALONIANS 2:8

There are several events previous to the second coming of Christ. The apostle speaks of some very great apostasy such as should give occasion to the revelation or rise of the lawless one. This, he says (v. 5), he had told them of when he was with them. No sooner was Christianity planted and rooted in the world than there began to be defection in the Christian church. It was so in the Old Testament church, and therefore it was no strange thing that after the planting of Christianity, there would come a falling away.

The apostle afterward speaks of the revelation of the lawless one. Here he seems to speak of his rise. He is called the lawless one, and he is the son of perdition, because he himself is devoted to certain destruction and is the instrument of destroying many others. The antichrist is some usurper of God's authority who claims divine honors. His rise is mentioned (vv. 6–7). There was someone who hindered—or let—until He was taken away. This mystery of iniquity was gradually to arrive at its height. While the apostles were yet living, the enemy came and sowed tares. The fall or ruin of the anti-Christian state is declared. The head of this anti-Christian kingdom is called the lawless one. The revelation or discovery of this to the world would be the sure presage of his ruin. The apostle assures the Thessalonians that the Lord will destroy him. The power of the Antichrist in due time will be totally and finally destroyed, and this will be by the brightness of Christ's coming.

Stir Up the Gift

For God has not given us a spirit of fear,
but of power and of love and of a sound mind.
2 TIMOTHY 1:7

Paul exhorts Timothy to do his duty (v. 6). The best men need reminding. Stir up the gift that is in them as fire under the embers. Use gifts and have gifts. He must take all opportunities to use these gifts, for that is the best way of increasing them. The great hindrance of usefulness in the increase of our gifts is slavish fear. Paul therefore warns Timothy against this. God has delivered us from the spirit of fear and given us the spirit of power and of love and of a sound mind: the spirit of power, or of courage and resolution; the spirit of love to God that will set us above the fear of man; and the spirit of a sound mind, or quietness of mind, for we are often discouraged in our work by the creatures of our own imagination, which a sober, thinking mind would obviate.

He exhorts him to count on afflictions and get ready for them. We must not be ashamed of those who are suffering for the gospel of Christ. Timothy must not be ashamed of good old Paul, who was now in bonds. The gospel is the testimony of our Lord; in and by this He bears testimony of Himself to us, and by professing our adherence to it, we bear testimony of Him and for Him. Paul was the Lord's prisoner. For His sake he was bound with a chain. If we are ashamed of either now, Christ will be ashamed of us later.

The Great Harvest

> "The Son of Man will send out His angels,
> and they will gather out of His kingdom all things that offend,
> and those who practice lawlessness,
> and will cast them into the furnace of fire.
> There will be wailing and gnashing of teeth.
> Then the righteous will shine forth
> as the sun in the kingdom of their Father."
>
> MATTHEW 13:41–43

This world will have an end. At harvest all is ripe and ready to be cut down; both good and bad are ripe at the great day. At harvest every man reaps as he sowed; every man's ground and seed and skill and industry will be manifested. The reapers are the angels, servants of Christ, holy enemies of the wicked, and faithful friends to all the saints. They are therefore fit to be the reapers. The reapers will be charged first to gather out the weeds. Though good and bad are together in this world, at the great day they will be parted. They will then be bound in bundles. Those who have been associates in sin will be so in shame and sorrow. They will be cast into a furnace of fire. They are fit for nothing but fire. There shall be wailing and gnashing of teeth, comfortless sorrow, and an incurable indignation at God.

All God's wheat will be lodged together in God's barn. They will then be secure, no longer exposed to wind and weather, sin and sorrow, no longer afar off but near, in the barn. The honor in reserve for the righteous is that they shall shine forth as the sun. Here they are obscure and hidden, their beauty eclipsed by their poverty, but then they shall shine forth as the sun from behind a dark cloud. Those who shine as lights in this world so God may be glorified shall shine in the other world, that they may be glorified.

Submit in Love

Therefore submit to God.
Resist the devil and he will flee from you.
JAMES 4:7

We are taught to submit ourselves entirely to God. Christians should forsake the friendship of the world and should by grace learn to glory in their submissions to God. We are subjects, and as such must be submissive, not only through fear but through love. Now, as this subjection and submission to God are what the devil most industriously strives to hinder, so we ought with great care and steadiness to resist his suggestions. "Resist the devil and he will flee from you." If we basely yield to temptations, the devil will continually follow us, but if we stand firm against him, he will be gone from us. Resolution shuts and bolts the door against temptation.

We have great encouragement to act thus toward God (vv. 8–10). Those who draw near to God in a way of duty shall find God drawing near to them in a way of mercy. If there is not a close communion between God and us, it is our fault, not His. He shall lift up the humble. If we are truly penitent and humble under the marks of God's displeasure, we shall in a little while know the advantages of His favor. He will lift us up out of trouble, or He will lift us up in our spirits and comfort us under trouble. The highest honor in heaven will be the reward of the greatest humility on earth.

The Roaring Lion

Be sober, be vigilant;
because your adversary the devil walks about
like a roaring lion,
seeking whom he may devour.
1 PETER 5:8

The apostle shows Christians the dangers of the enemy, whom he describes by his characteristics and names. He is an adversary, "your adversary." He is the devil, the grand accuser of all the brethren. He is a roaring lion, the fierce and greedy pursuer of souls. He "walks about. . .seeking whom he may devour," his whole design to devour and destroy souls.

It is the Christian's duty to be sober, to be vigilant, to be watchful and diligent to prevent the devil's designs and save their souls, to resist him steadfastly in the faith. It was the faith of these people that Satan aimed at. This strong trial and temptation they must resist by being steadfast in the faith.

Similar afflictions befell their brethren in all parts of the world; all the people of God were their fellow soldiers in this warfare. The devil is the grand persecutor, as well as the deceiver and accuser of the brethren. Sobriety and watchfulness are necessary virtues at all times, but especially in times of suffering and persecution. If your faith gives way, you are gone. The consideration of what others suffer is proper to encourage us to bear our own share in any affliction.

Sin

He who sins is of the devil,
for the devil has sinned from the beginning.
For this purpose the Son of God was manifested,
that He might destroy the works of the devil.
1 JOHN 3:8

Commission of sin is the rejection of the divine law, and this is the rejection of the divine authority, and consequently of God Himself. Jesus takes sin away that He may conform us to Himself, and in Him is no sin. Those who expect communion with Christ above should study communion with Him here in the utmost purity. He who lives in Christ does not continue in the practice of sin. Those who abide in Christ abide in their covenant with Him. They abide in the potent light and knowledge of Him, and therefore it may be concluded that he who sins has not seen Him or known Him. Practical renunciation of sin is the great evidence of saving knowledge of the Lord Christ.

The practice of sin and a justified state are inconsistent. It may appear that *righteousness* may in several places be justly rendered "religion," as in Matthew 5:10, "Blessed are those who are persecuted for righteousness' sake," that is, for religion's sake. To do righteousness then is to practice religion. The practice of religion cannot subsist without a principle of integrity and conscience. To commit sin is to live under the power and dominion of it, and he who does so is of the devil. Christ came into our world that He might conquer the devil. Sin will He loosen and dissolve more and more, until He has quite destroyed it. Let us not serve or indulge in what the Son of God came to destroy.

Apostasy

*Now the Spirit expressly says that in latter times
some will depart from the faith,
giving heed to deceiving spirits
and doctrines of demons.*

1 TIMOTHY 4:1

The prophecies concerning the Antichrist, as well as the prophecies concerning Christ, came from the Spirit. "Some will depart from the faith," an apostasy from the faith. Some, but not all, for in the worst of times, God will have a remnant.

One of the great instances of the apostasy is giving heed to doctrines of demons or concerning demons. The instruments of promoting and propagating this apostasy and delusion are that it will be done by hypocrisy of those who speak lies (v. 2), who have their consciences seared with a red-hot iron, who are perfectly lost to the very first principles of virtue and moral honesty. Another part of their character is that they forbid to marry, and that they command to abstain from foods, and place religion in such abstinence at certain times and seasons.

The apostasy of the latter times should not surprise us, because it was expressly foretold by the Spirit. The Spirit speaks expressly, but the oracles of the heathen were always doubtful and uncertain. In such general apostasies all are not carried away, but only some. Men must be hardened and their consciences seared before they can depart from the faith and draw in others to side with them.

Faith and Works

You believe that there is one God.
You do well.
Even the demons believe—
and tremble!
JAMES 2:19

Compare a faith boasting of itself without works and a faith evidenced by works by looking at both together, to see how this comparison will work in our minds. "You make a profession and say you have faith; I make no such boasts, but leave my works to speak for me." This is the evidence by which the Scriptures all along teach men to judge both themselves and others. And this is the evidence according to which Christ will proceed at the day of judgment.

Look on a faith of bare speculation and knowledge as the faith of devils. That instance of faith which the apostle here chooses to mention is the first principle of all religion. But to rest here and take up a good opinion of your state toward God merely on account of your believing in Him will render you miserable: "Even the demons believe—and tremble!" If you content yourself with a bare assent to articles of faith and some speculations on them, thus far the devils go. They tremble not out of reverence but hatred and opposition to that one God in whom they believe.

He who boasts of faith without works is to be looked upon as a foolish, condemned person (v. 20). Faith without works is said to be dead, not only as void of all those operations that are the proofs of spiritual life, but as unavailable to eternal life.

Believe Not Every Spirit

Every spirit that does not confess that
Jesus Christ has come in the flesh is not of God.
And this is the spirit of the Antichrist,
which you have heard was coming,
and is now already in the world.

1 JOHN 4:3

The apostle calls the disciples to caution and scrutiny about the spirits that had now risen. As to caution: "Beloved, do not believe every spirit; follow not every pretender to the Spirit of God." There had been real communications from the divine Spirit, and therefore others pretended to have the same experience. As to scrutiny, the examination of the claims that are laid to the Spirit (v. 1), the disciples are allowed to use their discretion. The reason is given for this trial: It should not seem strange to us that false teachers set themselves up in the church. The same thing occurred in the apostles' time.

He gives a test whereby the disciples may try these pretending spirits. They were to be tried by their doctrine (v. 2). He who confesses and preaches Christ does it by the Spirit of God. The sum of revealed religion is comprehended in the doctrine concerning Christ, His person and office. We see then the aggravation of a systemic opposition to Him and it. The anti-Christian spirit began early, but we have been warned that such opposition would arise, and the more we see the Word of Christ fulfilled, the more confirmed we should be in the truth of it.

False Apostles

For such are false apostles, deceitful workers,
transforming themselves into apostles of Christ.
And no wonder! For Satan himself transforms himself
into an angel of light.
Therefore it is no great thing if his ministers
also transform themselves into ministers of righteousness,
whose end will be according to their works.
2 CORINTHIANS 11:13–15

The apostle makes an apology for commending himself (v. 1). As much against the grain as it is for a proud man to acknowledge his infirmities, so it is against the grain for a humble man to speak his own praise. The apostle did this to preserve the Corinthians from being corrupted by the insinuations of the false apostles. He was jealous of them with godly jealousy. He had espoused them to one husband, and he was desirous to present them as a chaste virgin, pure and spotless and faithful, not having their minds corrupted by false teachers. He vindicated himself against the false apostles. They could not pretend they had another Jesus, or a different spirit, or a different gospel to preach to them (v. 4). But seeing there is but one Jesus, one Spirit, and one gospel preached to them and received by them, what reason could there be why the Corinthians should be prejudiced against him who first converted them?

The false apostles are charged as deceitful workers, and though they were the ministers of Satan, would seem to be the ministers of righteousness. Since Satan can turn himself into any shape and sometimes look like an angel of light in order to promote his kingdom of darkness, so he will teach his instruments to do the same. But it follows that their end will be according to their works.

Ashamed

*"For whoever is ashamed of Me and My words
in this adulterous and sinful generation,
of him the Son of Man also will be ashamed when
He comes in the glory of His Father
with the holy angels."*

MARK 8:38

Jesus tells us what men do to save their lives and gain the world. "For whoever is ashamed of Me and My words in this adulterous and sinful generation, of him the Son of Man also will be ashamed." The disadvantage that the cause of Christ labors under in this world is that it is to be owned and professed in an adulterous and sinful generation. Some ages, some places, are more especially sinful, as that in which Christ lived. In such a generation, the cause of Christ is opposed and run down, and those who own it are exposed to reproach and contempt, and everywhere ridiculed and spoken against. There are many who, though they cannot deny that the cause of Christ is a righteous cause, are ashamed of it. They are ashamed of their relation to Christ. They cannot bear to be frowned on and despised and therefore throw off their profession. There is a day coming when the cause of Christ will appear as bright and illustrious as now it appears mean and contemptible. They shall not share with Him in His glory then who were not willing to share with Him in His disgrace now.

The Saints Shall Judge

Do you not know that we shall judge angels?
How much more, things that pertain to this life?
1 CORINTHIANS 6:3

The apostle reproves the Corinthians for going to law with one another before heathen judges for little matters. The bonds of fraternal love were broken through. Christians should not contend with one another, for they are brethren. Bringing their matters before heathen magistrates tended to the reproach of Christianity. Therefore, says the apostle: "Dare any of you, having a matter against another, go to law before the unrighteous" (v. 1)? Here is at least an intimation that they went to law for trivial matters, for the apostle blames them that they did not suffer wrong rather than go to law. Christians should be of a forgiving temper, and it is more to their honor to suffer small injuries than seem to be contentious.

He lays before them the aggravation of their fault: "Do you not know that we shall judge angels?" And are they unworthy to judge the things of this life? It was a dishonor to their Christian character for them to carry little matters before heathen magistrates. When they were to judge the world, even to judge angels, it is unaccountable that they could not determine little controversies among themselves. Shall Christians have the honor to sit with the sovereign Judge, and are they not worthy to judge the trifles about which they contend before heathens?

Christ and Baptism

> *Jesus Christ, who has gone into heaven*
> *and is at the right hand of God,*
> *angels and authorities and powers*
> *having been made subject to Him.*
> 1 PETER 3:21–22

Noah's salvation in the ark upon the water prefigured the salvation of all good Christians by baptism. By saving baptism, the apostle means not the outward ceremony of washing with water, but that baptism wherein there is a faithful answer of a resolved good conscience.

The efficacy of baptism to salvation depends not upon the work done, but upon the resurrection of Christ. The sacrament of baptism, rightly understood, is a means and a pledge of salvation. "Baptism now saves us." The external participation of baptism will save no man without an answerable good conscience and life. There must be the answer of a good conscience toward God.

The apostle proceeds to speak of Christ's ascension and sitting at the right hand of the Father. If the advancement of Christ was so glorious after His deep humiliation, let not His followers despair, but expect that after these short distresses they shall be advanced to transcendent joy and glory. Upon His ascension into heaven, Christ is enthroned at the right hand of the Father. Angels, authorities, and powers are all made subject to Christ Jesus.

God's Care

*The angel of the LORD encamps
all around those who fear Him,
and delivers them.*
PSALM 34:7

"The angel of the LORD" (a guard of angels) "encamps all around those who fear Him," as a bodyguard about the prince, and delivers them. David would have us join with him in kind and good thoughts of God (v. 8). "Oh, taste and see that the LORD is good!" The goodness of God includes both the beauty and amiableness of His being and the bounty and beneficence of His providence and grace. He would have us join with Him in a resolution to seek God and serve Him, and continue in his fear (v. 9). "Oh, fear the LORD, you His saints!" Fear the Lord, that is, worship Him, and make conscience of your duty to Him in everything, not fear Him and shun Him, but fear Him and seek Him (v. 10).

To encourage us to fear Him and seek Him, it is promised that those who do so, even in this wanting world, shall want for no good thing. They shall have grace sufficient for the support of the spiritual life, and as to this life, they shall have what is necessary for the support of it from the hand of God. As a Father, He will feed them with convenient food. What further comforts they desire, they shall have, as far as Infinite Wisdom sees good, and what they lack in one thing shall be made up in another. What God denies them, He will give them grace to be content without, and then they will not want it.

Precious Fruit

*"To him who overcomes
I will give to eat from the tree of life,
which is in the midst of the Paradise of God."*
REVELATION 2:7

Advice and counsel is given to the Ephesians from Christ: Those who have lost their first love must remember whence they have fallen. They must compare their present with their former state and consider how much better it was with them then than now. They must repent. They must return and do their first works. They must, as it were, begin again. They must endeavor to revive and recover their first zeal.

This good advice is enforced and urged by a severe threat if it should be neglected. If the presence of Christ's grace and Spirit is slighted, we may expect the presence of His displeasure. There is an encouraging mention of what was still good among them (v. 6). Though you have declined in your love to what is good, yet you retain your hatred to what is evil. An indifference of spirit between truth and error, good and evil may be called charity and meekness, but it is not pleasing to Christ.

We have a promise of great mercy to those who overcome. We must never yield to our spiritual enemies, but fight the good fight until we gain the victory, and then warfare and victory shall have a glorious triumph and reward: They shall eat from the tree of life in the midst of the Paradise of God, not in the earthly paradise but the heavenly.

Thyatira

*"And he who overcomes,
and keeps My works until the end,
to him I will give power over the nations."*
REVELATION 2:26

Christ makes honorable mention of their charity (there is no religion where there is no charity), their service, their faith, that was the grace that actuated all the rest, their patience, and their growing fruitfulness. Their last works were better than their first. It should be the ambition and earnest desire of all Christians that their last works may be their best works.

He encourages them who keep themselves pure and undefiled. The seducers among them called their doctrines depths, profound mysteries, while Christ called them depths of Satan, satanical delusions and devices. How tender Christ is of His faithful servants. "I only require your attention to what you have received." If they hold fast faith and a good conscience until He comes, all the difficulty and danger will be over.

There will be an ample reward to the persevering, victorious believer: very great power and dominion over the rest of the world, and the knowledge and wisdom suitable to such power and dominion. "I will give him the morning star" (v. 28). Christ is the morning star; He brings day with Him into the soul, the light of grace and of glory.

Sardis

"He who overcomes shall be clothed in white garments, and I will not blot out his name from the Book of Life; but I will confess his name before My Father and before His angels."

REVELATION 3:5

Jesus begins with a very severe reproof to this congregation. Hypocrisy and a lamentable decay in religion are the sins charged against them. This church had gained a great reputation; it had a name as a flourishing church. Everything appeared well, but this church was not really what it was reputed to be.

Our blessed Lord does not leave this sinful people without some comfort and encouragement. He makes mention of the faithful remnant in Sardis, though it is small. God takes notice of the smallest number of those who abide with Him, and the fewer they are, the more precious in His sight. They shall walk with Christ in the white robes of honor and glory in the other world. Christ will not blot the names of His chosen and faithful ones out of this Book of Life. The names of those who overcome shall never be blotted out. Christ will produce this Book of Life and confess the names of the faithful who stand there before God and all the angels. How great this honor and reward will be!

Philadelphia

"Because you have kept My command to persevere, I also will keep you from the hour of trial which shall come upon the whole world, to test those who dwell on the earth."
REVELATION 3:10

Christ would make this church's enemies subject to her. Those enemies are described to be such as said they were Jews but were really the synagogue of Satan. Their subjection to the church is described. They shall "worship before your feet," shall be convinced that they have been in the wrong. How shall this great change be wrought? By the power of God in the hearts of His enemies and by signal discoveries of His particular favor to His church. They shall "know that I have loved you." Christ can show His favor to His people in such a way that their enemies shall see it and be forced to acknowledge it. This will, by the grace of Christ, soften the hearts of their enemies.

The gospel of Christ is the word of His patience. It is the fruit of the patience of God to a sinful world. After a day of patience, we must expect an hour of temptation. Those who keep the gospel in a time of peace shall be kept by Christ in an hour of temptation. Christ calls the church to persevere. "Hold fast what you have": You have been possessed of this excellent treasure; hold it fast. "Behold, I am coming quickly": I am coming to relieve those under trial, to reward their fidelity and to punish those who fall away. The persevering Christian shall win the prize from backsliding professors.

Soul-Winners Are Wise

The fruit of the righteous is a tree of life,
and he who wins souls is wise.
PROVERBS 11:30

This shows what great blessings good men are, especially those who are eminently wise, to the places where they live, and therefore how much to be valued. First, the righteous are as trees of life; the fruits of their piety and charity, their instructions, reproofs, examples, and prayers, their interest in heaven and their influence upon earth are like the fruits of that tree: precious and useful, contributing to the support and nourishment of the spiritual life in many. They are the ornaments of paradise, God's church on earth, for those whose sake it stands. Second, the wise are something more; they are as trees of knowledge, not forbidden but commanded knowledge. He who is wise, by communicating his wisdom, wins souls, wins upon them to bring them in love with God and holiness, and so wins them over into the interests of God's kingdom among men. The wise are said to turn many to righteousness, and that is the same with winning souls here (see Daniel 12:3). Abraham's proselytes are called the souls that he had gotten (see Genesis 12:5). Those who would win souls have need of wisdom to know how to deal with them; and those who do win souls show that they are wise.

The Commission

"Go therefore and make disciples of all the nations,
baptizing them in the name of the Father
and of the Son and of the Holy Spirit,
teaching them to observe all things
that I have commanded you; and lo,
I am with you always, even to the end of the age."
MATTHEW 28:19–20

The commission Jesus gives to those whom He sent forth is "Go therefore." This commission is given primarily to the apostles, the architects who laid the foundation of the church. It is not only a word of command but a word of encouragement: "Go, and fear not; have I not sent you?" They must go and bring the gospel to the doors of the nations. As an eagle stirs up her nest and flutters over her young to excite them to fly, so Christ stirs up His disciples to disperse all over the world. It is given to their successors, the ministers of the gospel, whose business it is to transmit the gospel from age to age, to the end of the world. Christ, at His ascension, gave the world not only apostles and prophets, but pastors and teachers.

What is the principal intention of this commission? To disciple all nations. "Admit them disciples; do your utmost to make the nations Christian nations." Christ the Mediator is setting up a kingdom in the world: Bring the nations to be His subjects. He is setting up a school: Bring the nations to be His scholars. He is raising an army: Enlist the nations of the earth under His banner. The work the apostles had to do was to set up the Christian religion in all places, and it was honorable work. The achievements of the mighty heroes of the world were nothing to it; they conquered the nations for themselves and made them miserable. The apostles conquered them for Christ and made them happy.

Saving a Soul from Death

*Brethren, if anyone among you
wanders from the truth,
and someone turns him back,
let him know that he who turns a sinner from
the error of his way will save a soul from
death and cover a multitude of sins.*

JAMES 5:19– 20

The epistle of James concludes with an exhortation to do all we can to promote the conversion and salvation of others. Be they ever so great, you must not be afraid to show them their error. Be they ever so weak and little, you must not disdain to make them wiser and better. If they err from the truth, whether in opinion or practice, you must endeavor to bring them back again. Errors in judgment and in life generally go together. If we are instrumental in the conversion of any, we are said to have converted them, though this is the work of God. If we cannot convert a sinner, we may pray for the grace and Spirit of God to convert and change them. We cannot be said to convert any by merely altering their opinions. We need to bring them to correct their ways. This is conversion. "He who turns a sinner from the error of his way will save a soul from death." By such conversion of heart and life, a multitude of sins shall be hidden. Though our sins are many, they may be hidden or pardoned. No matter how people contrive to cover their sin, there is no way to hide it but by forsaking it. Some make the meaning of this text to be that conversion prevents a multitude of sins. It is beyond dispute that many sins are prevented in others that a redeemed sinner may have had an influence upon.

Repentance

Then Peter said to them,
"Repent, and let every one of you be baptized
in the name of Jesus Christ for the remission of sins;
and you shall receive the gift of the Holy Spirit."
ACTS 2:38

Sinners who are convinced must be encouraged. Though their case is sad, it is not desperate; there is hope for them. Peter shows them the course they must take: Repent. This is a plank after a shipwreck. This was the same duty that John the Baptist and Christ had preached, and it is still insisted on: Repent, repent; change your mind, change your ways, that is, "firmly believe the doctrine of Christ, and make an open, solemn profession of this, and renounce your infidelity." They must be baptized in the name of Jesus Christ. Believe in the name of Jesus, that He is the Christ, the Messiah promised to their fathers. They must be baptized in His name for the remission of sins. This is pressed on each individual: every one of you. "Even those of you who have been the greatest sinners, if you repent and believe, are welcome to be baptized. There is grace enough in Christ for every one of you, no matter how many, and grace suited to the case of everyone."

He gives them encouragement to take this course. It shall be for the remission of sins. Repent of your sin, and it will not be your ruin; be baptized into the faith of Christ, and in truth you will be justified. Aim at this, and depend on Christ for it, and this you shall have. All who receive the remission of sins receive the gift of the Holy Ghost.

The Rewards of Ministry

But you be watchful in all things,
endure afflictions, do the work of an evangelist,
fulfill your ministry.
2 TIMOTHY 4:5

The comfort and cheerfulness of Paul, in the prospect of his approaching departure, might encourage Timothy. "I can look back upon my warfare with a great deal of satisfaction, so therefore be not afraid of the difficulties you must meet with. The crown of life is as sure to you as if it were already upon your head." The apostle looks forward to his approaching death and looks upon it as near at hand (v. 6): "I am already being poured out." Observe with what pleasure he looks back to the life he had lived. He did not fear death because he had the testimony of his conscience that by the grace of God he had in some measure fulfilled the duties of life. He had fought a good fight (v. 7); "I have kept the faith." We must fight this good fight and finish our course. To be able to speak in this manner at the end of our days will give us unspeakable comfort!

See with what pleasure he looks forward to the life he was to live hereafter. Let this encourage Timothy to endure hardship as a good soldier of Jesus Christ. There is a crown of life before us. It is called a crown of righteousness because our holiness and righteousness will be perfected there and will be our crown. This crown was not particular to Paul, as if it belonged only to apostles and martyrs, but to all those who love His appearing. It is the character of all the saints that they love His second appearing at the great day, love it and long for it. Their crown is laid up for them; they do not have it now, for here they are but heirs, but it is sure.

Baptism

Then Paul said, "John indeed baptized
with a baptism of repentance,
saying to the people that they should
believe on Him who would come after him,
that is, on Christ Jesus."
ACTS 19:4

Paul explains to those in Ephesus the true intent and meaning of John's baptism as principally referring to Jesus Christ. Those who have been left in ignorance or led into error by any lack of education should be compassionately instructed and better taught, as these disciples were by Paul. He admits that John's baptism was a very good thing, as far as it went. "John indeed baptized with a baptism of repentance." He shows them that John's baptism had a further reference: "They should believe on Him who would come after him, that is, on Christ Jesus." John's baptism of repentance was designed to prepare the way of the Lord, whom he directed them to: "Behold the Lamb of God" (John 1:36)! He was only the harbinger; Christ is the Prince. His baptism was the porch you were to pass through, not the house you were to rest in.

When they were shown their error, they thankfully accepted the discovery and "were baptized in the name of the Lord Jesus" (v. 5). It does not follow that there was any disagreement between John's baptism and Christ's, for those who were baptized there in the name of the Lord Jesus had never been so baptized before.

Plain Teaching

For Christ did not send me to baptize,
but to preach the gospel,
not with wisdom of words,
lest the cross of Christ should be made of no effect.
1 CORINTHIANS 1:17

The apostle gives an account of his ministry among the Corinthians. He thanks God he had baptized only a few of them. He is not to be understood as saying he would have preferred not to baptize at all, but he did not want to do so in the present circumstances. He left it to other ministers to baptize while he filled his time with preaching the gospel. This, he thought, was more his business. Ministers should consider themselves set apart to that service in which Christ will be most honored and the salvation of souls promoted, and for which they are best fitted. The principal business Paul did among them was to preach the gospel, the cross, and Christ crucified. This is what Paul preached, what all ministers should preach, and what all the saints live upon.

Paul preached "not with the wisdom of words, lest the cross of Christ should be made of no effect," lest the success should be ascribed to the force of art and not of truth, not to the plain doctrine of a crucified Jesus but to the powerful oratory of those who spread it. He preached a crucified Jesus in plain language and told the people that Jesus was the Son of God and the Savior of men, and that all who would be saved must repent of their sins and believe in Him. This truth shone out with the greatest majesty in its own light and prevailed in the world by its divine authority, without any human help. The plain teaching of a crucified Jesus was more powerful than all the oratory and philosophy of the heathen world.

Up and Down the World

And He said to them,
"Go into all the world and preach the gospel to every creature.
He who believes and is baptized will be saved;
but he who does not believe will be condemned."
MARK 16:15–16

This concerns the commission that Jesus gave the apostles to set up His kingdom among men by the preaching of His gospel. So far they had been sent only to the lost sheep of the house of Israel and were forbidden to go to the Gentiles or any city of the Samaritans. Now they are authorized to go into all the world and preach the gospel of Christ to every creature, every human being who is capable of receiving it. These eleven men could not preach it to all the world themselves, much less to every creature in it. They and the other disciples, with those who would be added to them, must disperse themselves and carry the gospel with them. They must make it their business to send those glad tidings up and down the world, with all possible fidelity and care as a solemn message from God to men and an appointed means of making men happy.

What is the summary of the gospel they are to preach? "Set before the world life and death, good and evil. Go and tell them that if they believe the gospel and give up themselves to be Christ's disciples, if they renounce the devil, the world, and the flesh, and be devoted to Christ, they shall be saved from the guilt and power of sin. He who is a true Christian shall be saved through Christ." Baptism was appointed to be the inaugurating rite by which those who embraced Christ owned Him. But "he who does not believe will be condemned." Even this is gospel: It is good news that nothing but unbelief will damn men.

Nothing Is Hidden

"Whatever I tell you in the dark,
speak in the light;
and what you hear in the ear,
preach on the housetops."
MATTHEW 10:27

"Whatever hazards you run into, go on with your work, publishing and proclaiming the everlasting gospel to all the world. This is your business; mind it. The design of the enemies is not merely to destroy you, but to suppress that." They must deliver their message publicly, in the light, and upon the housetops, for the doctrine of the gospel is what all are concerned with. The first indication of the reception of the Gentiles into the church was upon a housetop (Acts 10:9). There is no part of Christ's gospel that needs to be concealed; the whole counsel of God must be revealed. Let it be plainly and fully delivered.

The truths that are now hidden as mysteries from the children of men shall all be made known to all nations in their own language. The ends of the earth must see this salvation. It is a great encouragement to those who are doing Christ's work that it is a work that will certainly be done. This may also be seen as the revealing of the integrity of Christ's suffering servants. However their innocence is now covered, they shall be revealed. All their reproach shall be rolled away, and their graces and services, which are now covered, shall be revealed. Let Christ's ministers faithfully reveal His truths and leave it to Him to reveal their integrity in due time.

The Apostles Are Called

Then He appointed twelve,
that they might be with Him and that
He might send them out to preach,
and to have power to heal sicknesses and to cast out demons.
MARK 3:14–15

These verses concern Christ's choosing of the twelve apostles to be His constant followers and attendants. The rule He went by in His choice was His own good pleasure: He called whomever He wanted to call, not those we might have thought the fittest, but those He thought fit to call and determined to make fit for the service to which He called them. Christ calls whom He will.

The efficacy of the call was that He called them to separate themselves from the crowd and stand by Him, and they came to Him. Those whom it was His will to call, He made willing to come.

The end and intention of this call was that He ordained them, that they should be with Him constantly, to be witnesses of His doctrine, manner of life, and patience, that they might fully know it. They must be with Him to receive instructions from Him, that they might be qualified to instruct others. It would require time to fit them for that for which He designed them. Christ's ministers must be much with Him.

The power He gave them to work miracles was that He ordained them to heal sicknesses and cast out demons. This showed that the power Christ has to work these miracles was an original power, that He had it not as a servant, but as a Son in His own house. Our Lord Jesus had life in Himself and the Spirit without measure, for He could give this power even to the weak and foolish things of the world.

No Excuses

Jesus said to him,
"Let the dead bury their own dead,
but you go and preach the kingdom of God."
LUKE 9:60

This person seems resolved to follow Christ, but begs a day. The excuse he made was, " 'Lord, let me first go and bury my father' (v. 59). He cannot live for long and will need me while he does live. Let me go and attend to him until he is dead, and then I will do anything." We may see three temptations here. We are tempted to rest in a discipleship-at-large, in which we may be at loose ends and not come close. We are tempted to defer the doing of our duty and to put it off until some other time. When we have gotten clear of such a care or difficulty, then we will begin to think about religion, and so we are cheated out of all our time by being cheated out of the present. We are tempted to think that our duty to our family will excuse us from our duty to Christ. The kingdom of God and its righteousness must be sought and minded first.

Christ's answer was, "Let the dead bury their own dead, but you go and preach the kingdom of God." Christ would not have His followers or ministers act unnaturally; our religion teaches us to be kind and good in every relationship. But we must not make these duties an excuse from our duty to God. If the nearest and dearest relation we have stands in our way to keep us from Christ, it is necessary that we have a zeal that will make us forget father and mother. No excuses must be used against immediate obedience to the call of Christ.

Cease Not

And daily in the temple,
and in every house,
they did not cease teaching and
preaching Jesus as the Christ.
ACTS 5:42

The apostles bore their sufferings with invincible cheerfulness. When they went out, instead of being ashamed of Christ, they rejoiced that they were counted worthy to suffer shame for His name. They had never done anything to make themselves vile, and therefore must have been aware of the shame they suffered, but they considered that it was for the name of Christ that they were abused and that their sufferings should be made to contribute to the further advancement of His name.

They went on in their work with diligence. They were commanded by the authorities not to preach, and yet they ceased not to teach and preach. They preached every day, both publicly in the temple and privately in every house. Though in the temple they were under the eye of their enemies, yet they did not confine themselves to their own houses, but ventured into danger. Though they had the liberty of the temple, they also preached in every house, even the poorest cottage. They preached Jesus Christ, not themselves. This was the preaching that gave most offence to the priests, but they would not alter their subject to please them. It ought to be the constant business of gospel ministers to preach Christ crucified and glorified.

Unless They Are Sent

*How then shall they call on Him in whom
they have not believed?
And how shall they believe in Him
of whom they have not heard?
And how shall they preach unless they are sent?*

ROMANS 10:14–15

How necessary it was that the gospel should be preached to the Gentiles. This was why the Jews were so angry with Paul. He shows how needful it was to bring them within the reach of the promise. They cannot call on Him in whom they have not believed. Unless they believe that He is God, they will not call on Him by prayer. The grace of faith is absolutely necessary to the duty of prayer; we cannot pray properly without it. They who come to God by prayer must believe, but they cannot believe in Him of whom they have not heard. Some way or another, the divine revelation must be made known to us before we can receive it and assent to it; it is not born in us. They cannot hear without a preacher. Somebody must tell them what they are to believe. They cannot preach unless they are sent. How shall a man act as an ambassador without his credentials and his instructions from the one who sends him? It is God's prerogative to send ministers. Only He can qualify men for and incline them to the work of the ministry. But the competency of that qualification and the sincerity of that inclination must not be left to the judgment of every man for himself. This must be submitted to the change of those who are presumed the most able and are empowered to set apart those they find qualified and inclined. Those who are thus set apart not only may but must preach as those who are sent.

Willing Service

For if I preach the gospel,
I have nothing to boast of,
for necessity is laid upon me;
yes, woe is me if I do not preach the gospel!
1 CORINTHIANS 9:16

It is the glory of a minister to deny himself that he may serve Christ and save souls. This self-denial yielded Paul much more contentment than his preaching did. This is a duty expressly bound upon him. Those who are set apart to the office of the ministry must preach the gospel. Woe be to them if they do not. But it is not given in charge to all, nor any preacher of the gospel, to do his work without payment. It may be his duty to preach under some circumstances without receiving payment, but he has a right to payment. It may sometimes be his duty to insist on his salary, and whenever he forbears, he parts with his right.

Only willing service is capable of God's reward. Leave the heart out of our duties, and God abhors them: They are but the carcasses, without the life and spirit of religion. Ministers have a dispensation of the gospel committed to them. Christ's willing servants shall not lack their recompense, and His slothful and unwilling servants shall all be called to account.

What is the reward, then? "That when I preach the gospel, I may present the gospel of Christ without charge, that I may not abuse my authority in the gospel." It is an abuse of power to employ it against the very ends for which it is given. And the apostle would never use his power to frustrate the ends of it, but would willingly and cheerfully deny himself.

A Servant to All

For though I am free from all men,
I have made myself a servant to all,
that I might win the more.

1 CORINTHIANS 9:19

Paul asserts his liberty. He was freeborn, a citizen of Rome. He was in bondage to none, yet he made himself a servant to all to gain the more. He made himself a servant that they might be made free.

He accommodated himself to all sorts of people. To the Jews and those under the law, he came as a Jew. He submitted to it that he might prevail with them and win them over to Christ. To those without the law, the Gentiles, he behaved as one who was not under the bondage of the Jewish laws. In innocent things he could comply with people's usages for their advantage. He did not stand on privileges. To the weak he became weak, that he might gain the weak. He did not despise or judge them but became one of them. He denied himself for their sakes, that he might gain their souls. The rights of God he could not give up, but he might resign his own, and he very often did so for the good of others. A heart warmed with zeal for God and breathing after the salvation of others will not insist upon its rights and privileges.

Unsearchable Riches

To me, who am less than the least of all the saints,
this grace was given,
that I should preach among the Gentiles
the unsearchable riches of Christ.
EPHESIANS 3:8

How humbly Paul speaks of himself as "less than the least of all the saints." St. Paul, who was the chief of the apostles, calls himself less than the least. What can be less than the least? To speak of himself as little as could be, he speaks of himself less than could be. Where God gives grace to be humble, there he gives all other grace. While he magnifies his office, Paul debases himself. How highly he speaks of Jesus Christ: "the unsearchable riches of Christ." There is a mighty treasury of mercy, grace, and love laid up in Christ Jesus for both Jews and Gentiles. They are unsearchable riches, of which we cannot even find the bottom of. It was the apostle's business and employment to preach these unsearchable riches of Christ among the Gentiles. "God has granted to such an unworthy creature as I this grace, this special favor." It is also an unspeakable favor to the Gentile world that these unsearchable riches of Christ are preached to them. Though many remain poor and are not enriched with these riches, if we are not enriched with them, it is our own fault.

Paul's Preaching

I now rejoice in my sufferings for you, and fill up in my flesh
what is lacking in the afflictions of Christ, for the sake
of His body, which is the church, of which I became
a minister according to the stewardship from God
which was given to me for you, to fulfill the word of God.
COLOSSIANS 1:24–25

Paul was a suffering preacher: "I now rejoice in my sufferings for you." He suffered for preaching, and while he suffered in such a good cause, he could rejoice in the suffering. "And fill up in my flesh what is lacking in the afflictions of Christ." The suffering of Paul and other good ministers made them conformable to Christ. They are said to fill up what was behind the sufferings of Christ, as wax fills up the emptiness of a seal when it receives the impression of it. Or it may refer to his suffering for Christ. He was still filling up more and more what was behind or remained of them to his share.

He was a close preacher: "Him we preach, warning every man and teaching every man in all wisdom" (v. 28). When we warn people of what they do wrong, we must teach them how to do better. Warning and teaching must go together. Men must be warned and taught in all wisdom. We must choose the fittest times and accommodate ourselves to the different capacities of those we deal with. He aimed to present every man perfect in Christ Jesus. Ministers should aim at the improvement and salvation of each person who hears them.

He was a hard-working preacher: "To this end I also labor, striving according to His working which works in me mightily" (v. 29). As Paul laid himself out to do much good, so he had this favor, that the power of God worked in him more effectually.

The Apostles Go Out

So they went out and preached that people should repent.
And they cast out many demons,
and anointed with oil many who were sick,
and healed them.
MARK 6:12–13

The apostles' conduct in pursuance of their commission was that though they were conscious of their great weakness, yet, in obedience to their Master's order and in dependence upon His strength, they went out as Abraham did, not knowing where they went.

The doctrine they preached was that people should repent, that they should change their minds and reform their lives. The great design of gospel preachers and the great tendency of gospel preaching should be to bring people to repentance in a new heart and in a new way. They did not amuse people with curious speculations, but told them that they must repent of their sins and turn to God.

The miracles they did showed that the power Christ gave them over unclean spirits was not ineffectual, nor did they receive it in vain but used it, for they "cast out many devils" and "anointed with oil many who were sick, and healed them."

Speaking for the Lord

*"For the Holy Spirit will teach you
in that very hour what you ought to say."*
LUKE 12:12

Whatever trials the apostles should be called to, they would be sufficiently furnished for them and honorably brought through them. The faithful martyr for Christ has not only sufferings to undergo but a testimony to bear, a good confession to witness, and is concerned to do that well so that the cause of Christ may not suffer, though he suffer for it. If this concerns him, let him cast it upon God. When they bring you into the synagogues, or before magistrates and powers, to be examined about your doctrine, take no thought of what you shall answer in order to save yourself. If it is the will of God that you should survive, He will bring it about, that you may serve your Master. Aim at this, but do not perplex yourselves about it, for the Holy Ghost, as a Spirit of wisdom, "will teach you in that very hour what you ought to say" and how to say it, so that it may be for the honor of God and His cause.

The Helper

"But the Helper, the Holy Spirit,
whom the Father will send in My name,
He will teach you all things,
and bring to your remembrance
all things that I said to you."
JOHN 14:26

Christ comforts His disciples with two thoughts. They would be under the instruction of His Spirit. Christ would have them reflect on the instructions He had given them, "These things I have spoken to you while being present with you" (v. 25). What He had said, He did not retract. What He had spoken, He had spoken and would abide by it. Christ would find a way of speaking to them after His departure from them.

On whose account the Spirit would be sent stated "The Father will send in My name," that is, "for My sake." Jesus came in His Father's name; the Spirit comes in Jesus' name to carry on His undertaking.

On what errand the Spirit would be sent was "He will teach you all things." He will teach them all things necessary for them to learn themselves or to teach others, for those who would teach the things of God must first be taught by God themselves. He shall "bring to your remembrance all things that I said to you." Christ had taught them many good lessons that they had forgotten. The Spirit will not teach them a new gospel but bring to their minds that which they had been taught by leading them to understand it. The Spirit of grace is given to all the saints as a remembrancer.

Suitable Food

For though by this time you ought to be teachers,
you need someone to teach you again
the first principles of the oracles of God;
and you have come to need milk and not solid food.
HEBREWS 5:12

The Hebrews should have been so well instructed by now in the doctrine of the gospel that they could teach others, but "you need someone to teach you again the first principles of the oracles of God." In the oracles of God, there are some first principles that are easy to be understood and need to be learned. There are also deep and sublime mysteries.

There are in the church babies and persons of full age, and milk and strong meat are in the gospel. Those who are babies, unskillful in the Word of righteousness, must be fed with milk. Christ does not despise His babies; He has provided suitable food for them. There is also strong meat for those who are mature. The deeper mysteries of religion belong to those who are of a higher class in the school of Christ. Every true Christian stands in need of nourishment. The Word of God is food and nourishment to the life of grace. There are spiritual senses as well as natural ones. The soul has its sensations as well as the body; these are much depraved and lost by sin, but they are recovered by grace. It is by use and exercise that these senses are improved, made more quick and strong, to taste the sweetness of what is good and true and the bitterness of what is false and evil.

A Preacher's Duty

Speak these things, exhort,
and rebuke with all authority.
TITUS 2:15

This summary direction to Titus explains the matter and manner of ministers' teaching. Ministers are to teach the truths and duties of the gospel, of avoiding sin and living soberly, righteously, and godly in this present world. To teach these things they are to use doctrine and exhortation and rebuke with all authority. They are to speak, exhort, and press with much earnestness the great and necessary truths and duties of the gospel. Ministers must not be cold and lifeless in delivering heavenly doctrine and precepts, as if they were indifferent things; they must urge them with earnestness. They are to rebuke, convince, and reprove those who contradict or neglect the truth. "Rebuke with all authority," as coming in the name of God. Ministers are reprovers at the gate.

"Let no one despise you." Speak and exhort these things, press them upon all. With boldness and faithfulness, reprove sin and carefully look to yourself and your own conduct, and then none will despise you. The most effective way for ministers to secure themselves from contempt is to keep close to the doctrine of Christ and do their duty with prudence and courage.

Perhaps an admonition might be intended to the people, too. Titus, though young, should not be held in contempt by them.

Church Leaders

For a bishop must be blameless, as a steward of God,
not self-willed, not quick-tempered,
not given to wine, not violent, not greedy for money.
TITUS 1:7

A church leader should not be self-willed. The prohibition is wide, including self-opinion, self-love, making the self the center of all, also self-confidence and self-pleasing, set in one's own will and way. It is a great honor to a minister to be ready to ask and to take advice, to be ready to defer to the mind and will of others, becoming all things to all men, that they may gain some. "Not quick-tempered": How unfit are those to govern a church who cannot govern themselves. "Not given to wine": Moderate use of this, as of the other good creatures of God, is not unlawful, but excess is shameful in all, especially in a minister. "Not greedy for money," not entering into the ministry with base worldly views: Nothing is more unbecoming a minister, who is to direct his own and others' eyes to another world, than to be too intent upon this world.

On the positive side, a minister must be a lover of hospitality. Such a spirit and practice, according to ability and occasion, are very becoming examples of good works. Ministers should also love the good things and good men of the world. They should be sober, or prudent, a needful grace in a minister both for his ministerial and personal carriage and management. He must be just in civil matters, holy in what concerns religion, and temperate. This last comes from another word that signifies strength and denotes one who has power over his appetite and affections.

The Road to Damascus

"But rise and stand on your feet;
for I have appeared to you for this purpose,
to make you a minister and a witness
both of the things which you have seen
and of the things which I will yet reveal to you."
ACTS 26:16

Paul asked, " 'Who are You, Lord?' And He said, 'I am Jesus, whom you are persecuting' " (v. 15). Paul thought Jesus was buried in the earth and, though stolen out of His own tomb, was laid in another. Therefore he is amazed to hear Him speak from heaven, to see Him surrounded with all this glory. This convinced Paul that the doctrines of Jesus were divine and heavenly, not to be opposed but to be cordially embraced, and this is enough to make him a Christian immediately.

He was made a minister by divine authority. The same Jesus who appeared to him in that glorious light ordered him to go and preach the gospel to the Gentiles. What is said about him being an apostle is joined to that which was said to him by the road. He puts the two together here for brevity: "Rise and stand on your feet." He must stand up because Christ has work for him to do: "I have appeared to you for this purpose, to make you a minister." Christ makes His own ministers. He will manifest Himself to all those whom He makes His ministers, for how can those preach Him who do not know Him? And how can those know Him to whom He does not by His Spirit make Himself known?

Paul's Steadfastness

> *Therefore, since we have this ministry,*
> *as we have received mercy,*
> *we do not lose heart.*
>
> 2 CORINTHIANS 4:1

In this chapter, Paul's intent is to vindicate their ministry from the accusation of false teachers. He tells them how they believed and how they showed their value for their office as ministers of the gospel. Their constancy and perseverance in their work are declared. Their steadfastness was owing to the mercy of God, since the best men in the world would faint in their work and under their burdens if they did not receive mercy from God. Their sincerity in their work is vouched (v. 2). They had no base and wicked designs covered with fair and specious pretenses of something that was good. Nor did they in their preaching handle the Word of God deceitfully, but they used great plainness of speech. They manifested the truth to every man's conscience, declaring nothing but what in their own conscience they believed to be true. And all this they did as in the sight of God, desirous to commend themselves to God and to the consciences of men.

Reconciliation

Now all things are of God,
who has reconciled us to Himself through Jesus Christ,
and has given us the ministry of reconciliation.
2 CORINTHIANS 5:18

Reconciliation is an unquestionable privilege. Reconciliation supposes a quarrel or breach of friendship. Yet, behold, there may be a reconciliation. God has reconciled us to Himself by Jesus Christ. All things relating to our reconciliation by Jesus Christ are of God, who by the mediation of Jesus Christ has reconciled the world to Himself. He has appointed the office of the ministry, which is a ministry of reconciliation.

As God is willing to be reconciled to us, we ought to be reconciled to God. Though God cannot lose any quarrel, nor gain by the peace, yet by His ministers He beseeches sinners that they would be reconciled to Him. And for our encouragement to do so, the apostle subjoins what should be well known by us: the purity of the Mediator who knew no sin. The sacrifice He offered was that He was made a sin offering, a sacrifice for sin, that we might be made the righteousness of God in Him. As Christ, who knew no sin of His own, was made sin for us; we who have no righteousness of our own are made the righteousness of God in Him.

Serving, Not Ruling

*"He who is greatest among you,
let him be as the younger,
and he who governs as he who serves."*

LUKE 22:26

Our Savior tells the apostles that doing good is much more honorable than being great. A benefactor of his country is much more valued than a ruler of his country. Doing good is the surest way to be great. He would have His disciples believe that their greatest honor would be to do all the good they could in the world. If they have that which is the greater honor of being benefactors, let them despise the less, of being rulers.

"It was never intended that you should rule any other way than by the power of truth and grace, but that you should serve." Here is the rule Christ gave to His disciples: He who is greater among you, who is senior, let him be as the younger. Their age and honor, instead of allowing them to take their ease, binds them to double work. And he who is chief, let him be as he who serves. Here is the example that He Himself gave to this rule: "For who is greater, he who sits at the table, or he who serves" (v. 27)? He was ready to do any office of kindness and service for them; witness His washing their feet.

They ought not to strive for worldly honor and grandeur, because He had better honors in reserve for them: a kingdom, a feast, and a throne, wherein they should all share alike.

Faithful Service

With goodwill doing service, as to the Lord,
and not to men,
knowing that whatever good anyone does,
he will receive the same from the Lord,
whether he is a slave or free.
EPHESIANS 6:7–8

Christians should be sincere in their obedience, serving with faithfulness. They should have an eye to Jesus Christ in all the service that they perform to their masters, "doing service, as to the Lord, and not to men." Service done to their earthly masters with an eye to Him becomes acceptable service to Him also. They must not serve their masters with eye service—that is, only when their master's eye is upon them. Their Master in heaven beholds them, and therefore they must not act as men pleasers. A steady regard to the Lord Jesus Christ will make men faithful and sincere in every station of life. What they do, they must do cheerfully, doing the will of God from the heart, serving their masters as God wills they should. This is doing it with goodwill. Service performed with conscience and from a regard to God, though it be to unrighteous masters, will be accounted by Christ as service done to Himself. Let faithful servants trust God for their wages while they do their duty in His fear, "knowing that whatever good anyone does, he will receive the same from the Lord." Though his master on earth may neglect or abuse him instead of rewarding him, he shall certainly be rewarded by the Lord Jesus Christ, "whether he is a slave or free." Christ regards not these differences of men at present, nor will He in the great and final judgment.

Watching

*"Blessed are those servants whom the master,
when he comes, will find watching."*

LUKE 12:37

Those servants will be happy who shall be found ready when their Lord shall come. Blessed are those servants who, after having waited long, are then found awake and aware of His first approach, of His first knock. He will "have them sit down to eat, and will come and serve them" (v. 37). For the bridegroom to wait upon his bride at the table is not uncommon, but to wait upon his servants is not the manner of men; yet Jesus Christ, to show His love, served them when He washed their feet.

We are kept uncertain concerning the precise time of His coming so that we may always be ready. The master of the house, if he had known what hour the thief would come, though he were ever so careless, would have watched (v. 39). But we do not know at what hour the alarm will be given us and therefore are concerned never to be off our guard. Or this may intimate the miserable case of those who are careless and unbelieving in this great matter. We have notice of the day of the Lord's coming "as a thief in the night" (2 Peter 3:10), and yet do not watch. If men take such good care of their houses, let us be equally wise for our souls: Be ready, as ready as the master of the house would be if he knew what hour the thief would come.

The Apostles at Work

And with great power the apostles gave witness to
the resurrection of the Lord Jesus.
And great grace was upon them all.
ACTS 4:33

The ministers went on in their work with great vigor and success. "With great power the apostles gave witness to the resurrection of the Lord Jesus." The resurrection of Christ, rightly understood, will let us into the great mysteries of religion. By the great power wherewith the apostles attested the resurrection may mean the great vigor, spirit, and courage with which they published this doctrine; they did it not softly and diffidently, but with liveliness and resolution. Or it may mean the miracles which they wrought to confirm their doctrine, God Himself in them bearing witness, too.

The beauty of the Lord our God shone upon them: "Great grace was upon them all." Grace that had something great in it (magnificent and very extraordinary) was upon them all. Christ poured out an abundance of grace upon them. There were evident fruits of this grace in all they said and did. Some think it includes the favor they were in with the people. Everyone saw a beauty and excellency in them and respected them.

Our Redeemer

"For I know that my Redeemer lives,
and He shall stand at last on the earth;
and after my skin is destroyed,
this I know, that in my flesh I shall see God."
JOB 19:25–26

There is a Redeemer provided for fallen man—Jesus Christ. The word for *Redeemer* is used for the next of kin, to whom, by the law of Moses, the right of redeeming a mortgaged estate belonged. Our heavenly inheritance was mortgaged by sin; we are utterly unable to redeem it by ourselves, but Christ is kin to us, our closest kinsman, and He is able to redeem. He has paid our debt, satisfied God's justice for sin, and so has taken off the mortgage and made a new settlement. Our persons also need a Redeemer. We are sold for sin and sold under sin; our Lord Jesus has worked out a redemption for us and proclaims redemption to us, so He is truly our Redeemer.

Job believes in the happiness of the redeemed and his own title to that happiness. He knows how the body is corrupted by the grave but speaks of it without concern. The same power that made man's body out of common dust can raise it out of its own dust. He comforts himself with hopes of happiness on the other side of death and the grave. Soul and body shall come together again, and the body that must be destroyed in the grave will be raised again as a glorious body, a spiritual body.

In Flaming Fire

Our God shall come,
and shall not keep silent. . . .
He shall call to the heavens from above,
and to the earth,
that He may judge His people.

PSALM 50:3–4

When God comes to reprove them for their hypocrisy and to send forth His gospel to supersede the legal institutions, He shall shine out of Zion. The gospel, which set up spiritual worship, was to go forth from Mount Zion, and the preachers of it were to begin in Jerusalem. Zion is called "the perfection of beauty" because it was the holy hill, and holiness is indeed the perfection of beauty.

He shall come and not keep silent, but shall show His displeasure at them, and the partition wall of the ceremonial law will be taken down; this shall no longer be concealed. In the great day our God will come and not keep silent, but will make those who would not hearken to His law hear His judgment. His appearance will be majestic and terrible: A fire shall devour before Him. The fire of His judgments will make way for the rebukes of His Word, that the sinners of Zion might be startled out of their sins. When His gospel kingdom was to be set up, Christ came to send fire on the earth. The Spirit was given in cloven tongues of fire and introduced by a rushing, mighty wind; and in the last judgment, Christ shall come in flaming fire.

His Glorious Reign

Then the moon will be disgraced and the sun ashamed;
for the LORD of hosts will reign on Mount Zion
and in Jerusalem and before His elders, gloriously.

ISAIAH 24:23

Let not the free man glory in his freedom, any more than the strong man in his strength, for he knows not what restraints he is reserved for. But after many days they shall be visited, either in wrath or reservation to the day of execution, to the judgment of the great day (Jude 6). Or they shall be visited in mercy and be discharged from their imprisonment, and shall again obtain, if not their dignity, at least their liberty.

When the proud enemies of God's church are humbled, it will appear beyond doubt that the Lord reigns. When the kings of the earth are punished for their tyranny, then the whole world will see that God is King of kings and reigns as Lord of hosts in Mount Zion. God's ancients, the old disciples, the experienced Christians who have often gone into the sanctuary of God in Zion and Jerusalem, shall see more than others of God's dominion and sovereignty. Then it shall appear that He reigns gloriously, in such brightness and luster that "the moon will be disgraced and the sun ashamed," as the smaller lights are eclipsed and extinguished by the greater. The glory of the Creator infinitely outshines the glory of the brightest creatures.

Christ's Dominion

"Then to Him was given dominion and glory and a kingdom,
that all peoples, nations, and languages should serve Him.
His dominion is an everlasting dominion,
which shall not pass away,
and His kingdom the one which shall not be destroyed."
DANIEL 7:14

The kingdom of the Messiah shall be set up in the world, in spite of all the opposition of the powers of darkness. Daniel sees this in a vision and comforts his friends. The Messiah is called the Son of Man here, for He was made in the likeness of sinful flesh, was found in fashion as a man. "I saw one like the Son of Man." Our Savior seems plainly to refer to this vision when He says in John 5:27 that the Father has given Him the authority to execute judgment because he is the Son of Man. Some refer this to His incarnation, but I think it refers to His ascension (Acts 1:9). When the cloud received Him out of the sight of His disciples, it is worthwhile to ask where it carried Him. Here we are told He ascended to His Father and our Father, to His God and our God (John 20:17). He was brought near as our high priest who enters within the veil for us and as our forerunner. He is represented as having a mighty influence upon this earth. When He went to be glorified with His Father, He had power given Him over all flesh. With the prospect of this, Daniel and his friends are comforted that not only the dominion of the church's enemies will be taken away, but the church's head will have dominion given Him. His dominion shall not pass away. The church will continue militant to the end of time and triumph to the endless ages of eternity.

According to Their Works

> *"For the Son of Man will come in the glory
> of His Father with His angels,
> and then He will reward
> each according to his works."*
>
> MATTHEW 16:27

This verse discusses the assurance we have of Christ's glory at the second coming to judge the world. If we see things as they will appear then, we shall see them as they *should* appear now. "The Son of Man will come in the glory of His Father with His angels." To look upon Christ in His state of humiliation would discourage His followers from taking any pains or running any hazards for Him, but seeing the Captain of our salvation coming in His glory through the eyes of faith will animate us and make us think nothing is too much to do or too hard to suffer for Him.

"Then He will reward each according to his works." Jesus Christ will come as a Judge to dispense rewards and punishments. Men will then be rewarded, not according to their gains in this world, but according to their works, according to what they were and did, and the constancy of faithful souls will be recompensed with a crown of life. The best preparation for that day is to deny ourselves and take up our cross and follow Christ; for so we will make the Judge our Friend. The rewarding of men according to their works is deferred until that day. Here good and evil seem to be dispensed promiscuously, but in that day all will be set to rights.

False Christs

> *"Take heed that no one deceives you.*
> *For many will come in My name, saying,*
> *'I am the Christ,' and will deceive many."*
> MATTHEW 24:4–5

Jesus warns the disciples that before He comes there will appear false Christs coming in Christ's name, assuming the name peculiar to Him and saying they are Him—pseudo Christs. There was at that time a general expectation of the appearing of the Messiah; they spoke of Him as He who should come, but when He did come, the nation rejected Him. Those who were ambitious of making themselves a name took advantage of the people's expectations and set themselves up as Christs.

The false Christs and false prophets to come will have their agents and emissaries busy in all places to draw people to them. Then when public troubles are great and threatening, and people will be grabbing at anything that looks like deliverance, Satan will take the advantage. They will say, "Here is a Christ," or "There is one." The true Christ did not strive or cry, nor was it said of Him, "Here!" or "There!" Christ is All in all, not here or there, but He meets His people with a blessing in every place where He records His name. These false Christs will show great signs and wonders, but they will not be true miracles—those are a divine seal, and with those, the doctrine of Christ stands confirmed. It is not said, "They shall work miracles," but "They shall show great signs." They are but a show.

Preached in All the World

> *"But he who endures to the end shall be saved.*
> *And this gospel of the kingdom will be*
> *preached in all the world*
> *as a witness to all the nations,*
> *and then the end will come."*
>
> MATTHEW 24:13–14

Jesus foretells the preaching of the gospel in all the world. It is called the gospel of the kingdom because it reveals the kingdom of grace, which leads to the kingdom of glory. This gospel, sooner or later, is to be preached in all the world, to every creature. The gospel is preached for a witness to all nations, that is, a faithful declaration of the mind and will of God.

It is intimated that the gospel should be, if not heard, at least heard of throughout the then-known world before the destruction of Jerusalem. Within forty years after Christ's death, the sound of the gospel was "gone out to all the earth" (Romans 10:18). Paul fully preached the gospel from Jerusalem and around to Illyricum (Romans 15:19), and there the apostles were not idle. The persecuting of the saints at Jerusalem helped disperse them, so that they "went everywhere preaching the word" (Acts 8:1–4).

It is likewise hinted that even in times of temptation, trouble, and persecution, the gospel of the kingdom will force its way through the greatest opposition. Though the enemies of the church grow very hot and many of her friends very cool, yet the gospel shall be preached. Then the people who know their God shall be strengthened to do the greatest exploits of all.

Desolation

"And unless those days were shortened,
no flesh would be saved;
but for the elect's sake those days will be shortened."
MATTHEW 24:22

"Then there will be great tribulation" (v. 2). The ruin of Jerusalem was an unparalleled desolation such as was not seen since the beginning of the world or ever shall be. Many a city and kingdom has been made desolate, but never any with desolation like this. No wonder that the ruin of Jerusalem was an unparalleled ruin when the sin of Jerusalem was an unparalleled sin—even the death of Christ.

It was a desolation which, if it continued for very long, would be intolerable, so that no flesh would be saved. He does not say, "No soul shall be saved," for the destruction of the flesh may be for the saving of the spirit in the day of the Lord Jesus. But there is one word of comfort in the midst of all the terror: That for the elect's sake these days shall be shortened—not made shorter than what God had determined, but shorter than what He might have decreed, if He had dealt with them according to their sins. In times of common calamity, God manifests His favor to the elect remnant: His peculiar treasure, which He will secure. The shortening of calamities is a kindness God often grants. Instead of complaining that our afflictions last so long, if we consider our defects, we shall see reason to be thankful that they do not last always; when it is bad with us, it becomes us to say, "Blessed be God that it is no worse."

Separation

*"Then two men will be in the field:
one will be taken and the other left.
Two women will be grinding at the mill:
one will be taken and the other left."*
MATTHEW 24:40–41

When ruin came to Jerusalem, a distinction was made by Divine Providence, according to that which had been made before by divine grace, for all the Christians among them were saved from perishing. If we are safe when thousands fall to our right and left, are not consumed when others are consumed round about us, so that we are as sticks plucked out of the fire, we have reason to say it is a great mercy.

We may apply this to the second coming of Jesus Christ and the separation which will be made in that day. He had said before that the elect will be gathered together. Here it is applied to them who shall be found alive. Christ will come, unlooked for, and will find people busy at their usual occupations in the field and at the mill. And it speaks an abundance of comfort to the Lord's people. Are they humble and despised in the world, as the manservant in the field or the maid at the mill? They shall not be forgotten or overlooked in that day. Are they dispersed in distant and unlikely places where one would not expect to find the heirs of glory? The angels will find them. What a change it will be to go to heaven directly from ploughing and grinding. Are they weak and unable to move heavenward by themselves? They shall be taken. Those whom Christ has once laid hold on, He will never lose His hold of. Are they intermixed with others, linked with them in the same cities, societies, and jobs? Let not that discourage any true Christian. God knows how to separate the wheat and chaff on the same floor.

Inherit the Kingdom

" 'Come, you blessed of My Father,
inherit the kingdom prepared for you
from the foundation of the world.' "
MATTHEW 25:34

The acknowledging of the saints to be the blessed of the Lord is: "Come, you blessed of My Father." He pronounces them blessed, and His saying they are blessed makes them so. They may be reproached and cursed by the world, but they are blessed by God. All our blessings in heavenly things flow to us from God, as the Father of our Lord Jesus Christ (Ephesians 1:3). He calls them to come; this "come" is, in effect, "Welcome, ten thousand welcomes, to the blessings of My Father. Come to Me, come to be forever with Me. You who followed Me bearing the cross now come along with Me wearing the crown." We now come boldly to the throne of grace, but we shall then come boldly to the throne of glory.

The tenure by which they shall hold and possess this blessing is very good. They shall come and inherit it. It is God who makes heirs of heaven. We come to an inheritance by virtue of our sonship, our adoption: if children, then heirs. A title by inheritance is the sweetest and surest title. Saints in this world are as underage heirs, tutored and governed until the time appointed by the Father (Galatians 4:1–2). Then they shall be put in full possession of that which now through grace they have title to. Come and inherit.

Watch and Pray

*"But of that day and hour no one knows,
not even the angels in heaven, nor the Son,
but only the Father.
Take heed, watch and pray;
for you do not know when the time is."*

MARK 13:32–33

As to the end of the world, do not inquire when it will come, for of that day and that hour, no man knows. It is not revealed by any Word of God, either to men on earth or to angels in heaven. But then it says, neither does the Son know. Is there anything of which the Son is ignorant? There were those in primitive times who taught from this text that there were some things that Christ, as man, was ignorant of. They said, "It was no more absurd to say so than to say that His human soul suffered grief and fear." Christ, as God, could not be ignorant of anything, but the divine wisdom which dwelt in our Savior communicated itself to His human soul according to divine pleasure, so that His human nature might sometimes not know some things; therefore Christ is said to grow in wisdom.

"Your duty is to watch and pray. Take heed of everything that would indispose you for your Master's coming. Watch for His coming, that it may not be a surprise to you, and pray for that grace which is necessary to qualify you for it; you know not what the time is, and you are concerned to be ready for that every day, which may come any day."

Being with Christ

*"And if I go and prepare a place for you,
I will come again and receive you to Myself;
that where I am, there you may be also."*
JOHN 14:3

Christ gave His disciples a warning against having a troubled heart. How did Christ notice their concern? Perhaps it was apparent in their looks. At least it was intelligible to the Lord Jesus, who is acquainted with all our secret, undiscovered sorrows, with the wound that bleeds inwardly. He takes cognizance of all the trouble His people are in danger of being overwhelmed with. Many things concurred to trouble the disciples.

"If I go and prepare a place for you, I will come again and receive you to Myself; that where I am, there you may be also." These are comfortable words indeed. Jesus Christ will come again; this verse stresses the certainty of that. We say, "We are coming" when we are busy in preparing for our arrival, and so He is. He will come again to receive all His faithful followers to Himself. The coming of Christ is in order to gather us together to Him. Where He is, there they shall be also. This indicates that the quintessence of heaven's happiness is being there with Christ. "Where I am to be shortly, there you shall be shortly; where I am to be eternally, there you shall be eternally," not only spectators of His glory, but sharers in it. This may be inferred from His going to prepare a place for us, for His preparations shall not be in vain. He will not build and furnish rooms and let them stand empty. If He has prepared a place for us, He will prepare us for it, and in due time put us in possession of it.

Times of Refreshing

*"Repent therefore and be converted, that your sins may be
blotted out, so that times of refreshing may come from
the presence of the Lord, and that He may send
Jesus Christ, who was preached to you before,
whom heaven must receive until the times of
restoration of all things, which God has spoken by
the mouth of all His holy prophets since the world began."*

ACTS 3:19–21

The remission of sin is its blotting out. When God forgives sin, He remembers it no more against the sinner; it is forgotten, as that which is blotted out. We cannot expect our sins to be pardoned unless we repent of them and turn to God: no repentance, no remission. Hopes of the pardon of sin upon repentance should be a powerful inducement for us to repent. The most comfortable fruit of the forgiveness of our sins will be when the times of refreshing shall come. During times of toil and conflict, we cannot have that full satisfaction of our pardon that we shall have when the refreshing times come, which will wipe away all tears.

If you repent and are converted, you shall find no want of Him; some way or another, He shall be seen by you. We must not expect Christ's personal presence with us in this world, for the heavens, which received Him out of the sight of the disciples, must retain Him until the end of time. We must live by that faith in Him which is the evidence of things not seen. Yet it is promised that He shall be sent to all who repent and are converted. "You shall have His spiritual presence. He who is sent into the world shall be sent to you; you shall have the comfort of His being sent. The sending of Christ to judge the world at the end of time will be a blessing to you."

Censure None

Therefore judge nothing before the time,
until the Lord comes,
who will both bring to light the hidden things of darkness
and reveal the counsels of the hearts.
Then each one's praise will come from God.

1 CORINTHIANS 4:5

The apostle cautions the Corinthians against censoriousness, judging out of season, judging persons' future state or the secret springs and principles of their actions. To judge in these cases is to assume the seat of God. How bold a sinner is the severe censurer! How ill-timed and arrogant are his censures! But there is one who will judge the censurer and those he censures. This should make them cautious of judging others and careful in judging themselves. There is a time coming when the Lord will "bring to light the hidden things of darkness and reveal the counsels of the hearts." The Lord Jesus Christ will manifest the counsels of all hearts. He must know the counsels of the heart, or He could not make them manifest. We should be very careful how we censure others when we have to deal with a Judge from whom we cannot conceal ourselves. When He comes to judge, "each one's praise will come from God." Christians may well be patient under unjust censures when they know a day such as this is coming. But how fearful should they be of loading any with reproaches now whom their common Judge shall later commend.

Citizens of Heaven

For our citizenship is in heaven,
from which we also eagerly wait for the Savior,
the Lord Jesus Christ, who will transform our lowly body that
it may be conformed to His glorious body,
according to the working by which He is able
even to subdue all things to Himself.

PHILIPPIANS 3:20–21

Good Christians, even while they are here on earth, are citizens of heaven. This world is not our home; heaven is. The life of a Christian is heaven, where his home is and where he hopes to be shortly. It is good having fellowship with those who have fellowship with Christ and citizenship with those whose life is in heaven.

We look for the Savior from heaven: "from which we also eagerly wait for the Savior, the Lord Jesus Christ." We expect His second coming from there. At the second coming of Christ, we expect to be happy and glorified there: "who will transform our lowly body that it may be conformed to His glorious body." There is a glory reserved for the saints, which they will be instated in at the resurrection. The body is now at best a vile body, but it will be made a glorious body: "according to the working by which He is able even to subdue all things to Himself." It is a matter of comfort to us that He can subdue all things and the resurrection will be wrought by this power. Let this confirm our faith in the resurrection, that we not only have the Scriptures, which assure us it shall be, but we know the power of God that can bring it to pass. As Christ's resurrection was a glorious instance of the divine power, so will our resurrection be. And then all the enemies of the Redeemer's kingdom will be completely conquered.

Hidden with Christ

When Christ who is our life appears,
then you also will appear with Him in glory.
COLOSSIANS 3:4

Though we are free from the ceremonial law, it does not follow that we may live as we please. We must walk more closely with God. "If then you were raised with Christ, seek those things which are above" (v. 1). We must mind the concerns of another world more than the concerns of this. He who is our best friend has gone before to secure us heavenly happiness, and we should seek what He has purchased at so vast an expense.

Our true life lies in the other world. "For you died, and your life is hidden with Christ in God" (v. 3). The new man has his livelihood there. It is hidden with Christ; not hidden only from us as a secret, but hidden for us, denoting security. This is our comfort, that our life is hidden with Him and laid up safely with Him.

At the second coming of Christ, we hope for the perfection of our happiness. "When Christ who is our life appears, then you also will appear with Him in glory." Christ is a believer's life. He is the principle and end of the Christian's life. He will appear again. He is now hidden, but He will appear in His own glory and His Father's glory. We shall then appear with Him in glory. It will be His glory to have His redeemed with Him, and it will be their glory to come with Him. Do we look for such happiness? Should we not set our affections on that world and live above this? Our head is there, our home is there, our treasure is there, and we hope to be there forever.

The Trumpet of God

*For the Lord Himself will descend
from heaven with a shout,
with the voice of an archangel,
and with the trumpet of God.
And the dead in Christ will rise first.
Then we who are alive and remain
shall be caught up together with them
in the clouds to meet the Lord in the air.
And thus we shall always be with the Lord.*

1 THESSALONIANS 4:16–17

"The Lord Himself will descend from heaven with a shout." The appearance will be with pomp and power, with the voice of an archangel. The glorious appearance of this great Redeemer and Judge will be proclaimed and ushered in by the trumpet of God. The dead shall be raised, the dead in Christ rising first. Those who shall then be found alive will not prevent those who are asleep. They shall be caught up together with them in the clouds to meet the Lord in the air. Here is the bliss of the saints at that day: They shall always be with the Lord. The principal happiness of heaven is being with the Lord, seeing Him, living with Him, and enjoying Him forever. This should comfort the saints on the death of their friends. We and they, with all the saints, will meet our Lord and be with Him forever, no more to be separated either from Him or from one another. The apostle would have us comfort one another with these words.

Rewards

Since it is a righteous thing with God
to repay with tribulation those who trouble you,
and to give you who are troubled
rest with us when the Lord Jesus is revealed
from heaven with His mighty angels.

2 THESSALONIANS 1:6–7

Those who suffered tribulations were improved by their sufferings, were counted worthy of the kingdom of God (vv. 4–5). Religion, if it is worth anything, is worth everything, and those who have no religion at all or do not value it cannot find it in their hearts to suffer for it. In this future repayment, there will be punishment inflicted on persecutors. There is nothing that more infallibly marks a man for eternal ruin than a spirit of persecution. God will render a recompense and will trouble those who trouble His people. The reward for those who are persecuted is a rest that remains for the people of God, a rest from sin and sorrow. The future rest will abundantly repay all their present troubles. There is enough in heaven to balance all that we may lose or suffer for the name of Christ in this world. God's suffering people will lose nothing by their sufferings, and their enemies will gain nothing. The Lord Jesus will in that day appear from heaven, revealed with His mighty angels, and He will come in flaming fire as a refining fire to purify the saints and a consuming fire to the wicked. The effects of this appearance will be terrible to some and joyful to others.

He Remains Faithful

If we endure, we shall also reign with Him.
If we deny Him, He also will deny us.
If we are faithless, He remains faithful;
He cannot deny Himself.

2 TIMOTHY 2:12–13

To encourage Timothy in suffering, the apostle reminds him of the resurrection of Christ. The consideration of it should make us faithful to our Christian profession. The incarnation and resurrection of Jesus Christ, heartily believed and rightly considered, will support a Christian under all sufferings in the present life. Those who faithfully adhere to Christ, whatever it costs them, will certainly have the advantage of it in another world. If we are dead to this world, we shall go to live with Him in a better world, to be forever with Him. Those who suffer for Christ on earth shall reign with Christ in heaven. We are unfaithful to Him at our own peril. That man will be forever miserable whom Christ disowns at last. This will certainly be the issue whether we believe it or not. If we are faithful to Christ, He will certainly be faithful to us. If we are false to Him, He will be faithful to His threats. This is a faithful saying and may be depended on and ought to be believed.

Marks and Signs

But know this,
that in the last days perilous times will come.
2 TIMOTHY 3:1

Paul tells Timothy the marks and signs whereby these times may be known (vv. 2–4). Self-love will make the times perilous. Instead of Christian charity, which cares for the good of others, they will mind themselves only. When men are lovers of themselves, no good can be expected from them, as good may be expected from those who love God. When every man is for what he can get and for keeping what he has, this makes men dangerous. When men do not fear God, they will not regard man. Unthankfulness and unholiness make the times perilous. What is the reason that men are unholy and without the fear of God, but that they are unthankful for the mercies of God? Those who will not be bound by natural affection will not be bound by the most solemn leagues and covenants. They are slanderers. When men have no control of themselves and their own appetites, they are without self-control, they are brutal. That which is good and ought to be honored is generally despised, and men are generally treacherous, willful, and haughty, puffed up, behaving scornfully to all around them.

Death and Salvation

So Christ was offered once to bear the sins of many.
To those who eagerly wait for Him
He will appear a second time,
apart from sin, for salvation.

HEBREWS 9:28

The appointment of God concerning men contains in it two things. They must die once. This is a matter of comfort to the godly, that they shall die well and die but once; but it is a matter of terror to the wicked who die in their sin. After death they shall come to judgment. This is the unalterable decree of God concerning men: They must die, and they must be judged.

The appointment of God concerning Christ is that He must be offered once to bear the sins of many. He was not offered for any sin of His own; He was wounded for our transgressions. Christ shall appear the second time without sin for the salvation of those who look for Him. He appeared in the form of sinful flesh, but His second appearance will be without any such charge upon Him. This will be to the salvation of all who look for Him. He will then perfect their holiness, their happiness.

Strive for More Grace

Therefore gird up the loins of your mind,
be sober, and rest your hope fully upon
the grace that is to be brought to you
at the revelation of Jesus Christ.
1 PETER 1:13

Let the loins—or the strength and vigor—of your minds be exerted in your duty. Disengage yourselves from all that would hinder you, and go on resolutely in your obedience. Be sober, be vigilant against all your spiritual dangers and enemies, and be temperate and modest in all your behavior. Be sober minded also in opinion as well as in practice. The main work of a Christian lies in the right management of his heart and mind. The best Christians need to be exhorted to sobriety. A Christian's work is not over as soon as he is in a state of grace; he must still hope and strive for more grace. We must hope perfectly, and yet gird up our loins and address ourselves vigorously to the work we have to do, encouraging ourselves from the grace of Jesus Christ.

An argument to press them to holiness from the consideration of what they now are, children of obedience, and what they were when they lived in lust and ignorance. The children of God ought to prove themselves to be such by their obedience to God. The best of God's children have had their times of lust and ignorance. Persons, when converted, differ exceedingly from what they were formerly.

The Crown of Glory

And when the Chief Shepherd appears,
you will receive the crown of glory
that does not fade away.
1 PETER 5:4

The pastor's duty is described: to feed the flock by preaching to them the sincere Word of God. The pastors of the church must take the oversight thereof. They must be examples to the flock and practice the holiness they preach and recommend to their people. These duties must be performed from a willing mind that takes pleasure in the work, not for money but from an eager mind, regarding the flock more than the fleece, nor as being lords over God's heritage, tyrannizing over them. These poor, dispersed, suffering Christians were the flock of God. The rest of the world is a brutal herd. These are an orderly flock, redeemed to God by the Chief Shepherd. They are also dignified with the title of God's heritage, chosen out of the common multitude for His own people. They are God's people and should be treated with love, humility, and tenderness for the sake of Him to whom they belong.

In opposition to money, the apostle sets before them the crown of glory designed by the Chief Shepherd for all His faithful ministers. Jesus Christ is the Chief Shepherd of the whole flock and heritage of God. He is also the Chief Shepherd over all inferior shepherds. This Chief Shepherd will appear to judge all ministers and undershepherds. Those who are found to have done their duty shall receive from the Chief Shepherd "the crown of glory that does not fade away."

The Appointed Day

But the day of the Lord will come as a thief in the night,
in which the heavens will pass away with a great noise,
and the elements will melt with fervent heat;
both the earth and the works that are in it will be burned up.
2 PETER 3:10

The certainty of the day of the Lord is that that day has not yet come, but it assuredly will come. God has appointed a day, and He will keep His appointment. The suddenness of this day will come as a thief in the night, a time when men are sleeping and secure. The time that men think to be the most improper and unlikely, and when therefore they are most secure, will be the time of the Lord's coming.

The solemnity of this coming is described as "The heavens will pass away with a great noise, and the elements will melt with fervent heat; both the earth and the works that are in it will be burned up." All must pass through the fire, which will be a consuming fire to all who sin has brought into the world, though it may be but a refining fire to the works of God's hand. What a difference there will be between the first coming of Christ and the second! May we be so wise as to prepare for it, that it may not be a day of vengeance and destruction for us.

See Him as He Is

Beloved, now we are children of God;
and it has not yet been revealed what we shall be,
but we know that when He is revealed,
we shall be like Him,
for we shall see Him as He is.
1 JOHN 3:2

We have the nature of sons by regeneration. The glory pertaining to the sonship and adoption is reserved for another world. The sons of God must walk by faith and live by hope. The time of the revelation of the sons of God is determined: "But we know that when He is revealed, we shall be like Him." The sons of God will be known and made manifest by their likeness to their head. Their likeness to Him is argued from the sight they shall have of Him. "We shall be like Him, for we shall see Him as He is." All shall see Him, but not as He is to those in heaven. The wicked shall see Him in His frowns, but these shall see Him in the smiles and beauty of His face. Their likeness shall enable them to see Him as the blessed do in heaven.

The sons of God know that their Lord is holy and pure. Those who hope to live with Him must study the utmost purity; their hope of heaven will dictate and constrain them to do so. It is a contradiction to such hope to indulge in sin and impurity. As we are sanctified by faith, we must be sanctified by hope. To be saved by hope, we must be purified by hope.

He Comes

Behold, He is coming with clouds,
and every eye will see Him,
even they who pierced Him.
And all the tribes of the earth will mourn because of Him. . . .
"I am the Alpha and the Omega,
the Beginning and the End," says the Lord,
"who is and who was and who is to come,
the Almighty."

REVELATION 1:7–8

He will be the Judge of the world. This book, the Revelation, begins and ends with a prediction of the second coming of the Lord Jesus Christ. John speaks as if he saw that day: "Behold, He is coming," as sure as if you beheld Him with your eyes. "He is coming with clouds," which are His chariot and pavilion. Every eye shall see Him, the eye of His people, the eye of His enemies, every eye, yours and mine. He shall come, to the terror of those who have pierced Him and have not repented, and of all who have wounded and crucified Him afresh by their apostasy from Him, and to the astonishment of the pagan world. This account of Christ is ratified and confirmed by Himself. He is "the Beginning and the End." All things are from Him and for Him. He is the Almighty. He is the same eternal and unchangeable one.

You Were Slain

"You are worthy to take the scroll, and to open its seals;
for You were slain,
and have redeemed us to God by Your blood out of
every tribe and tongue and people and nation,
and have made us kings and priests to our God;
and we shall reign on the earth."

REVELATION 5:9–10

The apostle beholds the scroll taken into the hands of the Lord Jesus Christ, who was on the same throne with the Father. Christ, as man and Mediator, is subordinate to God the Father but is nearer to Him than all the creatures. Before He was called a lion; here He appears as a slain lamb. He is a lion to conquer Satan, a lamb to satisfy the justice of God. He appears as a lamb having seven horns and seven eyes, perfect power to execute all the will of God and perfect wisdom to understand it all.

No sooner had Christ received this scroll out of the Father's hand than He received the applause and adoration of angels and men, of every creature. The church begins the doxology, as being more immediately concerned in it. The object of their worship is the Lamb, the Lord Jesus Christ. They fell down before Him, gave Him the most profound adoration. The instruments used in their adoration were harps and bowls. The harps were the instruments of praise, and the bowls were full of incense, which signifies the prayers of the saints. "You are worthy to take the scroll, and to open its seals." They mention the grounds of this worthiness, yet they chiefly insist upon the merit of His sufferings; these more sensibly struck their souls with thankfulness and joy. They mention His suffering: "You were slain." The fruits of His suffering are redemption to God and high exaltation.

Righteous Wrath

And the kings of the earth,
the great men, the rich men, the commanders,
the mighty men, every slave and every free man,
hid themselves in the caves
and in the rocks of the mountains.
REVELATION 6:15

The tremendous events were hastening, several occurrences contributing to make that day and dispensation very dreadful (v. 13). It would be a judgment that would astonish all the world. The dread and terror would seize upon all sorts of men in that great and awful day. The degree of their terror and astonishment would prevail so far as to make them call to the mountains to fall upon them, and to the rocks to cover them. The cause of their terror was the wrath of the Lamb. Though God is invisible, He can make the inhabitants of this world aware of His awful frowns. Though Christ is a lamb, yet He can be angry, and the wrath of the Lamb is exceedingly dreadful. As men have their day of opportunity and their seasons of grace, so God has His day of righteous wrath.

Happiness after Tribulation

"They shall neither hunger anymore nor thirst anymore;
the sun shall not strike them, nor any heat;
for the Lamb who is in the midst of the throne will
shepherd them and lead them to living fountains of waters.
And God will wipe away every tear from their eyes."

REVELATION 7:16–17

The way to heaven lies through many tribulations, but tribulation shall not separate us from the love of God. The means by which they had been prepared for the great happiness they now enjoyed: This is the only blood that makes the robes of the saints white and clean. The blessedness to which they are now advanced: They are happy in their station, for they are before the throne of God night and day, and He dwells among them. They are happy in their employment because they serve God continually. They are happy in their freedom from all the inconveniences of this present life, from all want and sense of want. They hunger and thirst no more; all their wants are supplied. They shall never be scorched by the heat of the sun any more. They are happy in the love and guidance of the Lord Jesus: He shall feed them; He shall lead them to living fountains of waters. They are happy in being delivered from all sorrow. God Himself, with His own gentle and gracious hand, will wipe those tears away, and they would not have been without those tears when God comes to wipe them away. In this He deals with them as a tender father who finds His beloved child in tears. He comforts him, He wipes his eyes, and He turns his sorrow into rejoicing.

Never-Ending Rule

Then the seventh angel sounded:
And there were loud voices in heaven, saying,
"The kingdoms of this world have become
the kingdoms of our Lord and of His Christ,
and He shall reign forever and ever!"
REVELATION 11:15

Loud and joyful acclamations came from the saints and angels in heaven. They rose from their seats, fell on their faces, and worshiped God. They thankfully recognize the right of our God and Savior to rule and reign over all the world. They give Him thanks because He had taken to Him His great power. They rejoice that His reign shall never end. None shall ever wrest the scepter out of His hand.

There were angry resentments in the world at these actions of the power of God. "The nations were angry" (v. 18); their hearts rose up against God. They fretted against God and so increased their guilt and hastened their destruction.

The temple of God in heaven was opened. What was seen there was the ark of God's covenant. This was in the holy of holies; in this ark the tables of the law were kept. Before Josiah's time the law of God had been lost but then found, so in the reign of the Antichrist, God's law was laid aside. Now the Scriptures are opened; now they are brought to the view of all. What was heard and felt there were "lightnings, noises, thunderings, an earthquake, and great hail." By terrible things in righteousness, God would answer those prayers that were presented in His holy temple, now opened.

Forever and Ever

And he showed me a pure river of water of life, clear as crystal, proceeding from the throne of God and of the Lamb. In the middle of its street, and on either side of the river, was the tree of life.

REVELATION 22:1–2

The heavenly state is described as a paradise, a paradise in a city or a whole city in paradise. In the first paradise there were only two persons to behold the beauty of it, but in this second paradise whole cities and nations shall find abundant delight and satisfaction.

The river of paradise: Its fountainhead is the throne of God and the Lamb. All our springs of grace, comfort, and glory are in God, and all our streams from Him are through the Lamb. Its quality is pure and clear as crystal. . .giving life to those who drink of them.

The tree of life in this paradise: Such a tree was in the earthly paradise, but this far excels it. It is situated in the middle of the street and on either side of the river. This tree of life is fed by the pure waters of the river that comes from the throne of God. It brings forth many sorts of fruit—twelve sorts, and it brings forth fruit at all times. There is always fruit on it. The fruit is not only pleasant, but wholesome. The presence of God in heaven is the health and happiness of the saints.

This paradise is free from everything evil. There is no serpent there, as there was in the earthly paradise. The devil has nothing to do there.

There the saints shall see the face of God. God will own them, as having His seal and name on their foreheads. They shall reign with Him forever. All this shall be with perfect knowledge and joy, walking in the light of the Lord; and this not for a time, but forever and ever.

Scripture Index